REFERENCE

CH-R

To Josephine Taylor, my mother-in-law,
and Vincent Wrynn, my father,
who in their own ways so kindly remembered
that dreamers need to dream

First published in 1993 by Motorbooks International Publishers & Wholesalers, PO Box 2, 729 Prospect Avenue, Osceola, WI 54020 USA

Motorbooks International is a certified trademark, registered with the United States Patent Office

The information in this book is true and complete to the best of our knowledge. All recommendations are made without any guarantee on the part of the author or Publisher, who also disclaim any liability incurred in connection with the use of this data or specific details

We recognize that some words, model names and designations, for example, mentioned herein are the property of the trademark holder. We use them for identification purposes only. This is not an official publication

Motorbooks International books are also available at discounts in bulk quantity for industrial or sales-promotional use. For details write to Special Sales Manager at the Publisher's address

Library of Congress Cataloging-in-Publication Data
Wrynn, V. Dennis.
    Detroit goes to war: the American auto industry in World War II/V. Dennis Wrynn.
        p. cm.
    Includes index.
    ISBN 0-87938-773-4
    1. Advertising—Automobiles—United States—History—20th century. 2. Advertising, Magazine—United States—History—20th century. 3. Automobile industry and trade—Military aspects—United States—History—20th century. 4. Industrial mobilization—United States—History—20th century. 5. World War, 1930–1945—Equipment and supplies. I. Title.
HF6161.A9W79   1993
338.4'7692'097309044—dc20   93–7693

On the front cover: No vehicle more aptly symbolizes America's contributions to the war effort than the famous Jeep. The headline of this Willys-Overland ad that appeared in May 1942 was "Hot from the 'Lines' at Willys-Overland . . . Hell Bent for Victory."

On the back cover: Chevrolet promoted its military production in this ad that appeared in February 1945, and Fisher, in this 1943 ad, adapted its familiar company slogan, "Body by Fisher," to suit its wartime production.

Printed and bound in the United States of America

Contents

Acknowledgments

The childhood memories I retain of World War II are vivid, though episodic, and certainly have contributed to my lifelong interest in the conflict. My specific fascination with wartime advertising began while researching old magazines for a college term paper, but was revived several years later when my mother-in-law gave me her collection of magazines from the 1940s, 1950s, and 1960s. They featured events that had been important to her, and among them were a significant number of issues dating from World War II. In my mind, the impact of the magazines' advertising took precedence over the editorial content. Most notable, in both volume and content, were the ads cataloging the automobile industry's production contributions to the war effort, and my interest in them led directly to the publication of this book.

Thus, I am deeply indebted to my late mother-in-law, Josephine Taylor, for planting the seed, and to my many friends and family who have supported me in this project, especially when I was in danger of faltering. Foremost among them was my wife, Mary Jo, who progressed from sometime doubter to strong advocate. I also must thank my friends Perry Bradley, pilot and journalist, for his advice and cordial guidance; Bob Christian, whose friendship and insight, as well as experiences as a naval veteran of the war, were important to me; and Ray Lewis, Librarian to the US House of Representatives, for his in-depth knowledge and critical guidance as I prepared this book. In addition, I thank Florence Ogg of Northport, New York, for her valuable contributions.

Not to be forgotten are my friends at the Big Chicken Barn Books & Antiques in Ellsworth, Maine, and Jerry Coombs, owner of the Collectable Book Shop in Dover-Foxcroft, Maine, who were very helpful and cooperative in my search for period magazines. Archivist Brandt Rosenbusch at Chrysler Corporation, and Cathleen Latendresse at the Henry Ford Motor Museum in Dearborn, Michigan, very kindly provided me with important historical data, as did General Motors Corporation, which sent me a copy of the company's seventy-five-year history published in 1983. I would also like to thank the various automotive companies and their survivors for permission to use their advertisements in this book.

V. Dennis Wrynn
Fairfax Station, Virginia
September 1992

Introduction

Historians, economists, and social scientists have said for decades that advertising, aside from being the lifeblood of modern American commerce, is a mirror reflecting the nation's attitudes and moods, and a yardstick by which to measure the constant changes occurring in society. This viewpoint has not always been paramount, however, and the debate continues about advertising's role in the US economy.

The ad industry has often been vilified, due to both exaggerated product claims and the belief that it leads to unnecessary and profligate consumption and spending on the part of the populace. During the 1930s, movements were formed within the federal government to restrict or even abolish advertising, viewing it as an evil foisted upon the electorate by the manufacturers and capitalists. Through it all, the advertising industry has prospered. The company that doesn't advertise has little opportunity to place its product in public view, and is usually doomed to failure. Advertising was, and has remained, a vital tool for business, as well as an accurate reflection of the American way of life.

Print advertising was at its zenith in the years before television and instant communications. Newspapers certainly had their place; in early 1942, circulation was forty-two million copies on weekdays and thirty-three million on Sundays. However, the daily papers were best utilized selling local products to local markets. Magazines were the primary vehicle of corporate advertising. This colorful, attractive advertising mode caught the eye of millions of Americans who either subscribed or regularly purchased at their local newsstands the dozens of weekly and monthly magazines available to the public. The weekly magazines were read and re-read in households spanning the physical and economic breadth of the United States. American automobile manufacturers invested heavily in magazine product advertising in peacetime. The people of this nation have always had a love affair with their cars, and as the depression waned, they eagerly looked forward to their first glimpses of next year's new models, usually in October, in their favorite magazines.

In the late 1930s, when war in Europe appeared inevitable and while Japan pursued aggressive expansionist plans in Asia (particularly its attack on China) and the Pacific, the Roosevelt administration orchestrated support for the nations of Western Europe resisting Hitler. But the American people did not view world conflict as imminent. Advertising content understandably reflected little of these world tensions while the country was at peace. The American pursuit of shiny cars, elegant clothes, good whiskey, and clean breath prevailed, and it wasn't until after the National Selective Service Act was initiated in October 1940, that US industries started selling their wares by highlighting corporate involvement in the country's security.

The Japanese surprise attack at Pearl Harbor on December 7, 1941, unified the American people as nothing has since. Every family was affected. Out of a population of 132 million in 1940, 15 million Americans served in the armed forces during the war. Millions more worked on the home front. Industry and advertising charged into the war effort as well, and this was significantly reflected in the advertising copy of those years. There were many facets of civilian involvement in the conflict, most notably in war bond rallies, the entertainment industry, and all sorts of drives by local government, churches, and civic groups. The most constant reminder, however, was the weekly magazines, filled with stories about the war and page after page of patriotic advertising from every imaginable company and organization. Young children collected the ads, while parents reflected on them as their older children went off to fight. The ads were an image of Americans united, a force that contributed to the spirit and will needed to achieve victory. All of this was not lost on the magazine publishers, who soon realized that this intense civilian interest in war coverage gave them new prominence and galvanized their advertisers, who wanted their names and products displayed before the American public at that time as well as after the war ended. In 1944 the advertising industry increased its participation in print advertising by a whopping $100 million over 1942, despite a national paper shortage which affected both the quality and quantity of weekly magazines.

American car manufacturers were aware of the power of advertising, especially to an industry unable to sell their products due to wartime restrictions and shortages. Like many organizations, though, the auto industry was immersed in war production and had a significant, if unorthodox, story to tell. It also had the opportunity to reap the profits resulting from such maximum production. The Lend-Lease Act of 1941, which provided military vehicles and equipment to allied nations, as well as the needs of the American military, created insatiable production demands as the threat of war loomed closer.

The uniquely American automobile industry responded enthusiastically to the demands of a wartime economy, meeting the challenges of military production and strengthening the country's morale in a time of crisis. As part of the overall advertising effort during World War II, automotive advertising was a visual barometer of the nation's emotional state, and remains part of an unforgettable compendium of America and Americans at their finest. Later, when the end of the war was within view, it helped to prepare the country for a return to civilian ways and goods, especially cars.

Japan capitulated onboard the USS *Missouri* on September 2, 1945, three years and nine months after its initial aggression against the United States. The war was over, and the advertising industry had done its work well, leaving behind a dynamic catalog of America at war on the home front as well as around the world. Returning soldiers and civilians alike were starved for material goods, and eager to spend their war-induced savings. For many the purchase of a car was a dream long-denied, soon to be a reality in a nation at peace.

This book attempts to capture that spirit of enthusiasm, patriotism, sacrifice, dedication, even anger that infused an industry and a generation of Americans as they fought the second global war within the first half of the twentieth century. The images presented are the images of the times, without the dubious benefit of hindsight. Only the captions come from the present.

CHAPTER 1

Business as Usual: 1940–1941

The American economy between World War I and World War II reflected the best and the worst scenarios in a capitalistic society. The end of the Great War ushered in the "Roaring Twenties," a frenzied era of economic success and social excess. These were good years for the US automotive industry, as the car became integrated into the American way of life. It freed people from public transportation in the cities and from the horse and wagon in the rural areas. The railroad industry felt pressure from the automobile's growing popularity, but highway systems were not yet developed well enough, nor were automobiles reliable enough, to affect the premier position of the train in long-range travel. Car sales were truly remarkable, however. In 1927, Chevrolet recorded its first million-car calendar year, and Oldsmobile's sales rose from 44,000 in 1924 to more than 100,000 in 1929.

Conversely, this decade of wealth and plenty was followed by a devastating economic depression which curtailed spending and reduced the country's standard of living significantly. Auto manufacturers realized that the national mood was no longer frivolous, and their sales were dramatically reduced, a direct result of the lack of jobs and money.

Many automobile dealerships were forced to close due to these dismal conditions. Studebaker, the oldest company in the transportation industry, went into receivership in 1933, but survived due to the energy and perseverance of Paul Hoffman and Harry Vance, two visionary and highly organized executives. American Bantam, Graham, and Hupmobile ceased production by 1940, the latter two after a failed merger attempt, and Chrysler closed the books on the Viking and the Marquette, two cars the company had developed in the twenties. Hudson's annual production dropped from 114,000 cars in 1930 to 41,000 in

The 1940 Ford, designed by Bob Gregorie, was a real style-setter with a horizontal-bar grille, angled windshield, and (for the first time) sealed-beam headlights. In excess of 600,000 Fords, priced from $619 to $947, were produced, second only to Chevrolet. The American Airlines DC-3 featured here was the most popular and dependable commercial aircraft of its day, and is still flying in many places around the globe. Courtesy, Ford Motor Company

Illustrated: Packard One-Twenty Convertible Coupe, $1270* (white sidewall tires extra)

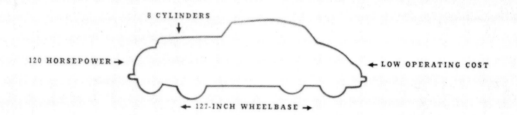

8 CYLINDERS

120 HORSEPOWER →

← LOW OPERATING COST

← 127-INCH WHEELBASE →

Meet Straight-Eight enthusiasm!

By COMPARISON with Packard 120 owner-enthusiasm, that of many car-owners is like a murmur to a shout.

For here is *one* eight that really gets under your skin. You'll sense this in the affectionate and highly personal way its owners refer to it.

To begin with, you may take the gentleman's word for it that *no other eight* belongs on the same road with the 1940 Packard One-Twenty. In smart new styling. In the thrill that waits in its throttle. In sheer luxurious comfort which stems from *extra length*. In year-'round upkeep costs—whose modest totals delight anyone with a sense of thrift.

But if you want to meet Straight-Eight enthusiasm at its height—hunt up a One-Twenty owner who has had his car long enough for any of the commoner service operations! *He'll* quote you figures which *prove* that One-Twenty service charges are smack in line with those of *much smaller* cars.

Better than all this, however, borrow a 1940 One-Twenty from your Packard dealer—*now!* Settle back, nudge the accelerator, and you'll witness a miracle of smooth and soundless flight! You're headed for that distant point where the roadsides draw together. And how soon you're past it—and gliding toward the next . . . the next . . . and the next.

Drifting home, you'll realize that this smart Packard takes exception to the rule that "All good times must end". They needn't, ever—in a One-Twenty.

PACKARD 120
$1038

AND UP. *Packard 110, $867 and up. Packard 120, $1038 and up. Packard Super-8 160, $1524 and up. Packard Custom Super-8 180, $2243 to $6300. *All prices delivered in Detroit. State taxes extra.*

ASK THE MAN WHO OWNS ONE

8

1933. By 1936 it was up to 136,000 but it dropped again in 1938 to 51,000 cars.

Still, in 1937 Packard produced 109,518 cars, the best year in its history. Two years earlier the company had made a very conscious decision to change from a strictly luxury priced line of motorcars to a new medium-priced car, namely the Packard 120, and its success was obvious.

Chevrolet had become the nation's most popular automobile by 1939, and came close to producing a million cars in both 1940 and 1941. Chrysler restyled all of its models in 1940, and DeSoto manufactured nearly 86,000 cars in 1941.

American industry in the late-thirties was recovering from the doldrums in part because a major war was brewing, and many countries in Europe and Asia demanded American production goods of all types. When President Franklin D. Roosevelt signed the Lend-Lease Act into law in 1941, the economy regained its health and was further strengthened by the demands of the US military establishment for all manner of war materiel.

As conflict erupted all over the globe and the US hastily attempted to upgrade its own military preparedness, the nation's auto manufacturers continued to improve their product lines. Car companies made considerable progress in the styling and performance of their new cars. Fenders on many models were integrated into the car bodies, and headlights were set into the body rather than atop the fenders. Running boards were shrinking or disappearing completely. As automotive styling evolved, cars took on a smoother look; their lines flowed with greater continuity rather than simply looking like several

sections pieced together to create a vehicle. But motorcar development was about to be interrupted.

Even as automotive production and other manufacturing surged at home, the ominous intrusion of global warfare signalled an end to peaceful civilian development of just about everything in the US, from motorcars to televisions, and zippers to refrigerators. Attention and energy had to be turned to the war effort. Some manufacturers, however, resisted involvement in the coming war—in *any* war, for that matter.

Prior to the outbreak of war, many American business and political leaders held legitimate isolationist positions, and their views were strongly supported by the majority of the population. Although the Allies won World War I, the hoped-for peace had been short-lived, creating a feeling of

frustration and betrayal among US citizens, so there was a distinct lack of enthusiasm for getting involved in another European war.

Henry Ford, founder of the Ford Motor Company, had long held pacifist views and was not much interested in producing military equipment for foreign governments. He and his wife Clara had been involved in "moral rearmament" during the twenties, essentially promoting peace and understanding based on personal Christianity. Joining Ford in his abhorrence of involvement in Europe's problems was Charles Lindbergh, a national hero since his solo trans-Atlantic flight in 1927.

After the war had started in Europe, Henry Ford agreed to build 6,000 Rolls-Royce aircraft engines for the US. Upon realizing that the engine contract actually was directly with Great Britain, however, he reneged. Ford was not willing to supply a foreign belligerent, saying he would produce military hardware for defense purposes only. The engine order went to the Packard Motor Car Company instead.

Ford produced aircraft components, but it was under a contract with the US government to develop and build a new 18-cylinder air-cooled aircraft engine. Although the Ford Motor Company soon became an integral part of the American defense community and accepted many more important contracts, Henry Ford steadfastly maintained that while he would certainly contribute to the nation's defense, he was firmly against involvement in anybody else's war. Thus as the thirties ended, a mixture of idealism and reality existed in the economic and political positions of many US business and elected leaders, and it hindered the creation of a national conscience and consensus regarding America's possible involvement in foreign conflicts.

More than two years of active warfare occurred in Europe before the United States entered the battle against the Axis powers as a direct result of the Japanese attack on Pearl Harbor. The September 1939 invasion of Poland was initiated by Germany and followed two weeks later by Russia. Within a week of the German aggression, the Wehrmacht (the German Army) was at the gates of Warsaw: The issue was never in doubt, and Poland was engulfed by the two most

The Dodge brothers sold their company to Chrysler Corporation in 1928, and in the early 1930s ran fourth in production in the automotive industry. By 1940, Dodge had fallen to sixth place, building 195,505 units, all featuring six-cylinder engines. They were priced from $755 to $1,170. Dodge was a steady, unspectacular, even dull automobile. Two-tone exteriors were never a great success. The two women shown here are rather disparate, from the chic woman in the sophisticated hat and shirtwaist dress to the young girl modeling a tea gown. Courtesy, Chrysler Corporation

Next page
For 1941, Plymouth changed its design to include a heart-shaped grille and "speedline fenders," and repositioned its battery under the hood for the first time. It also pioneered Chrysler's safety rim wheel, which was designed to save the tire in case of a blowout. The Plymouth engine produced 87 horsepower (hp) at 3800 revolutions per minute (rpm), and the company was third in production that year with 423,155 units. Courtesy, Chrysler Corporation

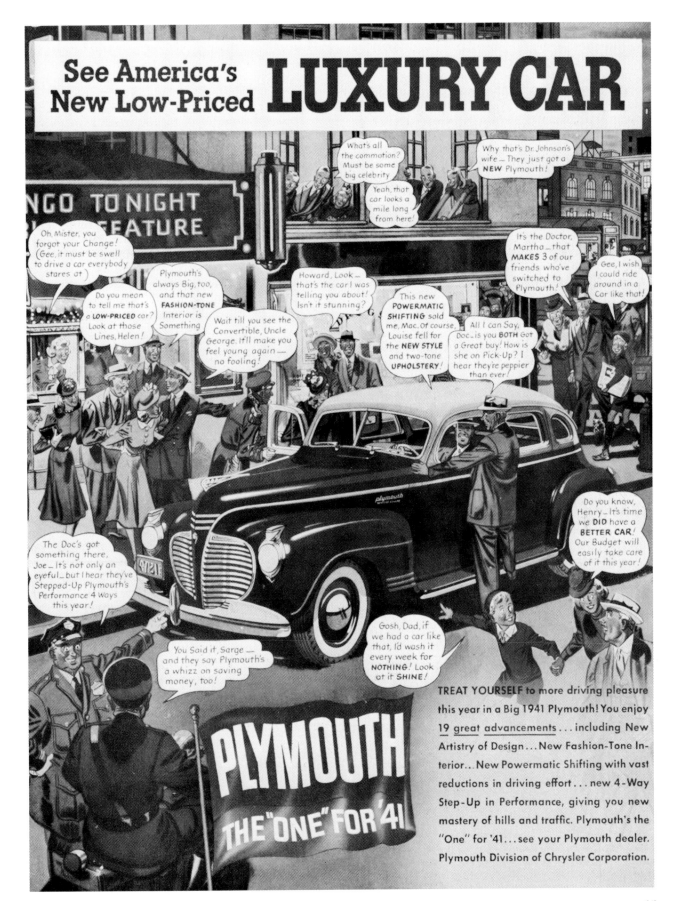

savage regimes in the modern history of Western civilization.

During the spring of 1940, following several months of inactivity in Europe, Denmark and Norway were invaded and defeated by Germany. The same horror befell Holland and Luxembourg in mid-May. Belgium, whose defense was the key to stopping this major German offensive, surrendered to the Wehrmacht on May 28. The evacuation by British forces from the beaches of Dunkirk in late May and early June was quickly followed by the Franco-German armistice on June 22, 1940. Britain stood alone. Only Sweden, Switzerland, Spain, and Portugal were not in the war. All the rest of Western Europe was dominated and occupied by Germany and its Axis partners.

Operation Sea Lion, code name for Hitler's planned invasion of England, awaited attainment of total air superiority by the Luftwaffe (the German Air Force), but this was thwarted by the Royal Air Force in the aerial Battle of Britain. Both air forces displayed incredible courage and determination in performing their assignments, but the failure of the Luftwaffe to achieve decisive victory, coupled with the curious peace proposals being bandied about (Nazi Deputy Rudolf Hess had parachuted into Scotland with a request to meet with Prime Minister Winston Churchill, which was righteously denied), caused Hitler to delay Sea Lion. With increased British naval activity in the channel and the proximity of severe fall and winter weather, the invasion was ultimately canceled.

Before the year ended, Germany occupied Rumania in order to control that country's oil fields. The British defeated the Italians in Libya, and the invasion of Greece by Italy was a failure. Hitler had to intercede in both arenas to protect his planned attack on Russia. Almost imperceptibly, the Axis war machine was finally meeting

Pontiac's Torpedoes featured a rounded hood, horizontal bar grille, and GM's pontoon fenders. In 1941 a fastback sedan was added, creating six separate series with six- or eight-cylinder engines. Prices ranged from $828 to $1,250, and production ranked fifth with 330,061

units. The Torpedo name reflected new styling, but also evoked a warlike mood in the country as conflict drew closer. Courtesy, Pontiac Division, General Motors Corporation

1941 MERCURY 8

The car that was right from the start!

From its very introduction, the Mercury 8 was *right*. It has caught the imagination of American motorists because it meets every qualification of what a big car should be—in size, in luxury, in power and performance—and adds real economy of operation that is a welcome satisfaction to every owner.

For 1941, there is a new and even bigger Mercury 8. Clean new streamlines emphasize its new long wheelbase and broadened body. Glass areas are enlarged to "picture window" proportions. Seats are wide and deep. There's a new zip to its get-away, a reassuring steadiness

in its commanding way on the road, and a swift obedience to commands that makes owners say, "You don't *drive* this car, you *guide* it!"

THE ONE BIG CAR THAT HAS EVERYTHING —PLUS ECONOMY

Keystone of the Mercury's amazing success is its remarkably efficient V-8 engine—the only one in its field. An engine so perfectly balanced with the car's weight that gasoline consumption is very low. Few cars of *any* size can match the brilliant gas mileage record of the Mercury. (Owners report up to 20 miles per gallon!)

A BRAND-NEW TRAVEL EXPERIENCE

Don't be satisfied until you've had the adventure of a Mercury Ride. Learn why this car has already earned the confidence of over 150,000 enthusiastic owners, and become such an outstanding success. Any Mercury, Lincoln or Ford dealer will arrange to have you drive the Mercury.

> ### THINGS YOU'LL LIKE ABOUT THE NEW 1941 MERCURY
>
> **NEW EXTERIOR BEAUTY.** A long, low car with wide body, superb streamlining. New bright colors.
>
> **BIG POWERFUL ENGINE.** Only V-8 in the lower medium price field. Brilliant acceleration and high sustained performance. Amazing economy!
>
> **LUXURIOUS INTERIORS.** Beautifully decorated in harmonizing colors. Wide seats. Resilient cushion pads of foam rubber.
>
> **EASE OF CONTROL.** Finger-Tip Gearshift. Velvet-action clutch and hydraulic brakes. Newly-designed, perfected stabilizer.
>
> **NEW RIDING COMFORT.** Long, flexible easy-action springs. Improved shock absorbers. Center-poise balance. The car rides like a dream.

THE BIG CAR THAT STANDS ALONE IN ECONOMY

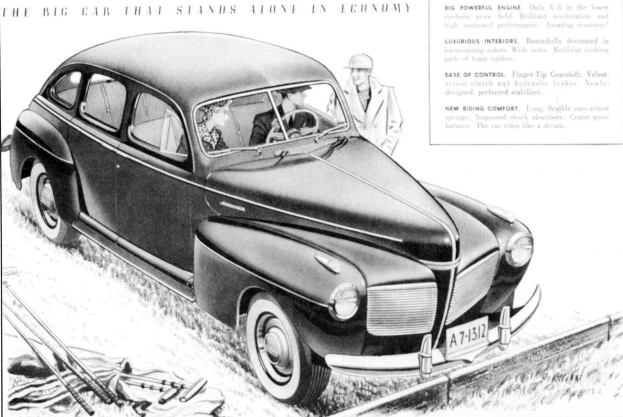

Mercury produced 81,874 cars in seven models in 1941, and called itself the "big car that stands alone in economy." Priced from $910 to $1,141, it still looked like a big *Ford. The convertible sedan was discontinued during the production year after only 1,000 cars had been built.* Courtesy, Ford Motor Company

NOW! SEE YOUR OLDSMOBILE DEALER FOR A

Hydra-Matic Drive!*

NO CLUTCH TO PRESS!

No clutch and no clutch pedal with Hydra-Matic Drive—no work for your left foot to do!

NO GEARS TO SHIFT!

No lever to manipulate. Simply set the control in "HI," and gears shift *automatically*

New low-priced Olds Special, stunning new Dynamic Cruiser, luxurious new Custom Cruiser—the 1941 Oldsmobiles are the newest of the new! And most sensational of all their new features is Oldsmobile's exclusive Hydra-Matic Drive—a combination of fluid coupling and *completely* automatic transmission! For a motoring thrill that's new and different, try real *no clutch, no shift driving*—today!

Car illustrated: Dynamic 6 Cruiser Four-Door Sedan, $1010. (Same model Eight, $1045.*) *Hydra-Matic Drive optional at extra cost.*

*Coupe prices begin at $852. Sedan prices start at $898, *delivered at Lansing, Michigan. Transportation based on rail rates, state and local taxes (if any), optional equipment and accessories—extra. Prices subject to change without notice.* A GENERAL MOTORS VALUE

OLDS PRICES BEGIN AT
$852*
FOR SPECIAL SIX
BUSINESS COUPE

STYLED TO LEAD
BUILT TO LAST

THE CAR *Ahead!* IT'S **OLDSMOBILE**

some resistance, but circumstances were still overwhelmingly in Germany's favor.

In the United States, 1940 was an election year and Franklin Delano Roosevelt (FDR) was returned to an unprecedented third term as president. The American people did not want anything to do with another European war, and Roosevelt had been cautious during his political campaign concerning military support for England. Now with the election behind him, he started to speak out against the Axis, warning that America's best defense was "the success of Britain defending herself." Lend-Lease was about to begin.

The United States may have been reluctant to get involved in the turmoil in Europe, but the country had not been asleep. Many of the weapons that would help ultimately to win the war, such as the M-1 rifle and the B-17 and B-24 bombers, were developed during the 1930s. The P-51 Mustang fighter was being developed for the British in the United States. Some American military and political leaders, more realistic and perceptive than their counterparts, tried to prepare for what they saw as inevitable. The Army War College had made a secret study in 1939 to prepare a defense of the Panama Canal and also Brazil in case Germany attempted to gain a foothold in Latin or South America. During the summer months there had been a general mobilization of the National Guard as well as the Navy and Marine reserves, and the military draft was initiated in October 1940. At the time, however, the United States still ranked nineteenth among the world's armies.

FDR asked Congress to authorize the Lend-Lease program so the US could help nations threatened by Axis aggression. In January 1941 Roosevelt declared the US as the "Arsenal of Democracy," and two months later Congress passed the Lend-Lease Act. A $7 billion appropriation permitted the lending of arms and equipment to allied nations. Great Britain was among the first nations to receive US aid, and the Soviet Union and China were also recipients.

Tanks, airplanes, Jeeps, arms, and ammunition were among the items delivered to allied

countries. The Lend-Lease program started before war had been declared, so there was some opposition to the plan from isolationists. The Mothers' Crusade Against Lend-Lease, for example, knelt in prayer as a group in front of the Capitol to urge Congress to repeal the Lend-Lease Act.

While Americans were reluctant to go to war, they did not mind profiting from the one in progress. Lend-Lease was a boon to the US manufacturing community, and with the availability of well-paying jobs, personal consumption of goods increased dramatically. Cars that had been nursed through the dark days of the Great Depression were turned in for the new models pouring out of Detroit. Prices certainly varied, from

Chevrolet was clearly the industry leader throughout the 1930s and into the 1940s, and 1941 was no exception, with 1,008,976 cars manufactured in the production year. Exterior running boards disappeared, and the hood opened from the front on all models for the first time. A new grille was introduced, and a "vacuum-power shift" sounded automatic, even if it wasn't. The 90hp "Victory" engine's name had a militaristic ring to it, somewhat fitting since Chevrolet in 1940 had signed its first contract to produce weapons for the US government. Models sold for $712 to $995—a great value for America's leading automobile. Courtesy, Chevrolet Division, General Motors Corporation

Five "Greats"
OF A GREAT NEW CHRYSLER CORPORATION CAR.

1941 DeSoto

ROCKET BODIES have spacious leg room, elbow room—deep, luxurious new Form-Rest Seats.

Enjoy {1} De Soto Fluid Drive with {2} Simplimatic Transmission— Automatic Shifting for all normal driving! {3} Low-slung Rocket Bodies! {4} New 2-Tone Interiors! {5} Chrysler Corporation **Quality**, **Economy**!

SB·742

"BUILT BY CHRYSLER CORPORATION" MEANS QUALITY

Fluid Drive
Formerly only on high-priced cars, now combined with Simplimatic Transmission, gives you Automatic Shifting for all normal driving
ASK FOR A DEMONSTRATION TODAY!

DE SOTO!...that's the name to remember—the car to watch—this year! It's a *big* car—a *wide* car—a long, *rakish, low-slung* car...with lines that are all action and beauty.

You can *see* and *feel* its quality...in the way it is designed and fitted throughout, in the velvety smoothness with which it handles.

It has every new and worth-while feature for '41. Drive it, and you'll see!

With Fluid Drive, you can stop, start, go all day without shifting or touching the clutch! A wonderful smooth surge of power at the getaway...flashing acceleration in traffic or on hills. Always that feeling of effortless, limitless power! And this beauty hugs the road...literally *smooths* out the rough spots. It gives you that solid, steady-riding "feel" you want.

Stop in today and see this big, impressive 1941 De Soto. Take it out on the road and try it. You'll find a rich, luxurious, wonderfully easy-handling car ...priced surprisingly low.

There are thirteen body styles — eight new solid colors...four beautiful two-tone combinations.

You have a choice of fine upholstery fabrics— two-tone interior color schemes. De Soto Division of Chrysler Corporation, Detroit, Michigan.

TUNE IN MAJOR BOWES, C.B.S., THURS., 9 TO 10 P.M., E.S.T.

16

the $300 Crosley to a luxury car that could cost $1,600. The mass-market automobile was firmly entrenched in the average American's vision of the good life. It had come about because of several factors. Initially, assembly-line manufacturing techniques had brought the car within the economic parameters of the average worker, but this was followed by the equally important concepts of installment buying, trade-in of the old car, and the excitement created by the new annual model every September or October.

During the 1920s car manufacturers were selling speed, flair, and the recklessness of the era, as personified in the famous Jordan Motor Car Company ad entitled "Somewhere West of Laramie," which extolled a Jordan model called the Playboy for "a broncho-busting steer-roping girl" who "loves the cross of the wild and the tame." The car was called "a brawny thing—yet a graceful thing for the sweep o' the Avenue."

When America's good times were replaced by the depression of the 1930s, automobile advertising took on a serious tone as people sought value for their scarce money. Included were ads featuring Walter Percy Chrysler, founder of the Big Three auto maker Chrysler Corporation, urging shoppers to "Look at All Three" (especially the Plymouth) when carefully comparing values in the search for a low-priced car.

In 1938, The Packard Motor Car Company ("Ask the Man Who Owns One") featured both monthly installments and trade-ins as down payments as the easiest and smartest ways to buy the car of your dreams. So did General Motors Corporation's (GM) Buick Motor Division ("Buick's the Beauty!") in 1939, offering a sedan for $51 less than the previous year with the catch phrase, "Easy on the eye—easy to buy—on General Motors terms!"

By 1940 the country's improving economy created a less serious approach, as the Chevrolet Motor Division ("First Again!") advertised its Fifteen-Footer, "the very longest of all lowest-priced cars!" for $659, a streamlined Royal Clipper.

In January, a Chevrolet became the 25 millionth car produced by GM and the division also received a US government defense contract to manufacture 75mm artillery shells, the first such contract awarded for war materiel.

In 1940 there was no doubt that the Chevrolet, with total calendar year production of 895,734 vehicles, was by far the number one car in America. In second place was Ford Motor Company with 599,175 cars produced, followed by Plymouth, Buick, Pontiac, Dodge, Oldsmobile, Studebaker, and Chrysler, all of which produced more than 100,000 cars each.

The new automobile models for 1941 arrived with great publicity in the fall of 1940. One model noticeable by its absence was General Motors' famous LaSalle, squeezed between the more expensive Cadillac and the less expensive Buick, and dropped from production after 1940.

Plymouth designated itself "The One for '41" and Pontiac introduced its line of Torpedoes, referring to the new bodystyling that did away with much of the boxy look of the 1930s. Oldsmobile trumpeted its Hydra-Matic Drive in a car that

The 1941 Ford was the biggest car the company had built thus far in its history, weighing 3,419lb with a 114in wheelbase, and offering six- or eight-cylinder engines. Priced at $684 to $1,013, the Fordor sedan was 7in wider than any previous Ford. Bigger fenders and a vertical grille were improved features on the 1941 Ford. In this ad, Ford highlighted its Rouge plant, one of the best known in the world. Courtesy, Ford Motor Company

Cuts your footwork in half!
Packard Electromatic Clutch

Illustrated: the new Packard One-Ten Deluxe Touring Sedan

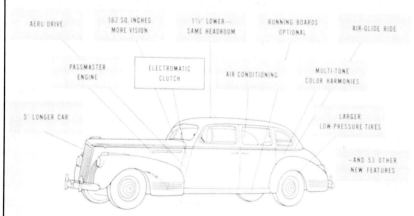

AERO DRIVE   162 SQ. INCHES MORE VISION   1½" LOWER— SAME HEADROOM   RUNNING BOARDS OPTIONAL   AIR-GLIDE RIDE

PASSMASTER ENGINE   ELECTROMATIC CLUTCH   AIR CONDITIONING   MULTI-TONE COLOR HARMONIES

5' LONGER CAR   LARGER LOW-PRESSURE TIRES   —AND 53 OTHER NEW FEATURES

ONCE YOU TOUCH THE STARTER of the new 1941 Packard, you've opened the door to amazement in motion—new and more effortless than you ever dreamed of!

For in this brilliant new Packard, your left foot loafs. It just goes along for the ride, *the car itself* operates the clutch.

The Packard Electromatic Clutch takes over the clutch operation . . . the letting-out and letting-in that used to keep your left foot so busy. This moderately-priced Packard optional feature has none of the defects that marred earlier self-operating clutches. It engages at *just the right rate*, neither too slow nor too fast. A combination of electrical and vacuum control does a smoother job of operating the clutch than you would do for yourself.

It has the further advantage of making the conventional foot-clutch available, if desired, by touching a button. And, in combination with the Aero-Drive, this Packard improvement not only eliminates footwork on the clutch—but reduces gear-shifting as well!

The Electromatic Clutch is only *one* of 64 bright new features that make the 1941 Packards the most exciting cars of the year. There's glamorous new Multi-tone beauty—inside and out—with no less than 261 color harmony combinations.

There's the Passmaster Engine, 10% more economical than preceding thrifty Packards. There's Aero-Drive*, giving you a dividend of *one mile free in five!* There's Air Conditioning* (a Packard *first*) which puts heat and humidity to rout with real refrigeration. There's Feather-light handling ease, Air-Glide ride, —and these are only the starting points!

Make no mistake, the new 1941 Packard is *new* from stem to stern. Longer, lower, lovelier, infinitely more luxurious, it's truly the Class of '41. See it now, and—*Ask the man who owns one!*

*Available at extra cost.

P. S.

Your Packard dealer has the good news about 1941 prices!

NEW PACKARD—the Class of '41

18

was "Styled to Lead–Built to Last." The company had a point: Hydra-Matic Drive, which was perfected in 1940, was a very successful automatic transmission, and was sold to many other auto manufacturers.

Chrysler marketed Fluid Drive for its cars. Some manufacturers, such as Ford, Mercury, Nash, and Hudson, did not offer automatic transmissions until several years after the end of World War II.

Autumn of 1940 also witnessed the closing of the New York World's Fair and the opening of the Queens Midtown Tunnel under New York's East River. In addition, the Japanese invaded French Indochina (leading ultimately to a total US embargo of commerce with Nippon [Japan]), and large-scale battles were fought in the North African desert between the British and the Italians. German submarine attacks on British ship-

Buick ranked fourth in 1941 production with 377,428 units—cars coming off assembly lines that during the war would produce Hellcats. Stressing its price as a solid investment, models ranged from $915 to $2,465 in twenty-six separate body styles. With aggressive president Harlow Curtice at the helm, Buick produced splendid cars. The bodies by Brunn have been called opulent, and featured the fastback look as well as headlights blended into the fenders. Transmissions were still standard, and the eight-cylinder Fireball Eight engines produced between 115 and 165hp. The Buick's massive grille would be a trademark for years to come. Courtesy, Buick Division, General Motors Corporation

Lincoln Zephyrs were available for $1,478 to $1,856 in 1941, and they remained the major model in the Lincoln line, although Continental was gaining in popularity. Total production was 21,994, meaning Lincoln output did not rank in the top sixteen US car makers. All of the models featured a V-12 engine that generated 120hp at 3500rpm. While several rivals were pressing the Zephyr, notably Buick, Oldsmobile, DeSoto, and Chrysler, its biggest competition was Cadillac, which built a luxury car for less money. Courtesy, Ford Motor Company

CAR OF THE TIMES... YOUR DE SOTO

HERE IT IS—the car that brings the future right down to today—your new *De Soto!*

Only De Soto, backed by Chrysler Corporation, could have conceived this superb car.

Notice that running boards are concealed... and new Airfoil Lights (concealed headlamps) are *invisible* by day.

You can express your own taste in fabrics and colors... De Soto's interiors are *personalized.*

And talk about performance! The new Powermaster Engine packs *115 horsepower!* And this extra power-margin is not all!

New *Fluid Drive and Simpli-Matic Transmission give No-Shift Driving that tops all previous

"bests"... with better-than-ever economy!

See this De Soto... see how it's styled *to stand out*—built *to stand up.* Your De Soto dealer will be glad to give you a demonstration.

Call or phone *now.* De Soto Division of Chrysler Corporation, Detroit, Mich. *Prices and specifications subject to change without notice.*

Hear Major Bowes' Hour, C.B.S., Thursdays, 9-10 P.M., E.S.T.

DEFENSE PRODUCTS OF CHRYSLER CORPORATION

Tanks • Anti-Aircraft Cannon • Reconnaissance Cars • Command Cars • Weapon Carriers • Troop Transports • Ambulances • Tent Heaters • Field Kitchens • Cantonment Furnaces • Marine Engines • Industrial Engines.

*AVAILABLE AT MODERATE ADDITIONAL COST.

NEW AIRFOIL LIGHTS — OUT OF SIGHT EXCEPT AT NIGHT

PERSONALIZED **INTERIORS** — COLOR-MATCHED TO YOUR TASTE

*FLUID DRIVE WITH SIMPLI-MATIC TRANSMISSION — NEW 115-H.P. PERFORMANCE

TOMORROW'S STYLE TODAY

ping were taking a terrible toll of lives, ships, and materiel.

American news services were full of stories about the war in Europe, and about the status of the country's defense establishment—which was described in mostly optimistic terms. All this was reflected in the media of the day. Magazines ran features on strategy and preparedness, and portrayed America's somewhat smug satisfaction with itself and its people, often to the detriment of the rest of the world, especially Asians.

One *LIFE* magazine article about the Navy mentioned that in Hawaii, "there are almost no white girls whom the sailors can meet, and since the average of the enlisted men are high school trained, ambitious and self-respecting, they do not want to have dates with native girls or underworld whites."

The advertising in these magazines, on the other hand, reflected little of the country's growing preoccupation with the world situation. To most corporations, it was just business as usual. Some shortages, such as silk stockings (needed for parachutes), were creeping into the economy, and little did the populace realize that liquor and gasoline would be in short supply in just a few years. There were also some indications of sugar hoarding during 1940, a vivid legacy and reminder of World War I which had ended a mere twenty-two years earlier. The possibility of actual conflict, however, still appeared far away. And as Americans are ever wont to do, when the good times roll, politics–however troubling–takes a distant back seat.

As 1940 drew to a close, the British were still valiantly withstanding German bomber raids on their cities, including fifty-seven straight night attacks on London during the fall months. While the threat of an invasion of "this blessed plot, this earth, this realm, this England" had diminished, the blitz continued, and 23,000 civilians died in England in 1940.

Hitler was wary of alienating American opinion, especially with his upcoming plans to invade Russia and create a two-front war. In addition to German-Americans and Irish-Americans who harbored no love for England, there were many Americans who extolled an isolationist stance. The loss of peace after World War I had left many people with a sense of betrayal by the politicians.

America Firsters, isolationists who wanted the US to stay out of any foreign conflicts, had a powerful and legitimate spokesperson in aviator Charles Lindbergh, certainly one of the best known and popular Americans of his day. But Roosevelt was powerful too, and he wanted desperately to aid the British, using his presidential authority to stretch the limits of neutrality. His concern with the Japanese and the Pacific appeared secondary.

Japan was eager to expand its Greater East Asia Co-Prosperity Sphere, specifically at the expense of the British and Dutch empires in the Pacific. For it to do so, America would have to be neutralized either politically or militarily. How well FDR understood Japan's determination and

Chevrolet produced only 258,795 units of the 1942 models, as civilian production halted on January 30, 1942. In the Special Deluxe series, only 1,182 convertibles and 1,057 station wagons were built. Priced between $760 and $1,095, its advertising slogan was "The Finest Chevrolet of All Time." Print ads continued to reflect a growing involvement in national defense and military production. Courtesy, Chevrolet Division, General Motors Corporation

Streamlining That Starts Away Down Deep

There's a definite feeling of depth and power in the flowing lines of the 1942 Lincoln-Zephyr, because its beauty is more than surface deep. ★ This modernness starts at the very core of the car! Built on an entirely new principle that sets it apart from other automobiles, the Lincoln-Zephyr is *naturally* streamlined right from its basic construction on through to its longer, lower appearance! ★ Free from excess weight... and with its V-type 12-cylinder engine more powerful than ever... this fine car gives you a different kind of ride. Relaxed on chair-high seats cradled amidships on longer, slow-motion springs, you skim along the highways with glider-like ease. ★ Interiors are roomy, more richly appointed this year. And the new Lincoln Liquamatic Drive with automatic gearshift* enables you to drive all day without shifting or even touching the clutch. ★ This is a good year to buy a better car. And the new Lincoln-Zephyr is truly the finest ever to bear the name. There's been no skimping on materials, no compromise with Lincoln traditions. The *quality* of the 1942 Lincoln-Zephyr also *starts away down deep!*

LINCOLN MOTOR CAR DIVISION, FORD MOTOR COMPANY
Builders of the Lincoln-Zephyr V-12, Sedan, Coupe, Convertible Coupe; the Lincoln Continental, Cabriolet and Coupe; the Lincoln-Custom, Sedan and Limousine.

*Optional at moderate cost

The Finest Lincolns Ever Built

Lincoln Zephyr V·12

The Zephyr still led production for Lincoln in 1942 with 6,118 units manufactured, compared to 336 Continentals and 113 Customs. Lincolns were priced from $1,650 to $3,075 and introduced a horizontal-barred grille, parking lights, and longer and higher fenders.

The rather expensive sport of deep-sea fishing is featured in this ad, not so subtly tying the ownership of a Lincoln to the thrills of the wealthy sports enthusiast. Courtesy, Ford Motor Company

resulting reactions to the US diplomatic and economic blockade of Japanese interests is a question often debated by historians. The reaction was aggression, and the question is legitimately asked whether Roosevelt expected this—or even essentially *welcomed* it—as a backdoor entry into the war in Europe.

But through all of this, 1940 was a good year for Americans. The war in Europe created a growing prosperity in the United States, and mobilization of the reserves as well as the draft created gaps in the civilian work force, helping some unemployed to find jobs. The bleak depression years were in the past, and all those young men on leave from the military for Christmas, this last Christmas before the war, made for a merry holiday time.

1941: Increased Involvement

Early in 1941, FDR went on the offensive. He introduced the Lend-Lease bill to Congress, and made speech after speech in support of Great Britain against Hitler's Germany. In his address to the opening session of Congress in 1941, FDR spoke of the necessity of securing the four freedoms: freedom of speech, freedom of religion, freedom from want, and freedom from fear, and followed each of them with the phrase "everywhere in the world." The president finished by saying, "To that high concept there can be no end, save victory."

There was no doubt where FDR stood regarding the war in Europe. The Lend-Lease Act, which Roosevelt signed barely thirty minutes after it passed Congress, gave him the power to wage economic war. England needed food. England needed ships. England needed war materiels. And America began to provide them.

In this last year before the war, Chevrolet would once again be the calendar year production leader with 930,293 cars, followed by Ford with 600,814 autos manufactured. The other 100,000 unit producers–Plymouth, Buick, Pontiac, Oldsmobile, Dodge, Chrysler, and Studebaker–stayed much the same as the previous year.

Defense contracts were starting to intrude on many aspects of civilian consumption by mid-1941. In April, Ford had produced the twenty-nine millionth car in its history, but it also had contracted with the government to manufacture reconnaissance cars and aircraft engines, helped develop the famous Jeep, built the B-24 bomber, and designed and built the Army's new tank, including the yet-to-be-developed engine.

The B-24 plant at Willow Run, Michigan, had a quota of 205 bombers per month, and aircraft engine and parts contracts held by Ford were valued at $480 million.

Packard for 1942 was selling fuel economy and lower prices along with Clipper beauty, warning the consumer of uncertain days ahead. Five different models accounted for 33,776 units before production stopped. Clipper styling had been so popular in 1941 that the company used the design almost entirely the following year. There was a $55 difference between the six- and eight-cylinder models, with overall prices ranging from $1,166 to $5,690. Courtesy, Dresser-Rand

The Willys-Overland Company won its first Army contract for the Jeep in July of 1941, calling for 16,000 Jeeps at $739 each. Pontiac was building military trucks, shells, and gun parts. Willow Run, near Ypsilanti, Michigan, and thirty miles from Detroit, had been a farm and orchard owned by Walter Wiard. Early in 1941, Ford representatives had bought the land as part of the planned site of the company's new bomber plant. Only Chrysler built a larger defense facility (near Chicago), and none would be as famous.

Encompassing an entire B-24 assembly line, the L-shaped Willow Run building cost $65 million and contained more than 1,600 pieces of heavy machinery. It was the largest assembly line in the country. Ultimately it reflected the brilliance of the American defense effort, but also many of the conflicts that arose from the social upheavals of the war years.

The demand for raw materials in this war economy led to changes in the food packaging industry since tin and metal were no longer available for cans. Dehydrated foods such as soup were packaged in paper. Aluminum foil became scarce, as did aluminum itself. Spam was born, and thrived as a badly needed meat import to Britain. Plastic became ubiquitous, replacing any number of natural resources like rubber, wood, leather, and tin.

The downside of this economic growth spurt was a significant rise in prices, and Roosevelt responded by creating the Office of Price Administration and Civilian Supply, known as the OPA. This office fixed priorities on literally everything, including rail and air transportation. Needless to say, the business community was not enamored and complained vociferously, but to little avail. Although the Roosevelt administration would not positively state that the country was on an unalterable track to war, it would appear from hindsight that this was the case. Certain civil liber-

ties, and quite a few corporate ones, would be curtailed in the name of national security.

Roosevelt had declared the North Atlantic to be American territory under American protection, and the Navy was actively escorting British convoys in that area. The president's offensive was gradually overwhelming his domestic enemies, and he was often abetted by the print media. When asked at a news conference why Charles Lindbergh, an Army Reserve colonel, had not been called up in the general mobilization, FDR made a reference to the untrustworthiness of the Copperheads, northern political opponents of Lincoln during the Civil War. They were generally regarded as traitors to the Union. The implication was clear: don't get in the way of the president's mission!

As a result of the Moscow-Berlin Nonaggression Pact, the president was also opposed by the American Communist Party, whose slogan was

Once again Pontiac featured the Torpedo, including ten new models as well as fifteen improvements, in this eye-catching double advertisement. The improvements include increased length and weight, but the point is made that the cars are "unchanged where quality and long life count most," inferring the need for longevity and dependability in uncertain times. Priced from $895 to $1,340, Pontiac's four major models accounted for 83,555 units for 1942. Civilian production ceased on February 10, 1942. Pontiac was already hard at work producing an antiaircraft gun for the US military. Courtesy, Pontiac Division, General Motors Corporation

24

"Keep America out of Imperialist War!" That all changed on June 22, 1941, when Germany launched Operation Barbarossa, the invasion of Russia by 120 divisions on a 2,000 mile front. Fighting was heavy, but the Germans advanced deep into the Soviet Union. This new war gave the British a respite from the Luftwaffe offensive, which now had to stage its aircraft eastward.

Prior to World War I, there had been rumors of a secret treaty between Japan and Mexico which would have given Japan a naval base at Magdalena Bay on the Pacific coast. The German Kaiser had predicted a war between the United States and Nippon, and in 1915 a Japanese warship was sighted in Mexican waters. This potential conflict cooled quickly, and Japan actually was one of the Allies during the Great War against Germany. Japan's reward was the League of Nations mandate to govern several German colonial possessions in the Pacific, known as the Mandated Islands. During the years between the world wars, many of these islands were heavily fortified by the Japanese and closed to foreigners.

In 1934, Japan had announced that in two years it was canceling both the 1922 Washington and 1930 London Naval Limitations Agreements. As a result, the Imperial Navy would build battleships with 18-inch guns, the largest in the world. During 1935 Japan quit the League of Nations after being condemned for its aggression against China. The Japanese Air Force had sunk the USS *Panay*, a Yangtze River gunboat on the China Station in 1937, reluctantly followed by a weak apology to the United States. The Empire of the Rising Sun–under the rule of the militarists, deeply suspicious and resentful of the West, and determined to improve its sources of raw materials by conquest–was serving notice that the Pacific belonged to Asia, especially Japan. Since the victory in the Spanish-American War, however, the United States believed that it too had a Pacific destiny.

Coexistence did not appear to be an alternative.

In July of 1941 America tightened the screws by refusing to sell scrap metal to Japan, as well as aviation fuel, iron ore, and a number of chemicals. Shortly thereafter, Japan was denied the use of the Panama Canal and Japanese assets in the United States were frozen. The oil embargo, which was supported by the British and the Dutch, was crushing as Japan needed to import 1,800,000 tons of oil a year to support its economy and military. There could be little doubt where this was going to end. Japan could not accept the humiliation of bowing to American demands. War became inevitable.

The Ford in 1942 was changed little from the previous year, the one exception being a lower, tighter front grille. Prices were up slightly, and ranged from $780 to $1,125. When production ceased on February 2, 1942, the company was already heavily into defense production, especially at Willow Run, a huge bomber factory in Ypsilanti, Michigan. This advertisement notes that "Now is the time when quality counts! We are glad to say that defense requirements have been met without a single reduction in the goodness of the car mechanically." Courtesy, Ford Motor Company

As the economic tempo quickened, certain products, such as automobiles, disappeared from the showrooms and used car lots of America. There wouldn't be any new ones for the duration, so the time to buy was now. Liquor became less

Next page
Studebaker had built wooden wagons used by the pioneers to cross the vast expanse of America during the westward migration in the nineteenth century. In this ad, the Studebaker is called "the car that anticipated the national defense situation" because of its economy and durability. Model year production for 1942 was 50,678, with three models priced from $744 to $1,276. Under the leadership of Raymond Loewy, famous in American marketing and advertising circles, Studebaker ranked eighth in production, and was involved in aircraft engine and truck manufacture, as well as Weasel personnel carriers in the South Bend, Indiana, plant. Courtesy, Dresser-Rand

Two leaders of the Studebaker quality vanguard—laboratory engineer O. K. Butzbach and experimental chassis foreman E. B. White.

Here's able motor assembler, Hedley Warrick, putting his more than 20 years of Studebaker experience to good account. Most Studebaker craftsmen are over 40 years of age.

For America's Defense

Studebaker is building an unlimited quantity of airplane engines, military trucks and other matériel.

The Studebaker Corporation

Studebaker builds cars and trucks that help keep the defense job moving

Low-cost transportation of high efficiency assured by brilliant engineering . . . expert craftsmanship . . . finest quality materials

THERE never was a time in American history when efficient transportation meant so much. Defense materials and defense workers must get to their destinations promptly. Millions of people, in all walks of life, depend upon motor vehicles for necessary travel—and for aid in earning a livelihood.

The situation is made to order for Studebaker, because Studebaker passenger cars, commercial cars and trucks stay on the job consistently and economically—day after day—regardless of the weather or the road conditions.

The car that anticipated the national defense situation

The economy and enduring soundness of the new 1942 President 8, Commander and Champion passenger cars—as well as the money-saving new Studebaker commercial cars and trucks—are a direct result of the brilliance of Studebaker engineering, the painstaking thoroughness of Studebaker craftsmanship and the relentless testing done in Studebaker's famed laboratories and on its great 800-acre million-dollar proving ground.

And thanks to the resourcefulness and research of Studebaker's engineering and production staffs, the traditional Studebaker standards of quality are being fully maintained.

This means that the Studebaker you buy today is a transportation investment that will still be paying you dividends—in savings and in satisfaction—on some far distant tomorrow.

New for now! This distinctive 1942 Studebaker Champion Custom Sedan, $840 delivered at factory—Built to traditional Studebaker standards of highest quality materials and craftsmanship. Engineered to deliver exceptional gasoline and oil mileage. Priced remarkably low. Equipped with many "extras at no extra cost." See it at your local Studebaker dealer's. C.I.T. terms.

HIGHEST QUALITY CAR IN LOWEST PRICE FIELD

PRICES BEGIN AT $810*

for a Champion Business Coupe

CHAMPION . . . $810 and up
COMMANDER . . $1108 and up
PRESIDENT 8 . . $1242 and up

*These are delivered prices at factory, South Bend, Indiana, as of October 1, 1941. Federal tax included. Prices and specifications subject to change without notice—but Studebaker quality will remain constant.

1

plentiful as alcohol was needed for torpedo fuel, gunpowder, and medicinal purposes. America was gearing up for conflict.

Conversely, in the midst of this national emergency that was proving so providential to the American worker, the economy came under attack by a series of union strikes. The steel industry was struck, as well as the auto manufacturers. The Congress of Industrial Organizations' (CIO) United Auto Workers (UAW) struck the Ford Motor Company, and Henry Ford was forced to negotiate with a union for the first time in his career. The strike ended on April 14, 1941, and the CIO-UAW became the bargaining agent for all the auto company workers.

Other strikes followed at the California shipyards, at a major military aircraft company, and in the lumber industry. The biggest strike of all was by John L. Lewis' United Mine Workers (UMW), who shut down the coal industry over the

issue of the closed versus open shop. Lewis ultimately agreed to arbitration by a board of which he was a member. Lewis won that arbitration on the night of December 7, 1941.

This curious mixture of optimism and war planning continued. New York Mayor Fiorello LaGuardia had been appointed head of civilian defense, and he poured his usual enthusiasm into it. At the same time, soldiers were writing "O.H.I.O." ("Over the Hill in October") all over the walls of military bases, but the 1940 draft bill was extended in August 1941, and a Gallup Poll indicated that 85 percent of those Americans polled felt war was coming.

Retired Air Corps Gen. Claire Chennault recruited American military aviators to join his American Volunteer Group, later known as the Flying Tigers, to fight for China against Japan. The Navy, facing a two-ocean war, had on active duty 115,000 officers and enlisted men aboard 17

For 1942 Plymouth redesigned its two lines, the Deluxe and the Special Deluxe, offering concealed running boards and a heavy horizontal grille. Its advertising slogan was "Buy Wisely–Buy Plymouth," and this ad touted Chrysler's broad military production. Plymouth's 1942 production was 152,427, with only 2,806 convertibles and 1,136 station wagons, priced from $812 to $1,145. Toward the end of production, which officially ended on January 31, 1942, materials ran short because of the war effort. Some Plymouths were shipped with wooden bumpers, some with reduced chrome (particularly fender trim) or chrome was painted black to achieve the "black-out" look. The armed forces impounded many Plymouths for official use. Courtesy, Chrysler Corporation

battleships, 8 aircraft carriers, and 58 submarines (plus 275 other ships).

Patriotism started creeping into magazine advertising late in 1941. Military preparedness and political freedom became themes, and the ads often featured famous people. Still, personal possessions and physical attractiveness were the overwhelmingly favored advertising topics, and continued to be so until well after the United States joined the war.

As in previous years, the automobile manufacturers featured next year's models in national advertising campaigns that got under way in September and October of 1941. Chevrolet called its vehicle "The Finest Chevrolet of All Time," and prominently displayed its defense contributions in its magazine advertising. Pontiac also included its defense aspects in new car ads (and called the ten new models Torpedoes for the second straight year), and Studebaker featured such involvement prominently in its advertisements.

Ford and Packard referred to the ominous sense of emergency in a more roundabout way,

talking about better value for the consumer's money and improved gas mileage. But the Lincoln Zephyr concentrated on its powerful V-12 engine and richly appointed interiors, a truly elegant car.

Plymouth's slogan for 1942 was "Buy Wisely," and the print ads included a short listing of Chrysler's contributions to national defense.

As the end of the year drew near, Chevrolet referred to its cars' victory performance and headlined that it was designed to "out-perform, out-save, out-last all other low-priced cars," while Ford's ads stressed the company's contributions to the nation's defense needs. The Cadillac Motor Division's advertising copy advised the buyer "to insure your family's motorcar needs for the duration of the emergency give them a Cadillac. It's good common sense for their protection."

Within a week after Pearl Harbor, Plymouth advertised that "The USA's Strength Is Power to Produce," and announced that "Plymouth Builds for America's Security."

The situation became tense. On December 4, just a few days before the attack on Pearl Harbor and the Philippines, the American automobile manufacturers were ordered by the government to cease all civilian programs and sharply reduce the use of chrome.

With the last year of peace in America coming to a close, the news from overseas was checkered. German Field Marshal Erwin Rommel had systematically defeated the British Army in North Africa, and Crete had also fallen, but in the oceanic war the German battleship *Bismarck* had been sunk, and the invasion of Russia had stalled outside Moscow with more than 200,000 German soldiers dead. On December 6, 1941, the Soviets took the offensive against the Germans, who were ill-prepared for a winter campaign.

When war finally came to the Hawaiian Islands at 7:55am on Sunday, December 7, it was certainly a surprise to most of the men and women stationed there. The death toll was 2,403, and half of the American battle fleet ended up at the bottom of the harbor. Fortunately, the carriers *Lexington, Saratoga,* and *Enterprise* were at

Another highly stylized view of the 1942 DeSoto, this time on a desert highway. As the probability of war loomed larger, DeSoto changed its advertising message slightly, emphasizing that it was "Built to Stand Up," while continuing to highlight Chrysler's contributions to the national defense. Courtesy, Chrysler Corporation

Next page
Chevrolet's message as 1941 drew to a close reflected the nation's anxiety and growing preoccupation with the threat of conflict, focusing in this ad on the longevity and "victory" performance of its cars, and highlighting the company's role in defense production. Even the ad's graphics—the border with stars under the headline—gives the ad a military look. General Motors became the biggest defense contractor in the United States, with some of the war materiels already in production highlighted in this ad. Courtesy, Chevrolet Division, General Motors Corporation

DESIGNED AND ENGINEERED
To Out·Perform, Out·Save, Out·Last
All Other Low·Priced Cars

The Finest
CHEVROLET
Of All Time

DESIGNED TO LEAD IN STYLING

Chevrolet alone of all low-priced cars has new "Leader Line" Styling, distinctive new "Door-Action" Fenders and new Body by Fisher with No Draft Ventilation.

DESIGNED TO LEAD IN PERFORMANCE

Chevrolet alone combines a powerful, thoroughly proved Valve-in-Head "Victory" Engine, Safe-T-Special Hydraulic Brakes, Unitized Knee-Action Glider Ride, and Extra-Easy Vacuum-Power Shift at no extra cost.

DESIGNED TO LEAD IN ECONOMY

Chevrolet is the most economical of all the largest-selling low-priced cars from the all-round standpoint of gas, oil and up-keep economy.

You'll find it every bit as far ahead in fleet, thrifty, Valve-in-Head "Victory" performance as it is in trim, modern, Fisher Body beauty

CHEVROLET MOTOR DIVISION, General Motors Sales Corporation, DETROIT, MICHIGAN

FOR
THE SERVICE OF
AMERICA

CHEVROLET AIDS
NATIONAL DEFENSE

MAKING MILITARY TRUCKS

MAKING AIRPLANE ENGINES

MAKING 75 MM. SHELLS

TRAINING MAINTENANCE OFFICERS

IT PAYS TO BUY THE LEADER AND GET THE LEADING BUY

5

Already-the 1942 Sensation!

THIS "MILLION DOLLAR BEAUTY" IS STEALING THE SHOW IN THE LOWEST-PRICE FIELD!

IMPORTANT! You can still buy a Nash for only one-third down, balance in 18 months—your present car may cover, or will apply at full trade-in value, on the down payment.

Specifications subject to change without notice.

Saving money was never so much *fun* before— 25 to 30 miles on a gallon of gas *at highway speed!*

ALL OVER AMERICA they're stopping and staring . . . looking at that massive front end . . . admiring those racing lines.

People *still* can't believe that this "Million Dollar Beauty" costs so little to buy and run.

● But already the word is coming back . . . from every highway . . . from thousands of new owners . . . *"Even a greater car than last year's sensational Nash!"*

They report 25 to 30 miles on a gallon at highway speed . . . trips of 500 to 600 miles on a *single tankful of gas!* (And you can imagine the money they're saving.)

They say that Four-wheel Coil Springing gives a ride un-

I'M USING **1/3 LESS** GASOLINE

500 to 600 Mile Trip on a Tankful

matched by any other car in their experience. They say that Two-way Roller Steering makes an amazing difference in traffic quickness, and parking ease.

No doubt about it, the 1942 Nash is the *news* in the lowest-price field.

It is the only car at the price that's built as a single piece—body and frame are *one welded unit,* 57% more twist-proof.

It's the only car that offers you a "Sedan Sleeper" Bed for summertime trips . . . a new

You Make Your Own Weather in a Nash

3 GREAT SERIES— 15 BRILLIANT MODELS

Greater than ever, too, are the 1942 Nash Ambassador "6" and "8". New engine development makes them more brilliant performers than ever. Still in the low- and medium-price fields!

Conditioned Air System to turn your winters into summertime comfort.

● In design, in features, and in economy—it's so far ahead of the times, it will be *new for years to come!* In every detail of construction, it's the *greatest car* that Nash has ever built.

Come down—put this "Million Dollar Beauty" through its saving paces!

New Kind of Body Built Like a Bridge

NASH

THREE NEW SERIES OF FINE MOTOR CARS

Sixes and Eights

sea and thus were spared the attack. For whatever reason, the Japanese did not bomb the main fuel depots on the Islands. Had they done so, those US ships still operable, including the carriers, would have been immobilized. The Japanese lost twenty-nine aircraft and five midget submarines, and suffered about 100 casualties. One midget sub commander was taken prisoner.

This sneak attack, which was modeled after the Japanese surprise attack against the Czar's fleet at the Battle of Port Arthur (in Lushun, China) opening the Russo-Japanese War in 1904, galvanized the American public like nothing before or since. Gone were all the arguments favoring isolationism. When the news was announced at the conclusion of a concert at Carnegie Hall in New York City, the audience stood and sang the "Star Spangled Banner." Everybody could remember for decades afterward just what they were doing when they heard the news, much like the reaction when John F. Kennedy was shot in Dallas in 1963.

On Monday morning, December 8, the military recruiting offices all across the nation had to turn volunteers away because they could not process the flood of applications. Later that day FDR gave his famous "Day of Infamy" speech to a joint session of Congress, and asked for a declaration of war against Japan. Congress readily agreed, with only one negative vote (Jeanette Rankin of Montana, who had also voted against World War I, but who now stood alone in her pacifism).

Three days later Germany and Italy, partners in the Axis, declared war against the United States. West Coast cities feared attack, and a black-out was haphazardly instituted. Japanese and Japanese-Americans made themselves scarce. Some were beaten up by home-front patriots. Later they were removed from coastal areas and sent to relocation camps. This also happened to large numbers of Germans and Italians, both foreign nationals and American citizens who were considered security risks.

All military leaves were canceled. Soldiers on their way home for the holidays were turned around in train and bus terminals and sent back to their units.

The US military leaders at Pearl, Adm. Husband E. Kimmel and Lt. Gen. Walter C. Short, were held accountable for the debacle, and both were relieved of command and forced to retire. Although congressional committees and partisan politicians would bicker for several years regarding responsibility for the military disaster and the actions of the two men prior to the attack, their careers were finished. Rumors surfaced that FDR and members of his cabinet knew much more about Japanese war intentions than they would ever admit. British historians studying recently declassified files report that Winston Churchill warned FDR on November 26 that the Japanese fleet was headed for Hawaii. This information was based on intercepts of a secret German code known to the allies as Ultra. American code breakers were reading the top-secret Japanese

Ford stressed its contributions to the nation's defense in this late 1941 advertisement. The message was that Ford was doing its part without diminishing the quality or its cars. Increased military production absorbed all the nickel available, and plastic dashboards and fixtures replaced those of zinc and chrome out of necessity. Many customers actually preferred the new look of plastic in their vehicles. Courtesy, Ford Motor Company

U.S.A.'s Strength is Power to Produce

★ A strong Automobile Industry is the backbone of National Defense.

★ What keeps the industry strong, keeps the nation strong. Keeping busy is the answer to that. Busy for defense. And busy for civilian needs.

★ Plymouth is fulfilling every U.S. defense requirement that has so far been assigned to it. Plymouth is pledged to do its utmost in every new defense production assignment.

★ Plymouth is also building under government allotment a reduced number of cars for civilian needs that in no way interferes with the No. 1 Job of defense production.

★ As long as Plymouth—and the entire automobile industry—is a healthy, vigorous business, you can expect only the finest for National Defense and for your own necessary transportation. If you need a new car, see and drive Plymouth.

PLYMOUTH
BUILDS FOR AMERICA'S SECURITY

This Plymouth advertisement was published on December 15, 1941, following too closely the attack on Pearl Harbor to have been altered in response to the onset of hostilities. Still, the copy reflects the state of tension existing in the country at the time. War had begun, and the American automobile industry was ready to do its part in the months and years ahead in order to ensure victory. The price, unpredictable in December of 1941, would be high. Courtesy, Chrysler Corporation

Purple Code for months, and reported that a fourteen-part message was being transmitted to the Japanese Embassy in Washington, with the last segment scheduled to arrive at 1:00pm (7:30am Pearl Harbor time) on December 7. Early in the message was the instruction to destroy all codes and ciphers upon receipt of the final message segment. In other words, after this message was received, there would be no further need for secret codes at the Imperial Japanese Embassy.

When a message warning of imminent hostilities was finally sent to the commanders at Pearl, it was transmitted "Deferred Precedence" by RCA Cablegram, instead of the much faster Navy transmitter available to the High Command in Washington.

Herr Hitler was surprised by the Japanese aggression. He had been trying unsuccessfully to induce Japan to attack the USSR from the Pacific, creating a two-front war for the Russians.

Hitler would now have the new American enemy to fight as a result of the Tripartite Pact with the Japanese, but without any new aid from his Nipponese allies in his fight against Russia.

The last three weeks of 1941 were disastrous for the Allied forces. Japan attacked rapidly and successfully down the Malay Peninsula, aiming for Singapore. Also invaded was the British Colony of Hong Kong, which surrendered on Christmas Day amidst unbelievable atrocities by the victorious Japanese. Murder and rape of noncombatants and prisoners were rampant. The Philippines were invaded on December 10, with much of the US Far East Air Force destroyed on the ground. American equipment and training for the new Philippine Army was woefully inferior, and by Christmas Gen. Douglas MacArthur had declared Manila an open city and retreated into the Bataan Peninsula.

Burma was attacked that month as well, and two British battleships, the *Repulse* and the *Prince of Wales,* were sunk by Japanese aircraft off the coast of Malaya. These ships had no friendly air cover, and even with their modern weaponry, could not successfully defend themselves against the enemy bombers. Wake Island was attacked on December 8, and an invasion attempt on December 11 was driven off. The Japanese returned on December 23 and successfully invaded the small atoll. All the American survivors of the battle, except for ninety-six civilian construction workers, were removed from Wake as prisoners. The ninety-six continued construction projects on Wake for the victors until October 1943, when they were executed en masse on orders from the Japanese commandant.

Prime Minister Winston Churchill arrived in Washington to address a joint session of Congress. At the Arcadia Conference late in December, England and America reiterated the war strategy of Germany first, somewhat of a surprise to the American populace, which had just witnessed the destruction of its Pacific empire by the Japanese.

The Christmas holidays in 1941 were not happy ones anywhere in the world. In the United States the people were approaching their "rendezvous with destiny" which was forecasted and, in the minds of some Americans at the time, precipitated by Franklin D. Roosevelt. However, isolationism was dead for the duration.

The automotive industry as it had always been conducted in the United States was about to come to a screeching halt, and it would be several years before the civilian population would see a new car on the streets of the nation. Dark days indeed...

DON'T tell it to the Marines—they KNOW!

*Emblem of the
United States Marine Corps*

WHAT'S BACK of that classic phrase "Tell It to the Marines"? Is it a touch of envy, perhaps? Is it admiration, in disguise?

The tough Marines don't give a hang. They just go on getting tougher. "From the Halls of Montezuma to the Shores of Tripoli" sing the Devil Dogs, and you get a glimpse of the colorful history of the United States Marine Corps—a history of brilliant service in many lands. In 95 of the years since the American Revolution the Corps has gone into action at the famous call "Send Marines!" They are *the soldiers that go to sea*—first on the war scene, *first to fight.*

If they'd let you visit the Marine Corps bases at Quantico, at San Diego, at Parris Island and Guantánamo, you'd see the Marines preparing your defense by ultra-

modern attack strategy—each division training to be its own self-contained expeditionary force, complete with planes and tanks and artillery, trucks and tractors, and engineer and supply services.

Today International Harvester, dedicating its effort to the cause of NATIONAL DEFENSE, pledges its trucks to the needs of the Armed Forces of the nation. Today the lessons of rugged, world-wide service—such service as Internationals have long been privileged to render the Marines—bear fruit of inestimable value. Wherever duty calls them in the emergency, Internationals shall play their part—Defenders all!

INTERNATIONAL HARVESTER COMPANY
180 North Michigan Avenue   Chicago, Illinois

INTERNATIONAL TRUCKS

The International Harvester (IH) Company was also hard at work building trucks for the military. In this advertisement the Marine Corps is demonstrating the half-ton weapons carrier, also used by the Army. Many of the half-ton carrier's functions were eclipsed by the Jeep, *which went into production in the latter half of 1941, but the Navy and Marines used IH trucks extensively in Pacific operations. The company also built crawler-tractors, halftracks, munitions, and guns.*
Courtesy, Navistar Archives

HOT FROM THE "LINES" AT WILLYS-OVERLAND..

HELL BENT FOR VICTORY

THEY'RE rolling off the teeming assembly lines at the Willys-Overland plants, in ever-increasing numbers—hell bent for Victory. "They" are the motorized mustangs of our modern mobile army—Willys-built Jeeps.

Climbing stiff grades, crashing streams, mud and sand—hauling men, guns and other vital materials —the Jeeps are getting more power, more speed, more action and durability out of a ton of steel and a gallon of gasoline, than has ever been done before.

It was the great Willys civilian engineering staff fresh from their fine triumphs in the Willys-American and Go-Devil engine, who collaborated with the Quartermaster Corps of the U. S. Army to create and perfect the jubilant Jeep.

But, proud as we are of this fine achievement, we are still a motor car concern—dedicated to the building of low-cost, dependable transportation for "the people" as thousands of thankful Willys car owners are realizing at this moment.

Willys-Overland Motors, Inc.

TODAY do your part. Conserve rubber and other materials vital to war equipment. Buy defense stamps and bonds. Pay taxes with a smile. Whatever the total price you pay, it will be as nothing compared to the value of continued Freedom...... TOMORROW, make your first new post-war car a Willys—"The Jeep in Civvies."

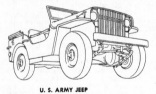

U. S. ARMY JEEP

WILLYS

MOTOR CARS  TRUCKS AND JEEPS

AMERICAR
the People's Car

The Willys Jeep became the most famous vehicle in World War II. It was used in every theater of war and added tremendously to the soldiers' mobility in rough terrain, transporting supplies, messengers, wounded personnel, and all manner of people performing the myriad tasks of war. The Willys-Overland Company alone could not produce the number of vehicles needed,

so the Ford Motor Company was given a production contract and became a major manufacturer of Jeeps during the war years. In this ad, the seeds of future sales are sown: "Tomorrow, make your first new post-war car a Willys—The Jeep in Civvies.' " Courtesy, Chrysler Corporation

The proudest assignment in our 90-year history

Studebaker BUILDS WRIGHT CYCLONE ENGINES FOR THE *Flying Fortress*

At flying fields throughout the world, airmen speak with unqualified admiration of the Flying Fortress, designed by Boeing and powered with mighty Cyclone engines. Studebaker, America's oldest manufacturer of highway transportation, welcomes the opportunity to work for victory with Wright, America's oldest builder of airplane engines. The same skill, the same Studebaker plus, that have gone into every Studebaker passenger car and truck, are today going into every implement of war being produced by Studebaker. We're proud of our assignments in the arming of our United States.

One of the most popular advertisements of its time, this ad was reprinted later in the war by popular demand. It featured an early war B-17E Flying Fortress bomber, which used Cyclone engines built by Studebaker. The B-17 was also known as the "Queen of the Skies" and was one of the legendary aircraft of World War II, with a reputation for surviving an enormous amount of punishment from enemy guns and planes, and somehow returning to base to fly and fight again. Courtesy, Dresser-Rand

First in the automotive industry to fly the Navy "E" with two stars, Fisher has also been awarded the Army-Navy "E" for its ahead-of-schedule tank production.

"Better than a rabbit's foot!"

Our fighting men have a tough job to do, and they are doing it. They are finding out, in all parts of the world, what they have to work with. They are the best judges of the weapons with which American industry is supplying them.

They know just how fast the General Sherman M-4 medium tank will go—how accurate that seventy-five is—and whether or not direct hits will bounce off the armor plate.

The test of action in actual service gives them the final answer—the only one that matters.

Here at Fisher, we want to make sure it's the *right* answer. That's

why we give our tanks, bombers, and anti-aircraft guns the best we've got in us. We're using every craft we've mastered, every special skill we've developed—and they add up to an impressive number—to give our armed forces that all-important edge.

Come the pinches, craftsmanship always counts. And it's only natural that our fighting men should rate such craftsmanship as "better than a rabbit's foot."

armament
BODY BY *Fisher*

DIVISION OF GENERAL MOTORS

Fisher built the M-4 Sherman tank at its Grand Blanc arsenal near Flint, Michigan. Originally armed with a 75mm cannon, the M-4 was upgraded with a 76mm cannon in an attempt to match opposing German tanks armed with the famous 88mm gun. It's doubtful that many American tankers chalked the Fisher logo on the fronts of their Shermans! Courtesy, General Motors

Uncle Sam's huge hand, the great American eagle, full-scale industrial production, and America's fighting soldiers in action surround the famous Jeep, a truly ubiquitous vehicle. Former President Dwight Eisenhower said it was one of the most important mechanical contributions to winning the war. Considering that the Jeep was in battle on fronts almost around the world, it was true that "The sun never sets on the fighting Jeep."
Courtesy, Chrysler Corporation

The versatile British Mosquito bomber, built by de Havilland, was very fast and also difficult to track on German radar due to its plywood construction. It was used extensively for both high-level reconnaissance and low-level bombing missions. With two 1,635hp engines and four 20mm cannons, the Mosquito flew at 408mph and carried a 4,400lb bomb load. One operational difficulty the plane experienced in Burma was the loosening of glued joints in the aircraft structure due to the region's high humidity and rains. The Mosquito used Hamilton Standard propellers manufactured by Nash-Kelvinator. Courtesy, Chrysler Corporation

Studebaker continued its father-son, home-front, and war zone connection in its advertising, this time in B-17 engine production. It appears that one Williams boy is in the infantry and the other is in the Army Air Force, while their father works the production line back home. This ad appeared in April 1943; Studebaker's anniversary year had come and gone, so there is no longer mention in ads of its ninety years of business. Courtesy, Dresser-Rand

Next page
Buick built the 1,200hp Pratt & Whitney engines that powered the B-24 Liberator bomber, four engine per plane. The aircraft's ability to fly long distances made it useful in the Pacific theater, where the difficulty of flying the B-24 in close formation, so necessary over Europe, was not as important. While the aircraft pictured does not have its guns installed, the Liberator was usually armed with ten .50 caliber machine guns and carried a crew of ten to twelve. The B-24 was also flown by the Navy as a patrol plane designated the PB4Y-1. Buick produced 1,000 aircraft engines a month during the war. Courtesy, Buick Division, General Motors Corporation

"GET UP THERE AND *SLUG!*"

It takes all kinds of planes to make an air force.

Sleek fighters. Swift interceptors. High-level bombers bristling with defensive armament.

And perhaps you'd like to know where, in this line-up, the B-24 Liberator fits in.

Well, it's swift. Not so long ago it made the headlines for the world's record Atlantic crossing — six hours, twenty minutes flying time.

Again, this plane's job is to carry a world-famed figure on missions of global strategy.

Sometimes you've heard about it in North Africa, or over the Channel, or peppering the long, battered boot that was Rome's glory.

"Liberator" to you, it's rapidly becoming "Nemesis" to the Axis—because this big, swift, four-engined ship with its broad belly full of bombs is ideal when the command is "Get up there—and slug!"

We're proud of the Liberator's record because we build its engines.

The four mighty Pratt & Whitney engines with which it starts in life come by the many-hundreds monthly from busy Buick plants.

We think a lot, as we build those engines, about the men who will ride beside them.

They get in the licks wherever there's a job to do. Just "git there fustest with the mostest" bombs.

They count a lot on their engines — both to get them over the target before they are spotted and to get them away from intercepting fighters.

So they count on us. And whatever it takes — *we're not going to let them down!*

BUICK DIVISION OF GENERAL MOTORS

The Army-Navy "E" proudly flies over Buick plants in both Flint, Mich., and Melrose Park, Ill., having been awarded to Buick people for outstanding performance in the production of better war goods.

WHEN BETTER AUTOMOBILES ARE BUILT BUICK WILL BUILD THEM

VICTORY THROUGH PROGRESS

NOW BLUEPRINTS ARE BORN
on the battlefield

THE lessons of this war come hard, fast and many, leaving no time for the measured, steady progress by which the automobile was perfected in peacetime.

So, close up behind our fighting men — close enough to know the sting of desert sandstorms, the taste of salt spray, the sound of overhead dogfights — General Motors maintains a staff of some 250 special field technicians and observers.

On every front, these men gather firsthand reports of General Motors-built war goods in action, assisting military men to find possible improvements in structure or design. From the reports they send back, blueprints for new and better instruments of victory can be shaped by home-front teamwork between

General Motors engineers and Army and Navy experts.

Such on-the-spot search for technological progress is but one instance of how General Motors carries out its fourfold wartime purpose — which is to increase the volume of war goods, to reduce costs, to make most efficient use of materials and to maintain high Army and Navy standards through constant enlargement of General Motors "know-how."

This "performance reconnaissance" represents a step taken primarily to hasten victory. It likewise serves to spur progress when victory is won. For from what is learned in the stern test of war are being gathered many lessons to make more bountiful the blessings of the coming peace.

GENERAL MOTORS
"VICTORY IS OUR BUSINESS"

PROGRESS THROUGH VICTORY

General Motors' generic advertisements announced "Progress Through Victory" as one of its 1943 slogans. GM led all American manufacturers in wartime production, and provided its own technicians to the military, as well as training 62,346 Army and Navy personnel at GM training centers in the United States. This full-color ad noted that "from what is learned in the stern test of war are being gathered many lessons to make more bountiful the blessings of the coming peace." Courtesy, General Motors

Some go Through – Some go Over !

Under the direction, and with the coopera-tion, of Army Ordnance—Cadillac has de-veloped, and is building, what have proved to be two of the most effective pieces of armament in the Arsenal of Democracy.

One is the M-5 Light Tank—a fast, quick, highly-maneuverable weapon, armed with a high velocity, 37 mm. cannon. This tough, speedy, hard-hitting tank is one of America's great "surprise weapons"—ideal for upsetting enemy formations. Like a speedy halfback, it darts through the slightest opening in the line,

or "runs the ends," as the need may be. It is almost as fast as a motor car.

The other is the M-8 mounting the Army's 75 mm. Howitzer cannon. Utilizing the same chassis as the M-5, it gives to demolition artillery a degree of mobility it has never known before. With this weapon, big guns can follow their targets—keep the position from which they can do the most good.

The two units that give these weapons their power and maneuverability were developed by Cadillac in peacetime: the Cadillac V-type

engine and the Hydra-Matic transmission.

The quickness with which these peacetime units were sent to war not only attests their inborn quality of design and construction—but it indicates the splendid manner in which Army Ordnance has utilized the nation's resources to astound the world with its armament program.

LET'S ALL

BACK THE ATTACK

Cadillac continued to build the M-5 light tank, while adding the M-8 tank destroyer to its production line. They both used the same chassis, but the M-8 mounted a 75mm pack Howitzer in an open turret. It carried forty-six rounds of ammunition. Cadillac built 1,778 M-8s between September 1942 and January 1944. The ad said the M-5 is "like a speedy halfback, it darts through the slightest opening in the line, or 'runs the ends,' as the need may be." Courtesy, Cadillac Division, General Motors Corporation

Chevrolet-built Pratt & Whitney engines power America's mightiest warplanes, including the C-82 Flying Boxcar, shown above.

CHEVROLET

America's Automotive Leader Gears All Its Resources to

THE BIGGEST TRANSPORT JOB OF ALL TIME"

on land ··· in the air ··· all around the world

BUY MORE WAR BONDS
HELP SPEED THE VICTORY

Chevrolet has produced more than 475,000 military trucks in three different types, serving our fighting men everywhere.

Popularly called the "Flying Boxcar," the twin-tailed C-82 Packet had a range of 1,000 miles and a maximum speed of 248mph, while carrying a crew of five. Its large rear cargo doors facilitated cargo loading and unload-ing. Chevrolet manufactured its Pratt & Whitney en-gines. Chevrolet also produced nearly half a million military trucks. Courtesy, Chevrolet Division, General Motors Corporation

The land-based B-25 Mitchell medium bomber was famous for its role in the Doolittle Raid against Tokyo, which was launched from the US carrier Hornet. Continuing in a tactical role, some B-25s were armed with a 75mm cannon for low-level attack missions. When fired, the recoil from the gun seemed to halt the aircraft in mid-flight for a split second. This ad had a box listing the "victims of this newest, heaviest form of aerial artillery." Courtesy, Oldsmobile Division, General Motors Corporation

Cadillac exhibited good timing with this ad in June 1944 since D-day, the cross-channel invasion of northern Europe, took place that month. The P-39 Airacobra in the center of this illustration was not as prominent in the European theater as the P-47 Thunderbolt or the P-51 Mustang. Courtesy, Cadillac Division, General Motors Corporation

Next page top
Chevrolet was a major manufacturer of military trucks, as GM provided 854,000 of them by war's end. In contrast, the Germans and the Russians depended on horse-drawn vehicles to carry much of their equipment. The Japanese also used animals for transport in the China and Burma campaigns, but most of the island battles did not require much in the way of land transport compared to Europe. Courtesy, Chevrolet Division, General Motors Corporation

Next page bottom
America's overwhelming military production might was evidenced in the output and diversity of just one auto manufacturer, namely Chevrolet. Amphibious vehicles, B-24s, C-47s and C-53s, trucks, naval guns, and anti-aircraft weapons represent Chevrolet's contributions to victory. The auto maker again listed its accomplishments in this July 1944 full-color, two-page ad. Courtesy, Chevrolet Division, General Motors Corporation

The US Army was very mobile, although most infantry soldiers remember a lot more walking than riding in trucks. In Europe, the speed of the American advance allowed the troops to bypass heavily defended areas and continue the penetration of Germany. Enemy cities and towns were usually decimated by air attacks and heavy artillery bombardments before the ground troops entered to finish the fight. GMC noted in this ad that although civilians couldn't yet buy new vehicles, trucks were available in the US to qualified commercial customers. Many GMC amphibian Ducks are still being used today, often as open-air tourist buses. Courtesy, GMC Truck Division, General Motors Corporation

International trucks used this garishly but patriotically painted civilian armored truck to promote the purchase of war savings bonds. They were issued in denominations of $25, $50, $100, $500, and $1,000. Americans bought them at 75 percent of maturity value, redeemable in ten years. Corporate investors could purchase in denominations up to $1 million. Brink's operated 600 International trucks in its fleet and clocked seven million miles a year. Brink's transported more than $125 billion in War Bond money in 1944. Courtesy, Navistar Archives

Next page
This B-24 was manufactured primarily for the Navy and was called the PB4-2 Privateer. Its modifications included a single tail fin and a 7ft fuselage extension, as well as improved stabilization and control. It also had two upper turrets (not shown) and was powered by four 1,350hp Pratt & Whitney engines built by Buick. The Navy received 739 Privateers but only seven, designated the YB24-N, were delivered to the Air Force before production was canceled. In this June 1945 ad, Buick's "When better automobiles..." slogan is back. During the war, it had been revised to read, "When better armaments..." Courtesy, Buick Division, General Motors Corporation

She's got four "B's" in her bonnets!

She comes of a long line of battle-tested veterans with a gallant record over Europe, Africa and the lands and waters of the Far Pacific.

Thousands have gone before her—to strike their mighty blows for freedom, and to make that name "Liberator" famed and feared the world around.

As you may have guessed from the headline—Buick powers the Liberator.

As of June first, Buick factories and Buick people have sent forth approximately 75,000 Pratt & Whitney aircraft engines, destined with few exceptions to find their places in the four nacelles of these far-ranging B-24 bombers.

It has been a proud assignment, and a solemn one.

For our pride has been tempered by the constant knowledge that men's lives sometimes would depend on the way we here at home did our share of the job.

So our pride isn't in the numbers—important though volume may be to victory. It's in the way letters have been coming back from men who fly these B-24 bombers—men who take time off from the grim chore of fighting to tell us that those "B's" in the Liberators' bonnets are making good.

There's something pretty wonderful about having such a great gang for friends.

Buick will be glad to furnish, without cost, a full-color reprint of this advertisement to those interested in this airplane. Write to BUICK MOTOR DIVISION, FLINT 2, MICHIGAN.

The Army-Navy "E" proudly flies over all Buick plants.

BUICK POWERS THE LIBERATOR

WHEN BETTER AUTOMOBILES ARE BUILT BUICK WILL BUILD THEM

Every Sunday Afternoon — GENERAL MOTORS SYMPHONY OF THE AIR — NBC Network

Bonds Buy Bombs — BUY MORE WAR BONDS

Other jobs on BUICK'S Work-Sheet

In addition to supplying all the engines for the Liberator, Buick is now producing the Pratt & Whitney engines shown at left. At the top is a heavy-duty power plant developed for use in the cargo-carrying twin-engine Douglas C-47. The engine...

THE HELLCATS ARE ON THE PROWL

BUICK BUILDS THE HELLCAT

THE Army calls them 76-mm. Gun Motor Carriages—designation M-18. But to Buick men who designed and built them, in cooperation with Army Ordnance—and to Tank Destroyer Command forces who fight in them—they're Hellcats.

The name fits.

They are tank-killers with the pace of a panther and the lethal strike of the king cobra.

They're so fast they run rings around anything but their brothers, and they master obstacles that stop other vehicles cold.

They can split an enemy tank at several miles—and thanks to springing born of Buick's work on your car, they can romp down roads at passenger car speeds.

And now they're on the prowl.

It has been twenty-odd months since we started work on these sluggers as answers to the vaunted Tiger tank. Twenty-odd months of designing, building, testing, perfecting.

More than a year ago they went into production, and several months ago we knew they were on their way, in quantities, to undisclosed battlefields.

They have shown what they can do there. They've added their force to the Great Effort—and because of them, American men have had the benefit of a harder-hitting weapon against tanks, pillboxes, strong points and machine-gun nests.

We're mighty glad that's so. Not just because this is a Buick baby. But because it's a good American weapon, built in our way, for use of our own kind.

More power to it, say we—and to those gallant men in uniform for whom we sweated it out!

WHAT IS THE "HELLCAT"?

The Hellcat is a 76-mm. Gun Motor Carriage bearing the Army designation, Model M-18. With 55 mph speed, maximum maneuverability, high fire power, and all-steel, center-guided tracks, it can smash tanks at several miles.

Designed and built by Buick in cooperation with the Ordnance Department, it has proved superior to latest versions of the German Tiger Tank in actual battle and is 30 mph faster. Special Buick-designed suspension, including knee-action principles, enables the Hellcat to fight running battles when necessary. It masters obstacles that stop other vehicles, fords water traps and streams and is almost as easy to run as an automobile.

Ordered on January 28, 1943 after demonstration of pilot models, the Hellcat has been in regular production since July, 1943. All allies have asked to be supplied with it.

YOU LEND A HAND WHEN YOU LEND YOUR DOLLARS ★ INVEST IN MORE WAR BONDS

[Buick will be glad to furnish, without cost, a full-color reprint of this advertisement to those interested in this important new weapon. Write to Buick Motor Division, Flint 2, Michigan]

BUICK DIVISION OF GENERAL MOTORS

Every Sunday Afternoon — GENERAL MOTORS SYMPHONY OF THE AIR — NBC Network

WHEN BETTER AUTOMOBILES ARE BUILT BUICK WILL BUILD THEM

The M-18 tank destroyer carried a crew of five and was armed with the 76mm gun used on late-model Sherman tanks. It also carried a .50 caliber machine gun. Buick built 2,507 of them from July 1943 to October 1944. A version known as the M-39 was used as an ammunition vehicle and as an armored personnel carrier. With its 400hp air-cooled gas engine, the Hellcat was capable of 50mph. It also incorporated torsion bar suspension. Courtesy, Buick Division, General Motors Corporation

The Army-Navy "E" flies above seven Fisher Body plants for excellence in aircraft production and from two others for tank production, while the Navy "E," with five stars, is flown by still another Fisher Body plant for its naval ordnance work.

STRICTLY SUPER

IT'S a great day for our side whenever our flyers sweep out over the target in those fleets of B-29 Superfortresses.

Of course, Fisher Body does not make the complete Superfortress. But it does make huge dorsal fins, horizontal stabilizers, rudders, elevators and ailerons. Yes, and flaps, wing tips, outboard wings and turret parts, too.

More than that, Fisher Body makes engine nacelles — using more than 18,000 jigs and tools to turn out the 3,000 parts that are required for each nacelle.

Fisher Body is proud of its part in building this great Boeing-designed ship. All the skills and techniques inherent in the Fisher Body organization are concentrated on giving superworkmanship to the Superfortress. Yet it is but one of many war jobs including big guns, delicate aircraft instruments, tanks, and assemblies for other bombers.

And you may be certain that as long as war equipment is needed, the fine crafts-manship symbolized by the "Body by Fisher" emblem will keep right on backing up the courageous crews who pilot these great superplanes.

• •

Every Sunday Afternoon
GENERAL MOTORS SYMPHONY OF THE AIR
NBC Network

armament
BODY BY *Fisher*

D I V I S I O N   O F   G E N E R A L   M O T O R S

Fisher Body was a major contributor to the B-29 Super-fortresses of the Twentieth Air Force, which began its campaign against Japan from India and then from China before shifting to the Mariana Islands. The young Chinese boy in this illustration is giving the "V for Victory" sign as he stands in solidarity with an American pilot. Courtesy, General Motors

46

YOU'LL BE "ON THE BEAM"...

There's a *Ford* in your future!

It's a picture that will have to wait. America has an important job to do before your smart, peacetime Ford can be produced.

... But when your new Ford does arrive, you'll be proud of it. For it will be big and roomy—have plenty of "go". Its styling will be youthful, beautiful.

Inside and out, it will be rich appearing —with many refinements. Naturally, it will be thrifty and reliable—as all Ford cars have been for more than 40 years. ... Yes, exciting new fun is in the offing for you. For some day the necessary word will come through. And we'll be ready to start our production plans. Un-

til that time, however, the full Ford resources will continue to be devoted to the needs of final Victory.

FORD MOTOR COMPANY

Ford's crystal ball featured a picnic, complete with a pretty young woman and her beau. The first lieutenant is wearing his pilot wings, an Air Force shoulder patch, and three decorations: the Distinguished Service Medal, the Distinguished Flying Cross, and the Asiatic-Pacific campaign medal. Pretty good! Yet the ad copy noted, "It's a picture that will have to wait. America has an important job to do before your smart, peacetime Ford can be produced." Courtesy, Ford Motor Company

These things will live

There will be a hush that deepens with the night as the noisy tremors of a world at war subside . . . Mankind again will live with dignity and pride in the clean atmosphere of triumph over tyranny . . . Hope is justifiably strong as another Yuletide draws near that a great new epoch in the affairs of men and nations may not be too far away—that out of the suffering and destruction of war will flower a lasting peace truly worthy of the sentiments men voice at Christmas.

STUDEBAKER

Part of America's life and traditions since 1852

Many Americans cherished an image of small-town America in winter as a special time, and Studebaker captured that feeling in this advertisement. The company seemed wary of stating the reason why Christmas is celebrated, instead referring to "the sentiments men voice at Christmas" that would hopefully create a lasting peace. Courtesy, Dresser-Rand

CHAPTER 2

Dark Days Indeed: 1942

The shock and humiliation of Pearl Harbor, magnified by the loss of so many American, British, and Dutch possessions to the Japanese in the Pacific, continued unabated into early 1942. The courageous defenders of the Philippines steadily retreated before the victorious Asiatic enemy, and German submarines determinedly sailed west across the Atlantic for the coastal shipping lanes of North America. There was great consternation that the mainland would be bombed and shelled (both these fears would come to fruition in the weeks and months to come), and reports of false sightings and attacks were commonplace.

What is really astonishing is that with all the rumor of war, and news of war, when hostilities actually broke out the United States did not impose a black-out on the East Coast cities for three months, giving German U-boats the opportunity to attack tankers and freighters from seaward at night with the vessels silhouetted against the coastal glare. Mayor Fiorello LaGuardia was afraid that German subs would come into New York Harbor, and one did just that on the night of January 15, 1942, as the crew spotted landmarks from an old tourist map. In the first six months of 1942 the U-boats stalking the Eastern seaboard sank more than 400 ships with the loss of 5,000 sailors' lives. There were only 20 ships detailed to the Navy's Eastern Sea Frontier, which extended more than 1,000 miles from Maine to the Carolinas, and not one of them was a destroyer, since all the available destroyers were assigned to convoy duty in the North Atlantic. None of the patrol craft could match the surface speed of a German submarine, and their surface weaponry was also inferior to a German sub's deck cannon. It would take a major naval effort by the Americans and the British to bring the situation under control.

In fact, it soon became necessary for many things to be brought under control from the government's point of view. The population was admonished not to hoard sugar, and the White House set the example by abolishing dessert for the duration. Civilians went to the end of the line when requesting airline and train reservations. The military, government employees, and business executives with war priorities rode first.

But the biggest blow was to private automobile ownership. Both gasoline and tires were rationed in early 1942 (actually, gas station owners in August 1941 had been ordered by the government to restrict sale hours in order to reduce consumption), and civilians were no longer allowed to buy new automobiles as the Office of Price Administration (OPA) banned their purchase.

Most of the few 1942 models available were impounded for use by the military. All non-military automobile production stopped by government order, and an OPA "Certificate to Purchase 1942 Model Passenger Car for Use" was required. A person or business holding such a certificate was authorized to buy "one 1942 model passenger car of any type," or one of two other types of cars: a 1942 model passenger car "with a list price over $1,500," or "of convertible type."

Next page
Advertisements for 1942 cars disappeared very quickly from the nation's magazines once war began. Oldsmobile produced only 66,303 production year models for 1942, before government decree closed down all auto manufacturing for the duration, ending the company's attempt to produce the B-44 featured here. As with all General Motors divisions, Oldsmobile was heavily involved in defense production, indicated by the additional inserts to this advertisement. On January 1, 1942, the Oldsmobile Motor Works became the Oldsmobile Division of General Motors, forty-six years after its founding by Ransom Eli Olds in 1896. Courtesy, Oldsmobile Division, General Motors Corporation

Only HYDRA-MATIC* *is* Completely *Automatic!*

DEFENSE
FIRST
WITH
OLDSMOBILE

SPECIFICATIONS SUBJECT TO CHANGE WITHOUT NOTICE

HYDRA-MATIC

NO CLUTCH TO PRESS !.. NO GEARS TO SHIFT !
SAVES *10* TO *15%* ON GAS !

No Clutch To Press! NOTHING "semi" or "half-way" about Hydra-Matic! Hydra-Matic is the *one* drive that goes *all* the way to make driving simpler, easier and safer. It banishes the entire conventional clutch mechanism—discards the clutch pedal completely. It does *all* of the shifting *all* of the time, throughout the four forward speeds. *That's* what it does for

you. Now, what does Hydra-Matic do for *performance?* It steps up take-off, peps up pick-up and smooths out open-road cruising. And, because four speeds forward permit reduced engine speeds, it cuts down gas consumption by 10 to 15 per cent. Try Hydra-Matic in the new Oldsmobile B-44—Six or Eight. It's the automatic drive that makes an automatic hit—and no other drive is like it!

*Optional at Extra Cost

YOU CAN ALWAYS COUNT ON
OLDSMOBILE B-44
IT'S QUALITY·BUILT TO LAST !

BETTER
LOOKING, BETTER
LASTING, BETTER BUILT!

CANNON and SHELL for the U.S.A.

To serve America's armament needs, Oldsmobile *right now* is engaged in the mass production of automatic cannon for fighting planes . . . turning out high-caliber artillery shell at the rate of thousands a day . . . and, at the same time, setting up for still further large-scale defense assignments. With facilities that remain, Oldsmobile is building the Olds B-44—but building it in limited quantities in order to release vital metals for other defense requirements. Thus, Oldsmobile contributes in two important ways to our country's armament program.

On February 2, 1942, the last civilian vehicle, a Ford with the serial number 30-337 509, came off the line. Ford's calendar year production was only 43,307 cars in 1942, and model year production was only 160,432 units. The previous year the company had built and sold more than 600,000 cars, while the more popular Chevrolet had sold 930,293 autos. In 1942, Chevrolet production dropped to 45,472 cars. Buick plummeted from 316,251 units in 1941 to 16,601 in 1942. Many of the automobiles manufactured in those last production days had parts that were painted instead of chromed because of wartime restrictions.

People just couldn't get a new car, and Detroit's assembly lines were converted to military production—except for a few that produced military staff cars. Ironically, all this was happening at a time when Americans were on the move as

never before, as the war economy became a reality. Both men and women were enlisting at a rapid pace, and the draft for men over eighteen years of age was in effect. Every imaginable industry geared up for war, and expansion was evident in every aspect of the economy.

Women were doing the job at home and on the farm, in stores, factories, and offices. A select group became civilian pilots for the military, ferrying aircraft where needed within the continental United States. Women also descended on the nation's capital in droves for jobs in the ever-expanding wartime government.

Workers of both sexes and all creeds and colors were desperately needed; President Roosevelt's ambitious production schedule for 1942 called for 60,000 airplanes, 45,000 tanks, and 20,000 antiaircraft guns, as well as 8 million tons of merchant shipping. The vast majority of the first three categories would be produced by Detroit, which possessed the technology and tech-

Chevrolet's Car Conservation Plan attempted to keep car dealerships open even though there were no new cars to sell. These outlets would be necessary after the war ended, but in the meantime they needed a plan to maintain their locations and, of course, a flow of cash for the dealers. Understanding that consumer car production wasn't likely to resume for quite some time, the auto makers encouraged thorough maintenance of existing vehicles. The mechanics certainly wore clean overalls! Courtesy, Chevrolet Division, General Motors Corporation

Studebaker appeared to be cautioning the American public that manufacturing conversion would not occur overnight. With ninety years of experience, and producing military equipment for the sixth time in a national emergency, Studebaker planned to be in the forefront of defense production. It certainly wasn't the way the company had hoped to spend its milestone anniversary year. Courtesy, Dresser-Rand

nique of mass production. In early 1942, 100 companies were responsible for 82.6 percent of the country's war production, with three companies responsible for 17.4 percent. By the end of the war, the automobile industry was responsible for 20 percent of the nation's war production by dollar volume.

All was not peaceful in Detroit, however. During the first ten months of 1942, there were more than 700 strikes ranging in length from two hours to twenty days, almost all of them illegal considering labor's pledge to FDR not to strike. There was much confusion and many hard feelings between management, labor, and the government, with the latter taking much of the blame

for work stoppages due to red tape and the many overlapping agencies that became involved in any dispute.

It became more and more apparent in the months to come that this would be a long war. (Great Britain and the Commonwealth had already been fighting for more than two years.) Axis flags flew over North Africa, much of the Pacific Basin and Asia, and almost all of Europe. The casualty rate in particular, and the loss of materiel were being harshly brought home to the American people, albeit without television, by the defeats being suffered in the Philippines. The outrages perpetrated against American and Filipino prisoners of war by their brutal and sadistic Japanese captors after the fall of Bataan in April 1942 did not become common knowledge for some time in the United States, sparing the soldiers' families for the moment. The same conditions prevailed for the Australian, British, and Dutch military and civilians who fell into Japanese hands. But for now, defeat was more than enough to digest. Horror and outrage would come later.

Mass precision manufacturing techniques had been perfected by the US automobile industry over the several decades prior to World War II, and resulted in a remarkable lessening in unit cost as defense production increased. Buick proudly reports that its conversion of farmland into a factory that produced its first aircraft engine in only 243 days was Buick's way of remembering Pearl Harbor. Women apparently were not yet a significant part of Buick's work force (although they would be eventually) because the copy read, "We men of Buick..." Buick also altered its corporate slogan in the ad to read, "When better war goods are built, Buick will build them." Courtesy, Buick Division, General Motors Corporation

General Motors urged all Americans to extend the lives of their cars by conserving rubber and gasoline through preventative maintenance done by the local authorized GM dealer. The company offered a free automobile users' guide to everyone who requested it, "aimed at hastening the day of final victory." In April 1942, about the time this ad ran, there were thirty-three million cars on America's highways. Courtesy, General Motors

On February 9, 1942, the country went on War Time, and everybody moved their clocks ahead one hour by government decree, expecting to save 700 million kilowatts of electricity a year. Other things started tightening up on the domestic front as well. Late in April, sugar was rationed for the general population, with registration for ration cards being administered by the nation's schoolteachers. In the months and years ahead, rationed items included red meat, butter, fats, and even some canned vegetables. It was necessary for each family member to register for a ration card and use ration books and stamps while shopping. However, restaurants were not rationed so if one had the money, and many people did, dining out was an alternative and civilians could still enjoy the munificence of the American farm.

With food shortages looming on the horizon, the government sought to reinstitute a First World War concept: the war gardens. The National Victory Garden Program was created under the US Secretary of Agriculture and its slogan was "Vegetables for Vitality for Victory," with much emphasis placed on family health. Everybody had a victory garden, and the local newspapers patriotically proclaimed their virtues of fitness and nutrition.

Service flags were hung in the windows of homes that had a relative in the military, and many homes had more than one star on the flag. Another small flag, with a gold star, also appeared in windows. It signified the death of a family member in the war, and soon chapters of Gold Star Mothers formed all across the nation. The cost of unremitting world war was becoming evident, and for several months military and administration officials did not release the total number of casualties being suffered in the field.

Early in the war there was still some hope for civilians to purchase new cars if they could qualify under the OPA (Office of Price Administration) eligibility rules listed in this Chevrolet ad. However, the few cars available were quickly allocated, and most Americans had to make do with what they were driving for the duration. When the US first got involved in the war, many cars still at dealerships were impounded for official use by the military and various government agencies. Courtesy, Chevrolet Division, General Motors Corporation

Featured in this stylized advertisement are the P-39 Airacobra fighter plane and the M-4 Sherman tank, both of which were supplied with ammunition manufactured by Oldsmobile. The P-39's performance did not measure up to other more famous American fighter aircraft, and was often used in a ground-support role. Thousands of them were exported to the USSR, where they performed valiantly for the Soviet Air Force. The Sherman tank was the main battle tank of the US Army throughout the war. Courtesy, Oldsmobile Division, General Motors Corporation

TRADE-IN YOUR GAS-WASTER
FOR A GAS-SAVER!

"GAS-SAVING SPECIAL" USED CARS

SUCH AS THESE
NEXT-TO-NEW 1940 AND '41 OLDSMOBILES!

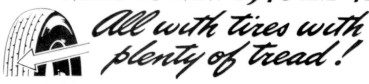
All with tires with plenty of tread!

HERE'S an opportunity that may not come again until the war is over. Oldsmobile dealers are offering a special selection of economy-conditioned, late-model used cars to replace the thousands of "gas-wasters" still on the roads. They're the last of the trade-ins on pre-war cars. They're cars bought back from men who joined the Service. They're 1940 and '41 models, with plenty of good, safe, dependable miles left in them. Many are Oldsmobiles! Every one has been tuned and adjusted to give you extra miles from war-grades of fuel. Every car in this special group has plenty of tread on its tires to last you a long, long time. Now is the time to think about what you'll be driving until new cars are built again. Now is the time to trade in your "gas-waster" for a *gas-saver!* Get the car that'll take you most miles per gallon, from your local Oldsmobile dealer. *No priority purchase certificates are necessary.*

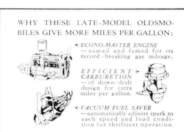

WHY THESE LATE-MODEL OLDSMO-BILES GIVE MORE MILES PER GALLON:

ECONO-MASTER ENGINE — named and famed for its record-breaking gas mileage.

EFFICIENT CARBURETION — of down-draft design for extra miles per gallon.

VACUUM FUEL SAVER — automatically adjusts spark to each speed and load condi-tion for thriftiest operation.

PLUS ALL THESE LONG-LIFE FEATURES

Electro-Hardened Aluminum Pistons; Completely Cooled Cylinders; Rifle-Drilled Connecting Rods; 100% Full-Pressure Lubrication; Heavy-Duty Air-Cooled Generator; Sturdy Fisher Body; Rigid X-Mem-ber Frame; Knee-Action Wheels; Modern Coil Springs All Around; 7-Bearing Hypoid Rear Axle; Super-Hydraulic Brakes; and (on many models) gas-saving, engine-saving, car-saving HYDRA-MATIC DRIVE!

OLDSMOBILE DEALERS
OF AMERICA

As the few 1942 model cars quickly disappeared from dealers' showrooms, Oldsmobile offered used "gas-savers" acquired from prewar trade-ins and men called up to active military service in trade for civilian "gas-wasters." All had been retuned to save gas and "had plenty of tread on their tires." Best of all, no priority purchase certificates were necessary. Courtesy, Oldsmobile Division, General Motors Corporation

54

Visiting nurses such as the one featured in this General Motors ad certainly needed transportation to make their appointed rounds, especially with so many doctors called into the military service. GM dealers offered their expertise in keeping cars on the road, and even restoring vehicles to "fresh usefulness." The focus of automobile company advertising was still in transition from peacetime needs to wartime production in the early summer of 1942. Courtesy, General Motors

Franklin Roosevelt was in his third term as president in 1942, the only chief executive many Americans had ever known. Oldsmobile featured him in this plea to spur production, while proudly acknowledging the efforts of its plant workers who were building the sinews of war. As the ad copy noted, some auto makers' production plants had been producing military equipment since early 1941, well before the US was directly participating in the fighting. Courtesy, Oldsmobile Division, General Motors Corporation

The government was well aware of the power of advertising, and during the Roosevelt years there had been various investigations and New Deal-inspired movements which questioned the desirability of an industry that promoted unnecessary and harmful consumption of nonvital goods at purported great cost to the purchaser. Some government officials viewed advertising as "sheer economic waste," according to a 1942 *Collier's* editorial. The US Treasury Department considered removing advertising as a legitimate business expense. Now the situation had changed dramatically. The War Advertising Council was formed in January 1942 as part of the Federal Office of War Information to unify national attitudes and opinions in favor of the administration's wartime and postwar goals. Mobilizing for victory included publicity for war bond drives, rationing, victory gardens, scrap drives, public acceptance of women in the military, volunteerism, and the need for vigilant security.

That same *Collier's* editorial extolled advertising as "a vital instrument of public service" and "a means of winning public support," while stating that "getting any idea clearly understood by millions and tens of millions of men and women is an appallingly vast undertaking."

It took several months for the ad industry and its clients to realign media campaigns and focus on wartime needs as well as propaganda symbols. This was evidenced by some very unimaginative advertising in the early part of 1942, which was remedied as the year progressed. In another article, *Collier's* stated that America's victories at the time were industrial rather than military, and that advertising needed to keep alive the great trade names of industry, symbols of enterprise that would ensure victory and energize the postwar world.

Needless to say, national magazines were just the right medium to handle the job. Automotive advertising was especially pressed to come up with interesting copy for civilian consumption.

Pontiac received the first armament contract given out before the war, and was well into production of the Swiss Oerlikon antiaircraft gun by mid-1942. The initial contract called for 19,100 weapons at $7,000 each for the Navy. Ultimately, Pontiac reduced the cost of the Oerlikon by 23 percent. The voluntary censoring of production figures in this ad immediately catches the reader's attention, and reinforces Pontiac's commitment to national security as well as production goals. Courtesy, Pontiac Division, General Motors Corporation

The aircraft pictured here, including the L-4 observation plane and the B-17 bomber, feature early war insignia. The red ball in the middle of a white star was removed to avoid confusion with Japanese markings, especially by the Australians, who shot at anything in the air early in the war. The tank is the medium M-3 Lee, which was limited by the lack of a full traverse turret, and was exported to Great Britain as the Grant. Also pictured is the ubiquitous Jeep.

Used cars were a topic while they were available from dealers, and car manufacturers also advertised that their dealers were the best place to perform maintenance on cars that had to last for the duration. Chevrolet proclaimed itself "Headquarters for Victory Service on All Makes of Cars and Trucks," providing any number of statistics about the nation's continuing dependence on cars and trucks, and thus on the services of the trained automotive mechanics available at the local Chevrolet dealership.

For many young people, the chaos and the energy of the war economy gave them a freedom they had never known at home. There was plenty of fun to be had, plenty of money to be made and spent, plenty of sex available and excitement to explore. Frank Sinatra was a matinee idol, Bing Crosby crooned, the bands played, and everybody partied after work and on the weekends. Eighty-five million people went to the movies every week, so the movie industry was having a wonderful war. Movies with a military theme would come soon enough, but most of the films in the theaters in early 1942 had been made during peacetime a few short months earlier.

Automobile manufacturers employed many of these mobile war workers, with Hudson and Pon-

Next page

The P-40F fighter, known as the Warhawk, was one of a series built by Curtiss Aircraft. Packard did a masterful job in producing the Rolls-Royce Merlin engine that powered it. While not as maneuverable as the Japanese fighters it often opposed, the P-40 possessed better armor, as well as self-sealing gas tanks and superior diving characteristics. Gen. Claire Chennault's Flying Tigers of the American Volunteer Group in China pioneered teamwork tactics that actually gave the P-40 an advantage against the Japanese in combat. The ad's headline was an adaptation of Packard's car-selling slogan, "Ask the Man Who Owns One." Courtesy, Dresser-Rand

Ask the man who *FLIES* one!

1. "I'll take this Warhawk any time for combat flying," said one Curtiss test pilot after taking up this latest thing in pursuit ships, the P-40 F. Army pilots are now using the *Warhawk* against the enemy. Whisking "upstairs" in a hurry is its specialty.

2. The Warhawk's terrific power makes only short take-offs necessary. That was a comment of another test pilot. The *Warhawk* climbs fast—and its Packard-built Rolls-Royce engine is the source of the power back of that fast-climbing performance.

3. It's a thrill to see a trio of Warhawks swoop down on an objective, shoot upward and "blossom out"—but no more thrilling than it is to the pilots! Fliers say this combination of plane and power makes the P-40 F a wonder of maneuverability.

4. Loaded with terrific striking force, moving with bullet-like speed, the *Warhawk* is the newest member of the famous Curtiss P-40 family.

It is powered by a Packard-built Rolls-Royce engine—the same design that powers the versatile, battle-tested Spitfires and Hurricanes of Great Britain.

These precision engines, as they flow in great numbers off Packard's continuously moving production line, are like jeweled watch movements—so fine and so finished is their workmanship.

This isn't unusual at Packard. Since the last war Packard has precision-powered equipment that rolls, flies, caterpillars, and scoots through water: cars, planes, tanks, record-breaking speedboats—and now the hard-hitting, fast-moving PT boats you hear so much about.

When the war is over, Packard will be making cars again—better cars and finer cars. For many advances in making wartime motors can be translated into automotive improvements—and they'll be there in your future Packard!

tiac building antiaircraft guns, Chrysler building tanks, and Studebaker turning out aircraft engines, as did Packard. The latter also provided engines for the romantic and speedy PT boat, made famous when a small number were used to successfully evacuate General MacArthur, his family, and staff from the Philippines in early 1942.

General Motors led all other producers with $1 billion in annual defense contracts. Ford manufactured aircraft engines at its Willow Run plant, which was so massive that motorcycles and cars were used by messengers on the immense assembly line.

Interestingly, although manufacturers were accused of war profiteering, in many instances mass-production techniques so necessary to automobile production brought about *savings* to the government for military equipment. Pontiac re-

duced the number of worker hours needed to manufacture an Oerliken antiaircraft gun from 428 to 346 hours, and reduced the cost of the weapon by 23 percent. An increase in production numbers allowed General Motors to cut the cost of Browning machine guns from $667 to $144 per gun. Ford's manufacturing techniques reduced the cost of a four-engined B-24 bomber from $238,000 in 1942 to $137,000 by 1944. Chrysler built the Swedish Bofors gun in ten hours per weapon, compared to 450 hours needed by the original manufacturer.

Unfortunately, the good news for major corporations involved in defense work did not usually mean the same for small retailers. Loss of employees to wartime demands and shortages of products and raw materials led to 300,000 US retailers closing down in 1942. By the end of the war, the number of closed businesses reached 500,000. War contracts did not help the business community in New York City very much, either. By November 1942, only seven firms there had

After successfully attacking a Japanese cruiser in Subic Bay in the Philippines during the early days of the war, Lt. John Bulkeley's PT boat used all three of its Packard engines to effect a getaway. It created quite an uproar, and a Japanese radio station in Tokyo reported America's new secret weapon, which was a "monster that roared, flapped its wings, and fired torpedoes in all directions." Bulkeley was awarded the Congressional Medal of Honor for successfully evacuating General MacArthur, his staff, and his family from Corregidor when President Roosevelt ordered the general to escape to Australia. Courtesy, Dresser-Rand

The P-38 Lightning was a twin-engined single-seat fighter which the Japanese called the "fork-tailed devil." When American intelligence intercepted the flight itinerary of Adm. Isoroku Yamamoto, supreme commander of the Japanese Imperial Navy, a squadron of P-38s intercepted his flight near Bougainville in the Solomon Islands. Yamamoto's aircraft was shot down and he was killed, and Japan lost its foremost military strategist. Courtesy, Oldsmobile Division, General Motors Corporation

defense contracts for a total value of $2.3 million, and the city still had 368,000 unemployed.

It was difficult to find housing near many of the huge defense plants, and even harder to find community services and the necessities of life, including food, cigarettes, and personal care items. Several months passed before many of these issues were resolved, including schools for the children of war workers, and some problems were never settled.

People drove their cars a lot, visiting Army and Navy camps, relocating for new jobs, and also just for the fun of it. They were yet to face the realities of gas and tire rationing, and were unhappy when the national speed limit was reduced to 35 miles per hour (mph) to conserve gas. Initially, gasoline was rationed in order to conserve rubber, but the successes of the German U-boats against coastal shipping, especially tankers, in the Atlantic soon made the shortage of fuel a reality.

When gas rationing took effect, most drivers could only qualify for an *A* sticker, which was good for five gallons of gas a week, while members of Congress got an *X* sticker, allowing unlimited consumption. Each business and farm vehicle was required to carry a "Certificate of War Necessity" issued by the "Office of Defense Transportation" to show that its use was "necessary to the war effort to the maintenance of essential civilian economy."

In some photos of car dealerships in the early 1940s, bird cages holding stuffed birds are seen hanging from the ceilings along with signs reading, "These birds were caught stealing gas."

On the plus side, there were fewer auto accidents as a result of driving restrictions, but there was also a serious reduction in gasoline tax collections, and communities that depended on tourism suffered from a lack of visitors all through the war years. One type of business that did profit from gas rationing was the small food store, usually located in the heart of a town or village. Before the war, these enterprises were being forced out by large supermarket chains. Now, they made a comeback because people could walk to them instead of driving, as was not often the case with the newer large markets.

A new phenomenon of the times was the arrival on American street corners of V- (for victory) girls. Mostly teenagers, these young women loitered around military bases and towns, offering themselves to the young sailors and soldiers for the price of a date. Detroit, Chicago, and Mobile, Alabama, had especially noticeable problems with V-girls. With parents caught up in the war, many young people had less supervision than usual, and the atmosphere of the times led some into reckless behavior. It was referred to by one author as "aggressive promiscuity," and it resulted in an increase in social disease and many unexpected war babies. In 1943, there was a 68 percent increase in the number of prostitution arrests over the previous year.

Adding to the domestic turmoil was the presence of many Japanese and Japanese-Americans on the West Coast and the fear of subversive activities on their part. This fear was also present concerning the activities of German-Americans and Italian-Americans, but their ethnic heritage was visually harder to determine, and they were more readily assimilated into the general population. During World War I, the Germans had per-

The job of feeding the civilian population, the military, and America's allies created a great strain on the country's agricultural community. Because so many men were called into the service, women, sometimes known as "tractorettes," joined the "land Army" to harvest the crops. Later in the war, German and Italian POWS were used for this task. Truck and tractor manufacturer IH even offered tractor operating courses for farm girls and women who would be working the fields. The US Department of Agriculture's slogan was "Food Will Win the War and Write the Peace." While there was only a 5 percent increase in the number of acres under cultivation, mechanization helped provide bigger harvests, and the number of tractors increased from 1,445,000 in 1939 to 2,072,000 by the end of the war. Farm income doubled between 1939 and 1943. Courtesy, Navistar Archives

formed many acts of sabotage against the American munitions industry, including the destruction of Black Tom Island, an eleven-acre munitions depot in New York Harbor that was utterly destroyed on Sunday night, July 30, 1916, by German saboteurs, who were not apprehended.

Thus there was precedent when on the night of October 11, 1941, in Fall River, Massachusetts, 12 percent of America's rubber stockpile was incinerated in a massive fire at the Firestone Rubber Company plant. Sabotage was suspected. The dearth of rubber for the war effort became a matter of pressing urgency during 1942. Japanese conquests had engulfed 92 percent of this raw material usually available to the United States from Southeast Asia, and the war couldn't be fought without it. Scrap drives were not successful (thousands of tons were collected, but most reclaimed rubber was useless for wartime materiel), so President Roosevelt appointed a commission to examine the problem and try to solve it. Synthetics eased the situation somewhat, but rubber remained a critical need throughout the war.

Civilians were required to have the tires on their cars and trucks inspected periodically. They

Willys-Overland created a series of ads featuring the Jeep in battle situations all over the world, in this case as part of the Russian Army's war against the Germans on the Eastern front. The Americar, which reportedly got 35mpg, is also promoted for qualified citizens in this ad. Courtesy, Chrysler Corporation

were also required to sell or donate any unmounted tires to the government as part of the "Idle Tire Purchase Plan."

Tires were used on cars and trucks well beyond their life expectancy, and that mileage—as well as tire wear and individual tire serial numbers—was checked at each inspection. Inspectors would sometimes order repair or recapping to extend tire life. In much rarer cases, drivers were given permission to buy new tires—if any could be found. A certificate labeled "Replenishment Part of Mileage-Rationing Program" authorized the purchase of new tires or repair of worn ones.

There was even a form labeled "Rubber Footwear Purchase Certificate" that authorized the purchase of shoes with precious rubber soles.

There were incidents of Japanese subversive activities and spying in the Hawaiian Islands and the Philippines before war started, and the Federal Bureau of Investigation (FBI) as well as military intelligence agencies were tracking the movements and activities of known Japanese agents on the West Coast for several months before Pearl Harbor. In fact, in the mid-1930s, well before the war, two Japanese nationals had been arrested by the FBI when they were caught sabotaging the radio-direction finder of a Pan Am Clipper. The plane was about to depart California for the Pacific on an early trial run when Pan Am was pioneering its trans-Pacific routes.

And in July 1938, what was considered the aviation world's first hijacking apparently occurred over the Pacific with the total disappearance of Pan Am's *Hawaii Clipper*. Since the Japanese had been very interested in the design of the Martin 130 aircraft, they were prime suspects. It didn't help their case when it became known that a Chinese-American with millions of dollars for China's government, then at war with Japan, was purported to be onboard the flight. Easily identifiable Japanese were looked on with suspicion by many Caucasian Americans.

In February of 1942, a Japanese submarine surfaced near Santa Barbara, California, and shelled an oil refinery, doing little damage. Other subs shelled the coasts of Oregon and Washington, and a Japanese plane flew two bombing missions in September of 1942 off a submarine (the plane could be dismantled and stored, then reassembled for missions) to drop incendiary bombs on the forests of Oregon in attempts to start major forest fires. Both efforts were unsuccessful.

In Detroit, a black-owned newspaper, the *Michigan Chronicle,* exposed the activities of a Japanese, Satohasi Takahashi, whose Black Dragon Society attempted to subvert the war effort there with appeals to black workers (there were approximately 150,000 blacks in Detroit in 1942) to join its Development of Our Own move-

CADILLAC

We're doing the job we're _best_ fitted to do!

It is Cadillac's good fortune that the job assigned to it in America's victory program is a job for which Cadillac is uniquely fitted by experience and tradition. For forty years the Cadillac organization has had but one guiding objective—"Craftsmanship a Creed . . . Accuracy a Law." . . . Today we are solely concerned with arming America. Cadillac tanks are now leaving the Cadillac factory in ever-swelling numbers. In addition, Cadillac is producing, as it has for nearly three years, vital precision parts of a famed aircraft engine. . . . But these different responsibilities have in no way altered Cadillac's basic methods. We are still working to the highest standards in materials and craftsmanship . . . still doing the same fine precision job we have always done. We are doing it faster and better, but it is our own type of craftsmanship—the thing we know best how to do.

CADILLAC MOTOR CAR DIVISION **GM** GENERAL MOTORS CORPORATION

The General Stuart M-3 light tank underwent several modifications by both the US and Great Britain, and ultimately was designated the M-5. Due to its riveted construction, any hit by an enemy projectile on the early models caused the rivet heads to fly off, creating casualties inside the tank. In the hands of an inexperienced driver, it could also easily "throw a tread" and be stuck in place. Served by a crew of four and armed with a 37mm gun plus five .30 caliber machine guns, the Stuart was originally powered by a Continental radial air-cooled 250hp engine. When that company could not maintain production, Cadillac stepped in and provided two V-8 engines in tandem, each 121hp, first for the M-3A3 modification, and later for the M-5 version. Courtesy, Cadillac Division, General Motors Corporation

Nash and Kelvinator had merged in 1937 to manufacture cars and refrigerators, but civilian production of both was suspended during World War II. Instead, Nash built Sikorsky flying boats and Hamilton Standard propellers, as well as bomb fuses and cargo trailers. The company's advertisements were aimed directly at the country's enemies, rather than at the pride of production trumpeted by most automobile manufacturers at this point in the war. Courtesy, Chrysler Corporation

This is another of Nash's hard-hitting ads, in this case illustrating the power of the Navy's F4U Corsair fighter against the Mitsubishi A6M Zero fighter. The Corsair was the first US fighter capable of exceeding 400mph. In wartime ads, Nash-Kelvinator always showed its peacetime products, a car and a refrigerator. Courtesy, Chrysler Corporation

ment. The purpose of the movement was to organize all people of color to revolt against whites. The FBI arrested Takahashi.

Many factors, including fear of invasion, economic greed, security concerns, racial prejudice, and hysteria were present when FDR signed the Civilian Exclusion Order on March 31, 1942, causing the evacuation of 70,000 to 100,000 (depending on whom you believe) alien Japanese and Japanese-Americans from the Red Zone, as the military areas of four western states were designated.

Contrary to beliefs of that day, however, most were not forcibly interned but were actually encouraged to leave their relocation camps. Approximately 25,000 of them did so, with 4,000 earning college degrees during the time, the condition being a signed agreement not to interfere with the nation's war effort. However, they could not enter the Red Zone in the western states where most of them had lived. Only those Japanese considered subversive were forcibly interned, mainly

at Tule Lake, California, where more than 18,000 were held and where 5,600 renounced their American citizenship.

One of the sadder aspects of this program is that very few of the loyal people who were relocated ever got their land and possessions returned to them. It is interesting to note, in light of the US government's decision to pay reparations to these Japanese evacuees, that of 25,655 aliens of enemy nationalities who were confined to Internment Centers by the US Department of Justice, 14,426 of them were of European descent while less than half, 11,229, were Japanese citizens and Japanese-Americans.

No plans have been made to compensate any of the Europeans involved. Approximately 13,000 other Japanese-Americans proved their loyalty by serving in the armed forces, but it should not be forgotten that a Japanese "fifth column" did exist in the United States and its territories prior to the war.

The Germans also were interested in penetrating the United States with saboteurs and in

Tens of thousands of big Studebaker Trucks move the men and supplies of war

AT the debarkation points and on the supply lines —at the fighting fronts and on the rough terrain behind them— big, multiple-drive Studebaker trucks are writing brilliant new chapters of transport history every day of this war.

Tens of thousands of them are on the job. And these rugged war trucks are pouring out of the Studebaker factories in so steady a stream that tens of thousands more soon will be moving the men and supplies of war on the far flung fronts of the United Nations.

From builder of commercial trucks in peacetime to one of the largest makers of military trucks in wartime is a logical transition for America's oldest manufacturer of highway transport. Once again, for the sixth time in a national emergency, Studebaker has answered the Government's call for the production of army transport on a large scale. And when decisive victory is achieved, finer, more economical Studebaker

trucks and commercial cars than ever before will be available for civilian use.

Today, Studebaker's world-famous craftsmen are bringing a new and more significant meaning to the traditional Studebaker watchword—*always give more than you promise.* And the job they're doing makes us justifiably proud of our assignments in the arming of our Nation and its Allies.

★ BUY U. S. WAR BONDS ★

Studebaker's
90th Anniversary
1852 · 1942

Studebaker builds Wright Cyclone Engines for the Boeing Flying Fortress, America's invincible dreadnought of the skies.

Studebaker was heavily involved in building military trucks as well as aircraft engines. American troops invaded North Africa in November 1942, and an enormous number of vehicles were required for the extended supply lines that were needed to carry the battle to the enemy. This ad contains a plug for eventual postwar cars ("And when decisive victory is achieved...") and urges readers to buy War Bonds. Courtesy, Dresser-Rand

the summer of 1942 landed two groups consisting of four men each by submarine, one group on New York's Long Island near Amagansett, and the other group on the beach near Jacksonville, Florida. The FBI captured them all within a few days before they did any damage. All of them had lived in the United States for a time, and were fluent in English. They were carrying explosives and $170,000. Two turned informer and received life sentences, but the other six were executed in the electric chair in Washington, D.C., and buried in unmarked graves.

Meanwhile, Gen. James "Jimmy" Doolittle and his Army Air Forces group comprising sixteen B-25s had bombed Tokyo and other major Japanese cities, flying their normally land-based bombers off the deck of the aircraft carrier *Hornet,* a feat not previously considered possible. FDR told the world that the planes had departed from Shangri La, the mythical kingdom in James Hilton's book, *Lost Horizon.* The planes flew on past Japan after completing their assignments, and when they ran out of fuel in a storm, the air-

Merchant convoys lacked sufficient military escort ships to provide security against enemy ships, submarines, and aircraft. In 1942 there were very few aircraft carriers and battleships available for convoy duty, making it necessary to equip the merchant ships with naval and antiaircraft guns. Pontiac's Oerlikon was in the forefront of these guns, and is depicted here in action against the German Luftwaffe. Pontiac's voluntary censorship is significantly decreased compared to earlier advertisements. The ad contains a "GM—Arms for Victory" logo and the phrase, "Victory is Our Business." Courtesy, Pontiac Division, General Motors Corporation

men parachuted into the night over China. Eight crew members fell into Japanese hands and were held as war criminals, suffering great hardships. Before their liberation in 1945, three had been executed by the Japanese and another had died of disease. A great majority of the fliers were helped to freedom by the Chinese. In retaliation, the Japanese devastated the provinces where this assistance occurred and killed 250,000 Chinese in an orgy of revenge.

The Doolittle Raid did a lot of good for American morale and was the first retaliation that the United States could claim after the series of defeats suffered in the first few weeks of the war. In May, the island fortress of Corregidor in Manila Bay fell when its exhausted and starving American defenders succumbed to Japanese bombardment and invasion. The fate of these men and

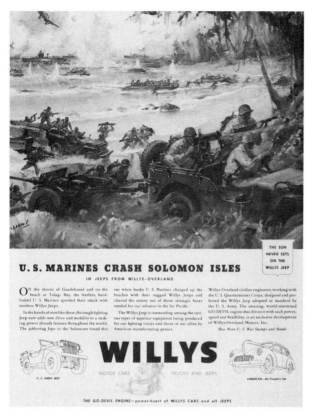

United States Marines invaded the Solomon Islands at Guadalcanal in August 1942. The Jeep in the forefront of this ad is carrying a .30 caliber water-cooled machine gun and towing a 37mm antitank gun. The Marines were woefully short of supplies on Guadalcanal due to the local superiority of the Japanese Navy and Air Force. US troops were initially on the defensive as the Japanese reinforced heavily, but went over to the offensive late in October. After several brutal engagements resulting in American victories, the last Japanese troops evacuated the island in February 1943. Courtesy, Chrysler Corporation

their fellow soldiers captured on Bataan in April—torture, brutality, and death for half of them (from 40 to 60 percent of the Allied military personnel captured early in the war died in captivity)—would not be known to the nation until several escapees brought out the news in 1943.

The Alaska-Canada Military Highway was built in 1942, and a 1,400-mile section from Delta Junction, Alaska, to Dawson Creek in British Columbia was completed in just over eight months by the US Corps of Engineers. The highway connected airfields that were used in the movement of 8,000 Lend-Lease aircraft being transferred to Russia for use against the German invaders, as well as to defend Alaska against the possibility of a Japanese attack. Fighting both the weather and geography, 19,000 soldiers and civilians using 11,000 machines finished the job, and the road was opened in November 1942.

On other fronts, the Allies were fighting back as well. Hitler resumed his offensive against Russia, but with less strength than his generals needed to predict victory. The Soviets absorbed tremendous casualties and endured terrible civilian suffering, stopping the Wehrmacht at the gates of Moscow and in the rubble of the siege of Stalingrad. The Germans were so deep inside the USSR that they couldn't maintain their supply lines, and the Russian winter also took an immense toll. By the end of 1942, the Russians were on the offensive and embarked on the road that would take them to Berlin.

Back in the United States, civilians were faced with the disappearance of many goods and services they took for granted. Some unique paradoxes were also created. While tire and gas rationing, as well as the suspension of new car sales to civilians, limited the availability of automotive travel, the immense increase in the civilian work force needed for wartime manufacturing (often in areas far from existing communities and transportation networks) expanded the transportation needs of the nation's workers. These often overwhelmed local resources and led to government encouragement of car-pooling and official pleas for self-discipline in the use of meager automotive resources. Along with the loss of the automobile was a ban or restriction on 300 products, including refrigerators (resurrecting the icebox), beer cans, coat hangers, bicycles, and toothpaste tubes. To get a new tube of toothpaste from the druggist meant turning in a used, empty one. With so many young men away in the service, it was hard to get chores done around the house and in small-town America. Soda-jerks, gas-jockeys, yard rakers, and grocery boys were all gone, and their sisters had left town also to become part of the war effort, making it tough to get babysitters!

Meanwhile, in North Africa in May, Field Marshal Rommel had forced the British back 300 miles to the gates of the Nile Delta in one week. But a second offensive in August was turned aside, and the Commonwealth troops under Generals Harold Alexander and Bernard Montgomery successfully counterattacked in October at the famous Battle of El Alamein. The Germans collapsed and by the end of 1942, Rommel had retreated a thousand miles. To add to the Axis problems and ultimately seal their fate in North Africa, the Allies in November launched a seaborne invasion of Northwest Africa, code named Torch, landing an American Army shipped directly from the States at Oran and Casablanca, which was followed by British landings a short while later farther east in the Mediterranean. This campaign marked Dwight D. Eisenhower's debut as commander of the American Expeditionary Forces in Europe, and helped create the reputations of Gen. George Patton and Gen. Omar Bradley.

In May of 1942, on the other side of the world, the US Navy had blunted Japanese aggression aimed at Australia and Port Moresby, New Guinea, at the Battle of the Coral Sea. Then in early June, one of history's most decisive naval engagements took place when the US Navy defeated the Imperial Japanese Navy at the Battle of Midway, sinking four Japanese carriers within minutes of each other and destroying 350 enemy aircraft. All of the enemy ships were sunk by naval aircraft, and the opposing fleets never came within range of each other's shipborne guns.

American ground forces were committed to battle in the Pacific when the Marines landed on Guadalcanal in the Solomon Islands in August. Initially the Japanese were taken by surprise, but then they fought back tenaciously. Guadalcanal became a savage land of sea and air battles, making the names of places like Henderson Field, Ironbottom Sound, and Bloody Ridge into familiar

bywords for courage and sacrifice in the United States.

At home gas rationing was fully in effect, having started on the East Coast but soon spreading across the country. A pleasure driver received five gallons of gas a week—one A stamp. This was reduced to three gallons a week in 1943, and for a short time in 1944, it was down to only two gallons a week. To qualify for a B sticker, a person had to use the car to commute to work, and supply exact mileage figures to the ration board. C stickers were for people who needed their cars to do their work, while E stickers were for the police, firefighters, doctors, news reporters, and others who qualified for "emergency" stamps. "X" stickers had no restrictions, and more than 200 Congressmen applied for these. The two latter sticker designations could usually get whatever they wanted, but Cs had to give an explanation.

It didn't take long for a black market for gasoline and tires to form. Some people, out of patriotism or out of thrift, put their cars up on blocks

Cooperation between management and labor was the theme of Packard's "Work to Win." War weariness had not set in, and most workers were eager to do their part for victory. The government created incentives for industry in the form of tax write-offs and postwar tax refunds, causing some critics to comment that companies *were getting rich from the war. But labor also profited mightily, as salaries and wages increased from $52.6 billion in 1939 to $112.8 billion in 1944. Many of the new workers recruited were unskilled, and wartime wages offered them a lifestyle never envisioned in peacetime. Courtesy, Dresser-Rand*

for the duration, but most car owners were too attached to their vehicles to give up easily, and there was usually somebody available to alleviate their fuel difficulties for a few bucks. Truckers had "T" stickers, and could usually get all the gas they wanted. Sometimes they abused that privilege. A trucker in Cheyenne, Wyoming, was convicted of trading 120 "T" stamps for four quarts of whiskey. A *Collier's* editorial entitled "Abide By The Rules" cautioned the civilian population that any serious fudging of the rules could cripple the home front, and lead to the exposure of the troops to "slaughter, capture and the loss of the war, and all through the fault of the people back home."

Store deliveries both from the factory and to the consumer were affected by gas rationing, and home milk deliveries in the East were reduced to every other day. Newspapers that traditionally produced two daily editions were reduced to a single edition. In the summer of 1942 the East Coast had literally no gas available, and desperate motorists would follow tanker trucks to filling stations in order to get in line to buy gas. The government estimated that highway use was only 20 percent of full capacity, evidenced by a corresponding drop in highway deaths. Over the Labor Day weekend in 1941, 423 people were killed in auto accidents, while in 1942 the toll was 169 dead.

It didn't take long for the criminal element to get involved in the gas shortage. The most common criminal behavior related to the fuel crunch was the counterfeiting of gas coupons even though the government printed the coupons on specially treated paper. At one point in San Francisco, more than three million gallons of illegal gasoline were sold in just a few days. The OPA admitted that 5 percent of the gas sold in the country was purchased illegally with fake

General Motors' Fisher Body Division made great contributions to the war effort, manufacturing an amazing array of defense materiel from aircraft instruments to tanks and ships. During the war GM operated 96 plants in 13 states, while cooperating with 20,000 outside suppliers and subcontractors. The company's "Body by Fisher" slogan was changed to "Armament by Fisher," and the ad notes that Fisher was the first automotive company to receive the Navy's excellence award for ahead-of-schedule production. Courtesy, General Motors

In late 1942, Studebaker launched an advertising campaign featuring fathers and sons working together for victory on the home front and in the military. The ads stressed the company's ninety-year history, its professional workmanship, and the fact that generations of the same families worked for Studebaker over the years. These are good examples of the auto makers keeping their names in front of consumers even though they had no civilian cars for sale. Courtesy, Dresser-Rand

The labor shortages created by the needs of the military were a stark reality in defense production, and this void was partially filled by unskilled labor, including women who had never been exposed to manufacturing before this time and blacks who migrated to the job locations. Late in 1942, Ford was proud to announce in this ad that there were 6,000 women employed at Wil- *low Run. Factories had to compete for available labor, and many plants were chronically short of needed workers. Because of maintenance needs in the field, it was also necessary for the manufacturers to train the military in these skills, further depleting the work force available at the factory.* Courtesy, Ford Motor Company

coupons, and that 15 percent of all "C" coupons in circulation were counterfeit. Gas stations would sell their existing stocks of fuel for more money than the price ceiling allowed, and then cover the profits by turning in counterfeit coupons to the OPA. Not every operator was willing to cooperate in these illegal ventures, and there were cases of coercion. One woman station owner was tortured with a burning torch, then robbed of the coupons already collected in her cash register as well as the cash on hand. Before the war ended, more than 4,000 stations lost their selling licenses, and 32,500 drivers lost their ration coupons due to illegal gasoline transactions.

Many young women, however, were exhibiting a higher level of patriotism than their fellow Americans involved in the black market. These women were joining the armed forces and taking on essential, but often mundane administrative jobs to free up men for combat. The women in the Army were known as WAACs (later changed to WACs), Navy women were WAVES, the Coast Guard called them SPARS, and in the Marines, everyone was a Marine, no gender difference. Many women confidently sought and gained recognition of their business abilities when peace returned.

In the meantime, there were plenty of things to do. Movies started to reflect the patriotic mood and the propaganda of a nation at war. *Mrs. Miniver* and *In Which We Serve* underscored the strength and indomitable spirit of our British allies, while others laughed at situations on the home front, and some were real tear-jerkers about the separation, sadness, and tragedy of war.

The musicians' union, the American Federation of Musicians, was on strike (1942—1944) due to a disagreement regarding royalties with the record companies, so no records using instrumentalists were being made in studios (some singers did fine work using other vocalists for back-

Women may have become important to the defense industry, but they were usually ignored by management. This ode to America's pilots is signed by the "men of Oldsmobile," with nary a word about the contributions made by the women on the assembly line. The message is called "a word from the men *who build the cannon you carry through the sky" (emphasis added). The featured aircraft is once again the P-39 Airacobra. Courtesy, Oldsmobile Division, General Motors Corporation*

A vivid *example of Nash-Kelvinator's contributions to national defense—including a warning that "the awakening is coming!" This aircraft, featured in its cargo-carrying role, is the VS-44A flying boat operated by American Export Airlines for the Navy. Known as the "Flying Aces," these aircraft flew the Atlantic nonstop throughout the war. Nash built subassemblies for the VS-44A. Courtesy, Chrysler Corporation*

ground). But there was still plenty of music in the dance halls, on the radio, and at the big-band concerts. Many romantic ballads like "I'll Be Seeing You" and "I'll Get By" were popular, but were easily overshadowed by Bing Crosby's stupendous hit "White Christmas," written for the 1942 movie *Holiday Inn.* There were also tunes like "Coming in on a Wing and a Prayer," "Praise the Lord and Pass the Ammunition," "Der Fuhrer's Face," and "You're a Sap, Mr. Jap." There was even one called "When Those Little Yellowbellies Meet the Cohens and the Kellys."

While music helped lighten the anxious mood of the American people in 1942, most civilians were working harder than ever to meet the demands of a wartime economy. The changeover requirements for industry were awesome, but the success of this conversion was equally awesome.

A prime example of this manufacturing professionalism was the Chrysler Corporation's plant at Evansville, Indiana, which before the war employed 650 people who built Plymouth cars and Dodge trucks. Within days of Pearl Harbor, the government contracted with Chrysler to manufacture three to five billion .45 caliber cartridges at the plant.

Employment rose to 12,650 workers at the facility, but fewer than five of them knew anything about ammunition. Nevertheless, the Evansville plant produced three billion .45 caliber cartridges, 500 million .30 caliber carbine cartridges, reconditioned 1,662 Sherman tanks, rebuilt 4,000 Army trucks, and manufactured 800,000 special tank tread covers, as well as completing several special ammunition projects. When the war ended, Evansville had just received a contract to build seven million incendiary aviation bombs. This type of breathtaking success, while not problem free, occurred all across the country as 1942 drew to a close.

The auto industry's advertising programs underwent dramatic changes during 1942 as well. With no new models to sell, the car companies sought ways to keep their names in front of the

From HUDSON ...for Fighting Men

Guarding vital convoy routes. Rapid-fire Oerlikon 20-m.m. anti-aircraft guns—mass-produced in the huge U.S. Naval Ordnance plant operated by Hudson—bark death to dive bombers before they reach their targets. OFFICIAL U.S. NAVY PHOTOS

Large facilities and long experience in building fine automobiles enable Hudson to contribute on a large scale to production of Army bombers. INTERNATIONAL NEWS PHOTO

Hudson has undertaken the manufacture of large numbers of husky, high speed Invader motors to power the landing boats with which American forces will carry the war to enemy-held shores. ASSOCIATED PRESS PHOTO

For many months Hudson has been in mass production of important units for the Wright Cyclone engine that powers the Curtiss-Wright Hell Diver shown here. RUDY ARNOLD PHOTO

Our plants are dedicated to war production... Our dealers to maintaining war transportation

VICTORY is the goal—but the road to that goal is WORK.

Bound for sea, air and land fronts around the world, a steadily growing stream of weapons and equipment is rolling today from Hudson factories.

Again and again, quotas have been raised, then exceeded—in the performance of contracts calling for the highest precision and finest workmanship. But we are far from satisfied. Constantly increasing production is our goal.

We are proud of the thousands of Hudson men and women who in peacetime designed and built more than 2,800,000 Hudson cars. They are now applying that same craftsmanship to the mass production of war materials, and investing over 10% of their pay in War Bonds.

We are proud, too, of the Hudson distributor and dealer organization—their service supervisors and mechanics. These have been classed by the Office of Defense Transportation as *essential workers*, to keep vitally needed automobiles "rolling" for the duration.

Hudson dealers have expanded their service facilities to meet the wartime needs of owners. They also have limited stocks of new cars which Uncle Sam has reserved for essential driving.

Your Hudson dealer invites you to call on him for the expert service that will prolong the life of your present car. He will also assist you with your application for a new 1942 Hudson, built for years of dependable service, and outstanding economy of gas, oil and tires.

HUDSON
MOTOR CAR COMPANY
33 Years of Engineering Leadership

Hudson was involved in producing the famous 20mm Oerlikon antiaircraft gun, as well as components for the B-26 medium bomber and engines for landing craft. The Helldiver featured in this ad was the successor to the Dauntless divebomber, made famous by its heroic exploits at the Battle of Midway. At this point in the war, the Helldiver was undergoing design modifications after the prototype aircraft was destroyed in a crash, and did not enter service until 1943. It was never beloved by the naval aviators who flew it. Courtesy, Chrysler Corporation

Willys featured China in this latest addition to its continuing series of ads recognizing the exploits of both America's troops and those of Allied nations using the fighting Jeep. In this battle-ravaged scenario, the soldier in the back of the Jeep is firing a Bren gun, the standard .303 caliber light machine gun of British and Commonwealth forces throughout the war. Courtesy, Chrysler Corporation

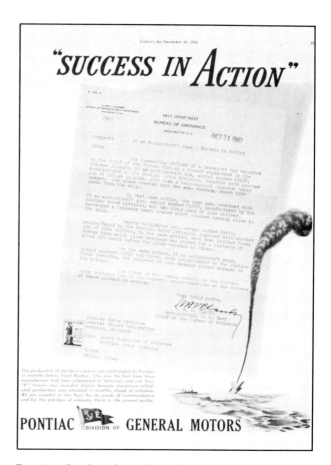

Pontiac displayed its Navy E banner for excellence, awarded for achieving maximum planned production ahead of schedule. The featured letter describing a successful action against the enemy was expected to be a morale booster for the Pontiac plant workers back home in Michigan. While some companies referred to Christmases past, present, and future in their December 1942 advertisements, the automotive industry largely ignored the religious holiday in favor of war talk. Courtesy, Pontiac Division, General Motors Corporation

public. Used cars and last year's models were highlighted, as well as the servicing of cars that needed to last for the duration of the war. When the Allies started regaining the initiative in mid-1942, advertising began to reflect the population's fortitude and pride, and also became somewhat pugnacious. Companies and their advertising agencies picked up this air of determination, and print ads boasted of both production gains and the general superiority of American soldiers and their machines over those of their evil enemies. Most personal invective was reserved for the enemy leadership, rather than the average civilian or soldier, and even then was addressed mainly by the government propaganda agencies. The Japanese, however, were often caricatured in corporate advertising as subhuman, even animalistic. Almost a year of active warfare had also allowed advertisers to plan campaign themes, some of which portrayed the military situation, others

the efficiency of production, and still others the American family as it overcame the dangers, sacrifices, and separations created by the war. Many of these campaigns changed in the months and years ahead as the political and military situations changed.

America was on an emotional binge as the war lengthened. Soldiers, sailors, and aviators were far from home: Hawaii, Australia, New Zealand, England, Iceland, North Africa, China, India. Excited and bored, happy and sad, exhilarated and afraid, these young men and women waited for what 1943 would bring, and while they waited, they wrote "Kilroy Was Here" on anything that wasn't moving–and some things that were.

CHAPTER 3

Kilroy Was Here: 1943

Nobody knows where the expression "Kilroy Was Here" originated, but it certainly became ubiquitous in the United States during the war, and wherever Americans were stationed around the globe. According to one story, James J. Kilroy was a shipyard inspector in Quincy, Massachusetts, who chalked "Kilroy Was Here" on equipment that he had inspected. However, this is unverified. Whatever its origins, "Kilroy" came to symbolize the presence of the American G.I., and joined a host of catch phrases so popular to propagandists and manufacturers of enthusiasm and patriotism. "Remember Pearl Harbor," "Loose Lips Sink Ships," "Back the Attack," "Buy More in '44" (the last two were to promote the sale of defense bonds), and "Don't You Know There's a War On?" were just a few of them.

It was desirable, actually *urgent,* from the government's point of view to focus the energies and the intellect of civilians on the nation's war goals, but this would prove difficult for the duration. There was certainly a sense of national purpose in clearing out the old and of revenge against a foreign culture that had attacked the United States and killed American boys and girls, but it was a major task, never really fulfilled, to motivate the general population regarding the end of imperialism and colonialism. FDR's vision of a postwar world free of these philosophies, as well as a United Nations forum to settle future disputes, did not enter into the thinking of an essentially isolationist population mainly interested in returning to the status quo.

Conversely, there was no lack of enthusiasm on the part of American automobile manufacturers to advertise their wartime production achievements. The vast array of equipment that poured forth from the nation's factories fueled the military machines of both the United States and its allies. Most of the automotive advertisements in

1943 featured defense production action against the enemy, with intermittent reminders that cars still on the road needed to be maintained through preventative maintenance for the duration.

Nash-Kelvinator (Nash and Kelvinator merged in 1937) pursued a different tactic, turning from depictions of military hardware to the trials of individual Americans caught up in the struggle. Paramount was their determination to achieve a final victory and return to a country that was fair and just, and worthy of their sacrifices. These ads were forceful and essentially political, a concept that the other auto manufacturers shunned.

Certainly old ways of manufacturing and doing business changed dramatically for many industries, including the car companies in Detroit. Among the many production methods that underwent change was the abandonment of hard steel dies in favor of soft steel dies, which were more adaptable to retooling. The insatiable demands of war accelerated during early 1943, when 86,000 aircraft were built in the United States, along with 1,949 ships. Shortages of many raw materials and scarce production necessities led to cooperative efforts among normally competitive companies. In the case of car manufacturers, this effort was organized as the Automotive Council for War Production, with George Romney as managing director. These enormous efforts began to show results on the battlefield, and while the enemies' strengths were still apparent and continued to take a heavy toll in both casualties and materiel, the toll did lessen as the year continued.

The submarine offensive against British and American shipping in the Atlantic continued to drain Allied resources, and was a prime example of German military strength. At the Casablanca Conference attended by Churchill, Roosevelt, and the two Free French leaders, Gen. Charles De

"Pass the Ammunition!"

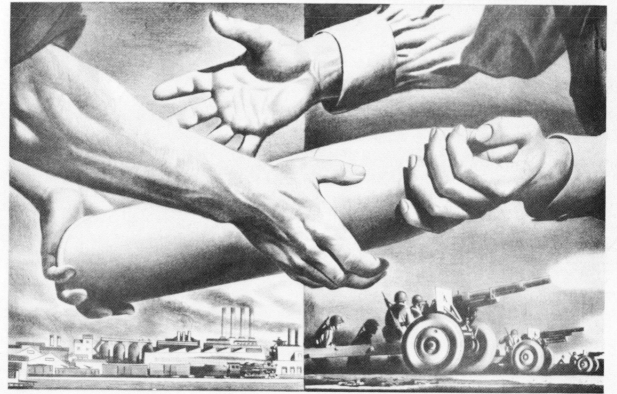

OLDSMOBILE WORKERS HAVE BEEN DOING IT FOR NEARLY TWO YEARS... BACKING UP OUR FIGHTING MEN WITH VOLUME PRODUCTION OF FIRE-POWER

AMERICA is "passing the ammunition" today to almost every corner of the globe. From the skilled hands of her millions of workmen... to the eager hands of her millions of fighting men... the planes and ships and tanks and cannon and shell are passing in a never-ending stream.

From Oldsmobile, for example, come automatic cannon for fighter planes—long-range cannon for tanks—shot and shell for tanks and the artillery. Oldsmobile is carrying out these vast assignments in close co-operation with more than 130 sub-contractors, working with them as an All-American "Keep 'Em Firing" team. They're part of the *free industry* of a *free country*, and they're working to keep it that way. "Let's pass the ammunition," American industry is saying, "and we'll all *stay free!*"

You Can Help "Pass the Ammunition" —Buy U.S. War Bonds and Stamps

KEEP 'EM FIRING!

OLDSMOBILE DIVISION OF GENERAL MOTORS
★ VOLUME PRODUCER OF "FIRE-POWER" FOR THE U.S.A. ★

In early combat action of the Pacific war, a US Navy chaplain exhorted the sailors at their battle stations to "praise the Lord and pass the ammunition," a phrase that quickly became a rallying cry and also a popular song on the home front. Oldsmobile apparently borrowed the well-known slogan to describe its manufacture of ammunition for the Army. Courtesy, Oldsmobile Division, General Motors Corporation

Gaulle and Gen. Henri Honore Giraud, the defeat of the German U-boats was given top priority. By early 1943 Germany had deployed more than 200 modern, operational submarines in the North and South Atlantic Oceans. The previous year had been devastating for the Allies' Atlantic convoys, which absorbed losses of approximately 500,000 tons of shipping a month.

This loss rate continued into early 1943, with the U-boats hunting in "wolf-packs." When one sub spotted a convoy, it would follow the slowly moving ships and call in the rest of the pack to make a mass attack, usually at night. The Allies countered with "hunter-killer" naval groups, utilizing both air and surface vessels equipped with much-improved radar. They were increasingly effective, and dramatically reduced the Allied tonnage lost to enemy submarines. During June, July, and August of 1943, the Germans sank 58 Allied ships and lost 79 U-boats in the process. In September and October, nine Allied ships in convoy were sunk out of 2,468 dispatched, while the Germans lost twenty-five more subs. The U-boats could be replaced, but the crews couldn't. The submarine threat had been neutralized, allowing the build-up of troops and materiel in Great Britain to continue at a massive rate.

Soviet Marshal Joseph Stalin had not attended the Casablanca Conference, saying he was too busy fighting Germans, and he received the disappointing message from the Anglo-American leadership that there would be no second front in Europe in 1943. Soviet war fortunes had taken a turn for the better–but at an immense cost in casualties and materiel. In early 1942 a desperate Stalin had tried to make a deal with Hitler, offering the Ukraine, White Russia, and parts of the Russian Federation in return for an armistice, but Hitler did not even deign a reply. Now the Russians, heavily supplied with Lend-Lease military equipment via the dangerous Murmansk and Archangel Arctic convoy routes, pushed the Germans back, regaining lost territories.

It was a ferocious war on the Eastern front, with frequent atrocities perpetrated by both sides and with no quarter given. Huge tank battles were fought. At the Battle of Kursk, southwest of Moscow, 1,500 Russian and German tanks were engaged. Here on the Eastern front the political enmity between Communist and Fascist clashed in brutal reality, with political police and commissars from both persuasions killing civilians by the thousands. The Soviets were temporarily halted by a German counterattack in May, but of longer range consequence was the discovery by the Germans of the mass graves of Polish prisoners of war executed by the Russians.

It was the type of revelation most likely to put a strain on Allied relations, as the Western

War bond drives were very successful in raising the funds necessary to prosecute the war, as well as for keeping excess spending capacity by civilians under control. As described in this Packard ad, war stamps could be purchased for pocket change and then converted into bonds when enough were accumulated. Packard injected a measure of fear into the message with its reference to the possibility of losing the war and the American automotive way of life. The Packard employee depicted in the sketch at the lower right notes that "if America doesn't win this war, I'll never be building Packard cars again, mister—and you'll never be buying them." Courtesy, Dresser-Rand

powers were ostensibly fighting to free Poland and the other captive nations of Europe (Free Poles were fighting in the Allied Armies, 400,000 under Soviet command and 200,000 in the West), and was indicative of the USSR's postwar plans for Eastern Europe. More than 10,000 Polish officers who were taken prisoner by the Russians were never heard from again after the spring of 1940. The overwhelming majority of them were reservists, the middle-class backbone of Poland's social, economic, and political hierarchy.

By murdering these officers, Stalin hoped to destroy the basis for resistance to a Communist takeover of Poland when the war was over. The bodies of more than 4,000 of these executed officers were found in the spring of 1943 in the Katyn Forest in eastern Poland, a name that became a byword for Russian mass murder and po-

The Toughest Fords Ever Built!

Hard-Hitting M-4 Tanks and M-10 Tank Destroyers
Built, Armored and Powered by Ford — Praised by Army
for Performance Under Fire!

This Sherman M-4 medium tank carried a 76mm gun and two .30 caliber machine guns. Later models carried a free-firing .50 caliber machine gun on top of the turret. The M-4s produced by Ford were powered by a 500hp V-8 gasoline engine. The M-10 tank destroyer incorporated the same chassis and engine as the M-4 tank. It had a full-traverse, open-topped turret and a crew of five, and featured a 3in gun. More than 6,400 M-10s and M-10As were built during the war. The box in the ad lists Ford's military products, but notes, "This list does not include other important Victory models now in production that cannot be named due to wartime conditions." Courtesy, Ford Motor Company

litical persecution in Europe. The Soviets tried to blame it on the Germans, but all evidence pointed to the Russian Secret Police. As a result of Polish accusations, the USSR broke off relations with the Polish government in exile located in London, and set up a puppet government in the area of Poland under Soviet control. The incident severely strained the Allied Alliance which was subordinated to the perceived greater task of defeating Hitler, but left little doubt in the minds of Western leaders as to the nature and ruthlessness of the Soviet cause. It was a ghastly war for those caught in the middle of it.

Elsewhere, the Germans started to experience the materiel and military weight of America's entry into the war. On January 27, 1943, the first American bombing raid on a German city, the port of Wilhelmshaven, was made by B-17s of the US Eighth Air Force flying out of England. Meanwhile, in North Africa, the Allied armies advanced on Tunisia. Field Marshal Erwin Rommel,

the "Desert Fox," counterattacked and inflicted a major but temporary defeat on the inexperienced American forces at the Kasserine Pass. Of 30,000 American soldiers in the battle, 3,000 were killed and wounded, and an additional 3,700 were taken prisoner, and hundreds of tanks, trucks, and artillery pieces were lost to the enemy. In April, however, the British and American armies linked up, and by May 13 the Germans had been driven from North Africa permanently.

Next page
This is an example of a General Motors public service ad with an additional plug for auto maintenance by GM dealers. Most Americans were rationed to five gallons of gas per week. Thousands of drivers had their gas ration cards suspended for pleasure driving when apprehended by OPA enforcement officials or the local police. Courtesy, General Motors

74

How many miles in a gallon of gasoline?

OUT of the need to save rubber, gasoline is rationed—necessarily in terms of gallons.

Your use of it, though, is measured in miles.

How are you going to get essential miles out of the fixed number of gallons that are available to you?

The size and kind of car you drive has much to do with this, but not everything.

Carburetor setting, spark plug condition, clutch action, tire pressure and numerous other things—including your driving habits—all help determine how many miles you get in your car from your gasoline.

Any General Motors car dealer can help you get top mileage by taking care of mechanical matters. He can help keep your car efficient, which is the basis for gasoline economy.

So why not take effective steps to get full mileage from gasoline? Let the GM dealer put and keep your car in most efficient condition—and show you how to handle it to stretch your regular ration.

Both are part of his job—and it's a job he *knows!*

★ ★ ★

The Automobile User's Guide answers your questions about taking care of your car and your tires in wartime. For a free copy see any General Motors dealer today or write Customer Research Staff, General Motors Building, Detroit.

GENERAL MOTORS DIVISIONS NOW PRODUCING:
Aircraft Engines • Airplanes • Airplane Parts • Bomber Sub-Assemblies • Military Trucks • Armored Cars • Rapid-Fire Cannon • Machine Guns • Diesel Engines • Shells • Tanks and Tank Parts • Propellers • Cartridge Cases • Gun Motor Carriages • Gun Mounts • Fire Control Devices • Electrical Equipment • And Many Other Wartime Essentials.

Working together for TOTAL VICTORY

GENERAL MOTORS

CHEVROLET • PONTIAC • OLDSMOBILE • BUICK • CADILLAC

Convert your car into a -

VICTORY CAR!

RE-ADJUST CARBURETOR
for greater economy

TUNE ENGINE
for smoother operation "under 35"

EQUALIZE BRAKES
to prevent excessive tire wear

RE-SET TIMING
for today's lower-octane gasoline

ALIGN WHEELS
to avoid "grinding off" rubber

SET UP CHARGING RATE
to prevent a run-down battery

CHANGE LUBRICANTS
to protect vital parts at today's low speeds

SWITCH TIRES
to distribute wear equally

ALL CARS WERE ENGINEERED FOR PRE-WAR DRIVING...THEY SHOULD BE RE-TUNED AND RE-ADJUSTED TO PROVIDE LONG-LASTING, THRIFTY WARTIME TRANSPORTATION

THE car you drive today has *two* jobs to do. First, it must meet your own essential driving needs. Second, it must help meet the vital transportation needs of America. It's doubly important, then, that your car be kept in perfect shape ... conditioned to do those jobs right. You may not be eligible to buy a new car ... but everybody is eligible to have his present car converted to a "Victory Model." It's just as easy as it ever was to go to your Oldsmobile dealer for a tune-up. He tunes your car for *today's new type of driving*. He adjusts it for

maximum efficiency at "35 and under." He tunes it for maximum economy on today's lower-octane gasoline. And he helps you protect it against the ill effects of low speeds and limited driving —such as run-down battery, neglected tires, diluted lubricants, sticky valves. Drive in to your Oldsmobile dealer's today ... whatever make of car you own ... and drive out a "Victory Car."

Convert your dollars to Victory dollars — Buy War Bonds and Stamps

THIS IS WHAT WE MEAN BY A "VICTORY CAR"

IT'S ANY MAKE OF CAR— WAR-CONDITIONED TO GIVE YOU—

MAXIMUM ECONOMY

LONGER TIRE LIFE

SMOOTHER PERFORMANCE
at wartime driving speeds

GREATER DEPENDABILITY
for essential driving needs

LONGER CAR LIFE
so that it will be serving you and your country for the duration!

OLDSMOBILE DEALERS of AMERICA

☆ *IN SERVICE FOR THE NATION* ☆

In the Pacific war during the first month of 1943, the island of Guadalcanal was finally wrested from the grip of the Japanese. It had been a protracted, bloody struggle, and in the early days a near defeat for the United States when a series of naval battles in which the Japanese prevailed (the waters around Guadalcanal were known as Ironbottom Sound because of all the sunken ships) left the American troops on the defensive, undermanned and poorly supplied. Over a period of several months, the US forces took the initiative and destroyed the enemy's resupply and com-

bat efficiency. Decimated, starving, and sick, the few surviving Japanese evacuated Guadalcanal, giving the Americans the forward bases needed in the Solomon Islands to prosecute the war. In May and August, the American Army invaded Attu and Kiska in the Aleutians, originally taken by the Japanese a year earlier. The necessity for this isolated campaign was more psychological than strategic, as the Aleutians are exceedingly close to (and part of) Alaska and the North American mainland. The next targets on Gen. Douglas MacArthur's list were Bougainville and Cape Gloucester on New Guinea, successfully invaded and conquered by his command in August of 1943. From then on, the Japanese were on the defensive.

Back home, the civilians were caught up in a whirlwind of change unprecedented in the nation's history. People were on the move, entering the military services and seeking higher paying jobs. It is estimated that fifteen million people crossed state lines for employment reasons during

While still a leader in the production of the 20mm Oer-
likon antiaircraft gun, Pontiac received a contract for
the bigger, Swedish-designed Bofors antiaircraft gun.
Its ceiling was 5,000 feet and its maximum range was
32,000 feet, while firing 120 rounds per minute from
four-round clips. If a shell didn't hit a target within
seven seconds, it automatically detonated. Also featured

in this ad are the aerial torpedoes being dropped from a
Grumman Avenger, and the M-5 Stuart light tank. To
link the company to the pursuit of freedom, the Liberty
Bell is hung from the "T" in Pontiac at the top of the ad.
Courtesy, Pontiac Division, General Motors Corpora-
tion

"COMIN' IN ON A WING AND A PRAYER!"

Used with permission of the copyright proprietor, Robbins Music Corporation

THEY HAVE TO BE BUILT RIGHT

"COMIN' in on a wing and a prayer" was the message the radio man sent ahead to his field in Tunisia. And this tough U. S. Marauder bomber, though riddled by anti-aircraft fire, did come in to a safe landing.

In Hudson plants, where we build fuselage sections for these daredevils of the air, we know how much depends on our work. It is one of our many important tasks that call for split-hair precision, at top production speed.

Against these exacting jobs, Hudson has put more than 30 years of experience in building automobiles that could *take it*—keep on going, under hard and constant punishment.

These cars today are proving their in-buil stamina. Ably serviced by a nationwide organization of Hudson distributors and dealers, they are part of the mighty transportation fleet that keeps us rolling to Victory.

Dishing Out Disaster to the Axis! *Wings for Helldivers . . . fuselage sections for Army Marauder bombers . . . components for Wright Cyclone engines! These are some of the important jobs on which Hudson is now in large-scale production for the Air Forces. High precision work—all of it! Finish dimensions of pistons, for example, must be accurate within 10 millionths of an inch, and weight within 4 hundredths of a pound.*

Aviation Division Awarded Army-Navy "E" for High Achievement in War Production.

Buy U. S. War Savings Stamps and Bonds

HUDSON
MOTOR CAR COMPANY
DETROIT, MICHIGAN
34 Years of Engineering Leadership

Itching for Action! *Engines, as well as men, must "come through" when American invasion forces stream from transports to beach. The engineering and manufacturing experience that produced a generation of famous Hudson automobile engines is now devoted to building large numbers of husky Hudson Invader engines to power Allied landing boats.*

32 Out of 35 Jap Dive Bombers Downed in Less Than 30 Minutes! *That's the amazing record of U. S. battleship gunners in a recent Southern Pacific action. We are proud of the fact that their batteries included 20-mm. Oerlikon anti-aircraft guns built in the U. S. Naval Ordnance plant operated by Hudson.*

OUR PLANTS ARE DEDICATED TO WAR PRODUCTION...OUR DEALERS TO MAINTAINING WAR TRANSPORTATION!

78

Previous page
The title of this advertisement was a popular World War II song, in this case illustrating a badly damaged B-26 Marauder returning from a raid during the North African campaign. Hudson manufactured fuselage assemblies for this 310mph medium bomber. While considered difficult to fly, this aircraft suffered the lowest loss rate of all US bombers. Courtesy, Chrysler Corporation

the war, and the number of working women leaped from twelve to eighteen million. Executives responding to the nation's need for their special experience, training, and skills were known as "dollar a year men" because they temporarily gave up their corporate positions (but not their salaries) to join the government for a token salary of $1 per year. Washington, D.C., was a madhouse, and housing was impossible to procure. Several movies featured this theme with comedic results.

With so much money being made by so many people, the government instituted the first withholding tax in 1943, and a whole new class of taxpayers was created from people who had never paid taxes before. Wartime romances flourished. One Elvira Taylor of Norfolk, Virginia, was apprehended after marrying six sailors for their allotment checks. Women like Taylor were known as "Allotment Annies" who preyed on lonesome servicemen. The pain and uncertainty of separation led to many a "Dear John" letter being mailed to the far corners of the world where Americans were serving. Poor, uneducated people left the rural countryside to take high-paying, assembly-line defense jobs in northern and western cities. These relocations precipitated permanent changes in the country's demographics.

The massive Ford Motor Company plant at Willow Run, Michigan, was probably the most famous example of the upheaval and dislocation caused by the wartime economy. Construction began in the spring of 1941, and ultimately included seven concrete runways, 109 acres of aircraft hangars, and 80 acres of factory buildings. Planners had to revise the original factory design so that the complex did not spill over into an adjoining county, creating tax and regulatory difficulties. Production of B-24 bombers began in November 1941, but the first aircraft wasn't completed until September 1942.

In January 1943, the Willow Run plant, which encompassed 1,600 machine tools and 7,000 jigs, produced 31 B-24s, reaching a production figure of 190 aircraft in June of that year. People finally stopped referring to the plant as "Willit Run?" Among the factory workers at Willow Run were several midgets whose size permit-

Oldsmobile urged the general public to preserve the nation's cars, so necessary in a war economy stressed by shortages of vehicles, gasoline, and rubber. At the same time, by patronizing an Oldsmobile dealer for preventative maintenance, it helped him keep his doors open until he once again had cars to sell. Most of the airplanes illustrated in the background of this ad were more artistic than realistic. Courtesy, Oldsmobile Division, General Motors Corporation

ted them to work inside the massive wings of the huge planes.

Ford's B-24 test pilots referred to the plant technicians as "plow mechanics" because of their unfamiliarity with airplanes, but the pilots agreed that these workers produced technically fine equipment. Unfortunately, the living quar-

Next page
Throughout World War II, the US Coast Guard bravely managed the landing craft and invasion beaches for the Army and Marines. At Guadalcanal, superior enemy naval units forced the American transports and supply ships to retreat out of harm's way, which created a shortage of troops and supplies in that desperate fight. In this ad, the Coast Guard saved a damaged barge containing vital supplies by towing it to safety with a Jeep, and at the same time fighting off enemy aircraft with a .50 caliber machine gun mounted on the back of the same Jeep. Courtesy, Chrysler Corporation

U. S. COAST GUARD GIVES JAPS THE OLD "ONE-TWO"

IN JEEPS FROM WILLYS-OVERLAND

ters available to the average worker could not be referred to as "fine." The arrival of large numbers of new employees created havoc in local communities, and Ypsilanti, nearby to Willow Run, was no exception. The lack of services available to these transplanted defense workers, including schools, stores, housing, and entertainment, as well as electricity, water, and sewers, caused dissatisfaction among the new arrivals and placed a great strain on area officials and resources.

Local communities were concerned that when the war ended, they would be faced with "ghost towns" left behind by the departed workers, and rejected plans formulated by the federal government for a permanent development called Bomber City. Instead, the Public Housing Administration erected fifteen buildings for 3,000 tenants in the early months of 1943, naming these dormitories and small houses Willow Village.

Soon after, a mobile home park opened with a thousand trailers moving in immediately. Often, shift workers shared a room; while one worked, the other slept. By the end of 1943, Willow Village, with its paper-thin walls, iceboxes, and coal stoves, housed 15,000 people, but the Willow Run plant employed more than 42,000. As a result, more than 50 percent of Willow Run's employees commuted great distances, in many cases thirty miles in each direction from Detroit. Car-pool restrictions demanded that commuter cars be fully loaded, and unlucky workers had to take a bus in both directions. Unfortunately, initial prewar planning had not considered tire shortages and

A somber atmosphere is evoked in this ad describing the many automotive failures that could occur without proper maintenance. However, the tires look fine and the headlights are working, so the first few admonitions in the advertising copy don't appear to pertain to this car. Chevrolet was one of the first automobile companies to advertise wartime maintenance as a necessary measure of national defense. This ad urged drivers to "see your Chevrolet dealer. Let him help make your car outlast the war." Courtesy, Chevrolet Division, General Motors Corporation

US servicemen who were overwhelmed by the enemy in the early days of the war on Wake Island and Guam, and those who surrendered on Bataan and Corregidor in the spring of 1942, were treated brutally by their Japanese captors. The harshness of their condition became known when three American officers escaped from the Davao Penal Colony, a POW camp in the Philippines, in April 1943, and reached Australia in July with their report of cruelty, torture, and murder. Not many POWs received mail from their families as depicted here. Nash-Kelvinator focused on the human element in war, and initiated an advertising campaign that emphasized the suffering and sacrifice of individual Americans caught up in the maelstrom. The ad urged, "Keep their spirits up! Write letters regularly to Fighting Men at Home and Overseas." Courtesy, Chrysler Corporation

LIFE, LIBERATORS AND PURSUIT OF THE AXIS

Take a gang of young Americans — alert, eager, vital —

Train 'em, groom 'em, wrap 'em in flying clothes and give 'em a big B-24 Liberator to fly —

Brief a target for them someplace where the Japs are thick, or where enemy factories cluster, ripe for the fall of a big stick of bombs —

Take all that, lump it together, and you've got the big purpose for which tens of thousands of workers in quiet Flint and suburban Melrose Park are working night and day.

Buick men, schooled and traditioned in doing things the good way, who in the past year or so have learned to do things even better than before.

Forgemen, machinists, lathe men, en-

gineers, metallurgists, production wizards — all of them joined together now in just one real aim: To come closer and ever closer to absolute perfection in the making of a mechanical thing.

What they make is the Pratt & Whitney engines that are original equipment on the Liberator.

VICTORY IS OUR BUSINESS

war goods

What they make it with is the finest of materials, the best and latest of machinery, the fine, patient, insistent skill of people good at their jobs and proud of it.

Some day they won't be building war goods any more. They'll be back instead producing things to make life sweeter, liberty more meaningful, the pursuit of happiness easier.

But they're not thinking about that — yet. They've got a job to do for those guys swathed in flying suits whose work it is to drop the bombs that pave the way for Victory Day.

It's their biggest job ever, and they're making it their best. They want the crew to know, whenever they see a Buick name plate on their Liberator engine, that they've got something *good* to help 'em do their work!

WHEN BETTER AUTOMOBILES ARE BUILT BUICK WILL BUILD THEM

Buick may be excused for its play on the words from the first paragraph of the Declaration of Independence as it boasted of its involvement with production of the B-24 Liberator bomber. With a range of 2,200 miles and an 8,000lb bomb load capability, it was superior to the B-17 in these respects. However, the B-24 was difficult to fly in tight combat formation and could not sustain as much battle damage as the B-17 Flying Fortress. It also never achieved as much recognition from the general public and the media as did the Fortress. Courtesy, Buick Division, General Motors Corporation

gas rationing when Willow Run was on the drawing boards.

Conditions were even worse for blacks in the migrant work force. In the Detroit area most of them lived in a slum called Paradise Valley, which it wasn't. The city's housing commission branded 50.2 percent of their residences as substandard, compared to 14 percent for white people. There were inequities in pay and opportunity as well, with blacks representing less than 1 percent of the work force in 55 out of 185 major defense plants. At one Packard plant, 3,000 white workers walked out in protest when three blacks were promoted. Events such as these did not bode well for America's future race relations.

Socially, there was not much to do around Willow Run. With little transportation available but a lot of money to spend, the pursuit of sex and alcohol became the mainstays of social life for single workers, as it was in many defense communities. The Orange Lantern Bar, located between the plant and Willow Village, was open–and packed–from eight in the morning until seven at night, selling its twelve cases of rationed whiskey a week. A reporter for *Daily Variety* called nearby Detroit "Baghdad on Lake Michigan," a wide-open town.

Another area of social and economic disruption on the home front was labor peace, never very stable in prewar twentieth century America. During April, United Mine Workers president John L. Lewis took thousands of his members out on strike and refused President Roosevelt's order to return to work.

In May, 25,000 Chrysler plant workers went on strike as well as 52,000 rubber workers in Akron, Ohio, and 2,000 workers in Toledo where the famous Willys Jeep was built. Also in May, 1,000 employees struck a roller bearing plant in Ohio, 2,000 auto workers walked out in Toledo, 1,900 struck a ball-bearing plant in upstate New York, and 400 steel workers in Kentucky struck for a 23 percent raise. There was a bus drivers' strike in Utica, New York, a transit workers' strike in Baltimore, and a milk drivers' strike in New York City.

In its June 7 issue *LIFE* magazine said, "...it is true that some of their [labor] leaders, notably John L. Lewis, would have difficulty in passing an examination at the bar of patriotism." It would appear that many Americans still had a preoccupation with their own needs, and national sacrifice would have to take a back seat.

Billboards were erected outside some factories to keep track of the number of employees absent from work each day or the number of man hours lost due to a day's absenteeism. "Don't be a Hiro-Hitler helper by being an absentee," one such board read. "Uncle Sam lost [the previous day's number of] man hours yesterday."

Problems in the work force continued, with relocation being a constant weakness. In one month at Willow Run, Ford hired 2,900 new workers while 3,100 existing employees went elsewhere. In July 1943, the numbers were 3,078 hired and 3,614 departed. At year's end, the absentee rate was 17 percent, and only 35,000 jobs were filled out of 58,000 available.

Nash-Kelvinator did not overlook those who waited anxiously at home to hear from their loved ones, in this case a wife and children. Nash was determined that the war must not be allowed to change its vision of prewar America, a hope that was dashed with the first rifle shot and bomb blast. Copies of this message were available free for the asking to send to "someone overseas." Courtesy, Chrysler Corporation

While Ford was a major manufacturer of the B-24 bomber, the company also produced engines for the B-26 Marauder featured here, along with the P-47 Thunderbolt, the PV-1 patrol plane, and the C-46 cargo air- *craft. Ford manufactured Jeeps, tanks, and air assault gliders as well. All were important contributions to America's war machine. Courtesy, Ford Motor Company*

Ultimately, parts of the B-24 assembly line were relocated to other Ford plants, and the company agreed to hire more women to work the line, something it had been reluctant to do earlier in the war. Ford was even slower in hiring blacks. Still, there was great progress in the technology of the workplace. Ford executives proudly pointed out that the company's specially manufactured machinery for building the center wing section of the B-24 bomber reduced the operation from a "36 man, 1,500 hour job to three men working 26 minutes." American industry would not return to many of its old ways when this war ended.

As mentioned earlier, victory gardens had been robustly embraced by the civilian population, and by the end of the war twenty million Americans with gardens of all shapes and sizes had grown one-third of all the fresh vegetables consumed in the country during the conflict. In New York City, 40,000 tons of vegetables were reportedly grown in 168,000 gardens. The best commercially produced food was still reserved for the

troops, with no butter or sugar available on the home front and powdered milk for everybody. SPAM, an acronym for spiced ham, was a canned meat readily available and both praised and condemned by Americans at home and abroad. It helped make "meatless Tuesdays" easier to bear. While shoe leather and zippers were hard to come by, most clothing was pretty much available during 1943, although diversity of styles and colors was lacking. An exception was ladies' nylon stockings. Silk stockings had been replaced prior to 1941 by nylons, and now all the nylon produced

Next page
Plymouth did very little magazine advertising during the war years, subordinating itself to its parent company, Chrysler. In this advertisement, the image flashes back to Plymouth's prewar production line, and hints optimistically of future Plymouths in a world at peace. This was Plymouth's straightforward request not to be forgotten by the public. Courtesy, Chrysler Corporation

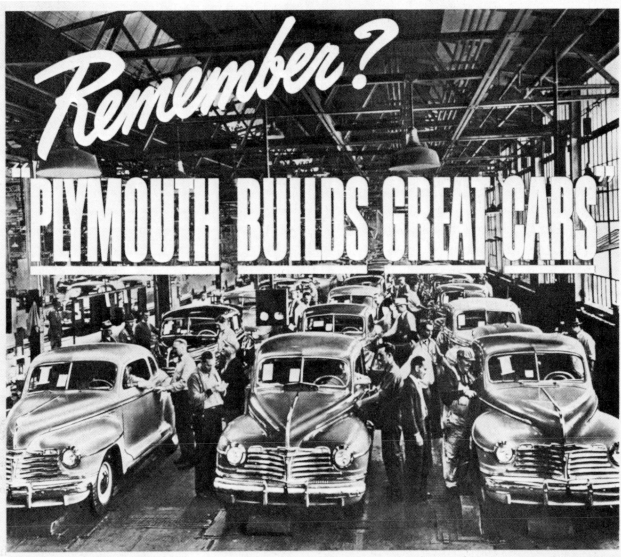

Remember?
"PLYMOUTH BUILDS GREAT CARS"

Pre-war view of Plymouth's half-mile long assembly lines—long since changed to war production.

THEY REMEMBER WELL, who find the promise of quality on which they chose a Plymouth has been fulfilled in generous measure. Plymouth economy and long life are more talked about in these days than ever before.

And Plymouth owners can well expect that the engineering "know how" and high-precision manufacturing technics—which produced a great car for them—are broadly and intensively engaged today in war production.

The huge Plymouth plants, where half-mile long assembly lines once turned out upwards of 600,000 great cars a year, are now vast volume production centers contributing heavily to Chrysler Corporation's many important war contracts.

Foundation of the saying "Plymouth Builds Great Cars" was the fact—proven among some three million Plymouth owners. The reputation follows these cars where they are sought today by second, third, fourth-hand buyers. The reputation is remembered when people talk about the new car they will buy after the war.

Meanwhile, present Plymouth owners are fortunate in the nationwide service and parts availability through Plymouth dealers everywhere. Indeed, car owners of other makes, too, are securing competent service from those Plymouth dealers.

And meanwhile, the thought—"Plymouth Builds Great Cars"—has so many living representatives on the streets and highways, so many devoted witnesses among the public that even several years of building tank, airplane and cannon assemblies, and no cars, in the Plymouth plants could not obliterate its meaning in the automotive world—nor the promise it holds with peace.

PLYMOUTH... *Division of Chrysler Corporation*

WAR BONDS ARE YOUR PERSONAL INVESTMENT IN VICTORY

Horsepower Wins Wars

Tractors powered by Chrysler Industrial Engines are extensively used by our Armed Forces for pulling airplanes into and out of hangars and repair shops as well as for other hauling jobs around air bases.

CHRYSLER AIR RAID SIREN

MILITARY victories culminate on the field of battle. They begin at the forge, the factory, the shipyard, and on the farm.

Thus the horsepower that contributes to the efficiency of war-time manufacture, agriculture or essential construction is contributing to victory just as surely as that which motivates actual fighting units.

The Chrysler Division, Chrysler Corporation, contributes horsepower both to the fighting and to the preparations for fighting. Its industrial engines are being applied to more than a score of essential uses directly connected with the war effort.

Among these uses are to furnish power for airport tractors, airport gang mowers, arc welders used in many kinds of con-

CHRYSLER MARINE TRACTOR

[BUY U. S. WAR BONDS AND STAMPS]

struction, generator sets for firing cannon, industrial lift trucks, emergency fire-pumpers, air raid sirens, air compressors for a variety of uses, farm tractors, farm combines, mechanical shovels and buses.

BOFORS ANTI-AIRCRAFT GUN

In some cases, the United States Government is specifying Chrysler Industrial engines as the power plants in equipment it orders. They are meeting the drastic requirements of the Army, Navy, Marine Corps, Coast Guards, O.C.D. and O.D.T.

for all kinds of service at home and abroad.

Power, flexibility, and smoothness are combined in these engines. Their Super-finished parts insure long life and economy of operation under the most exacting conditions of widely diversified programs.

Chrysler tank, automobile and marine engines by the thousands also are playing an important part in our vast wartime transportation.

CHRYSLER FIRE PUMPER

CHRYSLER
DIVISION OF CHRYSLER CORPORATION

WAR PRODUCTS OF CHRYSLER DIVISION: Industrial Engines . Marine Engines . Marine Tractors . Navy Pontoons
Harbor Tugs . Anti-Aircraft Cannon Parts . Tank Engine Assemblies . Tank Parts . Airplane Wing Panels
Fire Fighting Equipment . Air Raid Sirens . Gun Boxes . Searchlight Reflectors

THE NATIONWIDE CHRYSLER DEALER ORGANIZATION OFFERS OWNERS SERVICE FACILITIES TO MEET THEIR WARTIME TRANSPORTATION NEEDS

Although Chrysler manufactured Army tanks and anti-aircraft guns, a female war worker was the centerpiece for this advertisement, which showcased several wartime products that had civilian adaptations. Aston-ishingly, with victory so far in the future, some companies were already laying the groundwork for peacetime sales. Courtesy, Chrysler Corporation

SCRATCH ANOTHER "Impossible"

ONE of the toughest assignments ever put up to the Ordnance Department of the U. S. Army had to do with this seemingly simple item shown here.

It is a shell case for a 75-mm gun. Ordinarily it is made of easily-worked brass. But brass was desperately scarce. The tough and urgent job was to make it instead from a billet of plain, ordinary, run-of-the-mill steel like this:

To work in our fast-firing 75's, this shell case must have certain definite and dependable characteristics, and no maybes about it.

It must be *exactly* right as to size.

It must not be one iota too hard at any point, lest it crack in firing, nor one iota too soft, lest it expand and jam the breech block.

It must stand repeated firings and remain reloadable.

The job of working out the method of accomplishing this was a long and puzzling one that called for many minds and much experimenting.

But today these cases are coming from Buick plants at a rate that runs in the hundreds of thousands every month.

And they are coming out true in every respect to the rigid Army specifications which obviously must apply to such important materiel.

So you can scratch off another "impossible" as an accomplished fact.

You can chalk off millions of pounds of precious brass saved for other vital military jobs where no alternate material can be used.

And you can go ahead and buy more War Bonds confident that this and like forms of American industrial will-to-win are making each Bond buy the utmost for Victory.

BUICK DIVISION OF **GENERAL MOTORS**

A shortage of brass for many large-caliber shells necessitated the use of steel as a replacement. It was not an easy task for civilian manufacturers to produce military hardware with substitute materiels and still maintain the exceedingly fine tolerances required for the final product. In addition, the military wanted to reload

these steel shells for re-use on the battlefield, and this added to their quality requirements. Buick was justly proud of its role in this conversion, and told the story in a full-color ad. Courtesy, Buick Division, General Motors Corporation

was going to war, mainly for parachutes. Silk was scarce because most of it came from Japan. Both were replaced by rayon, another synthetic not appreciated by women for their legs, and this shortage created a memorable lament of the times. Some women resorted to leg make-up, painting a line up the backs of their calves to imitate the seam of an unavailable stocking.

The year 1943 was also the year that "Lucky Strike Green Goes to War." This was one of the most successful advertising campaigns ever launched, and it led to a 38 percent increase in "Luckies" sales in six weeks. Interestingly, the ads did not appear in the print media but were confined to radio spots and cardboard inserts in cigarette cartons. Many products were advertised in different magazines to attract different groups of consumers, then as now. The *Saturday Evening Post* and *Collier's* were family-oriented magazines with many short stories, while the more sophisticated *LIFE* magazine contained

more news items and photo essays. There was scarcely an organization or company that did not try to jump on the patriotic bandwagon to sell its products, and some of them really stretched the imagination. Nobody wanted his or her patriotism questioned!

With North Africa secured, the Allies turned their eyes toward the Italian peninsula, to appease both Stalin's demands for a second front and Churchill's strategic vision of an attack northward through what he termed "the soft un-

Next page
Dodge was a major manufacturer of ambulances for the US military, and also provided thousands of trucks for the war effort. Like Plymouth, another Chrysler division, Dodge was not a major wartime advertiser, yet the company was heavily involved in defense production, including parts for the 40mm Bofors gun. Courtesy, Chrysler Corporation

DODGE DEPENDABILITY
on the battlefronts...

ONCE again Dodge dependability is being proven on the battlefronts of the world. Again, Dodge is demonstrating its fundamental strength, resourcefulness and dependability.

Dodge owners throughout America take personal pride in the striking facts — that Dodge Trucks were the first combat vehicles ashore with American soldiers when the invasion of Africa took place. They were also the first military vehicles to penetrate the wilderness road to Alaska.

The twenty-eight year history of Dodge is one of precision craftsmanship applied to automotive vehicles in time of peace, and then re-applied to the arms and munitions of war whenever America's need requires.

The Dodge record of today is a greatly enlarged repetition of its outstanding performance three decades ago when General Pershing himself gave commands from a Dodge vehicle, and when basic parts of the famous French 75 cannon had their American production in the original Dodge plants.

Today finds Dodge factories and Dodge dealers again intimately joined in the total effort of the war. Again the factories are producing, in whole or in part, arms, munitions, instru-

ments and many varieties of combat vehicles for war. The Dodge dealers, at the same time, are everywhere helping to maintain, with factory engineered parts and approved service, Dodge cars and trucks in essential use.

[WAR BONDS ARE YOUR PERSONAL INVESTMENT IN VICTORY]

DODGE
DIVISION OF CHRYSLER CORPORATION

On almost every battlefield the Red Cross on thousands of Dodge vehicles tells its own moving story. These vehicles of mercy are almost beloved by medical staffs, nurses and patients for their unfailing dependability.

Dodge again fulfills an historic role with its sturdy vehicles of war. Dodge trucks were the first ashore with American troops when the invasion of Africa occurred and first, also, to penetrate the wilderness road to Alaska.

Twenty-eight years of dependability has qualified Dodge to do intricate and delicate manufacturing jobs. There is no better war example than the fabrication of vital parts for the famous Bofors anti-aircraft gun.

Dodge ability to handle precision manufacturing is exemplified by the Gyro-Compass. Mass production of this dependable instrument helps fighting and cargo ships navigate more safely. *Gyro-Compass shown during test in Dodge Plant.*

derbelly of Europe." In order to secure the flanks of such an incursion, the Allies invaded the island of Sicily in July of 1943 and conquered it after thirty-eight days of hard fighting. It was here that Gen. George Patton added to his reputation by slapping an American enlisted man said to be suffering from combat fatigue. The incident almost cost Patton his command, but Supreme Commander Eisenhower saved him, realizing that Patton was the premier American general in the European theater. That same month Italian dictator Benito Mussolini was forced to resign by his own Fascist government council, and with his departure went the Italian resolve to continue the war.

Another Italian significantly affected in the summer of 1943 was a pilot named Guido Rossi.

Flying a captured American P-38 fighter, he was able to shoot down an unsuspecting B-17 named "Bonnie Sue" whose pilot, Harold Fisher, was the only survivor. Vowing revenge, Fisher painted the name and face of Rossi's wife (the woman lived in Allied-occupied territory) on his replacement B-17 and continued to fly his assigned missions. Some weeks later, Rossi intercepted Fisher's aircraft and queried the American over his radio regarding the plane's nickname. Fisher answered by saying that it was named for the woman with whom he was living, so angering the Italian that he made a rash attack on Fisher's plane and was shot down. Rossi became a prisoner of war, and

Lockheed's P-38 Lightning was powered by two 1,745hp engines manufactured by the Allison Division of General Motors, and armed with a 20mm cannon built by Oldsmobile. It could also carry 4,000lb of bombs or ten 5in rockets and fly at more than 400mph. The P-38 was responsible for the destruction of more Japanese aircraft in the Pacific than any other type of Allied aircraft. Print ads like this one appearing in August 1943 used drawings and paintings rather than photographs, and it's noted that "this illustration [is] based on actual combat officially reported from the South Pacific." Courtesy, Oldsmobile Division, General Motors Corporation

The M-5 Stuart light tank mounted a 37mm cannon and used two Cadillac 121hp V-8 gasoline engines. It could travel at 40mph. In contrast, the German Mark IV tank featured a 75mm gun and a 300hp gas engine with a top speed of 26mph. It was far heavier at 25 tons than the M-5 at 15 tons. The clean-shaven G.I.s in this advertisement are all armed with the .45 caliber Thompson sub-machine gun with 50-round drums of ammunition, highly unusual for standard infantry usually equipped with the M-1 Garand. Actually, the Army used 30-round straight clips with the Thompson because the drums could not withstand the rigors of combat, and were also quite heavy when fully loaded. Courtesy, Cadillac Division, General Motors Corporation

When life hangs on **millionths** of an inch

The P-40 Warhawk, pictured here, was used extensively in China, the Pacific, and the North African campaign. Its 1,200hp Rolls-Royce engine was very reliable, and the aircraft could sustain heavy battle damage and still return to base. It could not match the enemies' top fighters in performance, but was first made famous by the Flying Tigers of the American Volunteer Group in China, who adopted tactics that utilized the P-40's best operational characteristics. These intrepid aviators also painted sharks' mouths on the noses of their aircraft. More than 14,000 P-40s were built during the war. Packard also manufactured engines for the British Mosquito and Lancaster bombers. Courtesy, Dresser-Rand

Fisher was awarded the Distinguished Flying Cross. (Fisher was killed flying the Berlin Airlift in 1948.)

On September 3 Italy signed an armistice with the Allies, the same day that British Gen. Bernard Montgomery launched his invasion of that country. These landings were followed by an American amphibious attack at Salerno, Italy, under Gen. Mark Clark on September 10. Meanwhile, the Germans had rushed troops into Italy to forestall the Allied advance, and they did a good job. Lost opportunities and miserable weather turned the Italian campaign into an Allied stalemate, although it did tie up thousands of elite German troops and provided advance airbases for the bombing of the Third Reich. However, the Germans' defensive position known as the

True Yesterday—

PLYMOUTH BUILDS GREAT CARS THE "R...

In Trust for Tomorrow

PLYMOUTH DIVISION OF CHRYSLER CORPORATION
"BUY WAR BONDS AND STAMPS FOR VICTORY"

Another "don't forget us" ad from Plymouth. By September of 1943, when this ad appeared, Plymouth's advertising was aimed at the postwar consumer, with barely a mention of the ongoing hostilities. Many Americans shared this optimistic attitude, which is remarkable considering that the cross-channel attack on Europe had not yet occurred, and the retaking of the Pacific was in reality in its infancy. Courtesy, Chrysler Corporation

Gustav Line across central Italy stopped the Allies cold in October.

The air war against Germany and occupied Europe started in earnest during 1943, with the Royal Air Force (RAF) providing carpet bombing at night and the United States attempting precision strategic bombing during the daytime. In 1942 it had become British doctrine that the RAF

Next page
DeSoto's contribution to the powerful B-26 medium bomber was in fuselage and nose section manufacture. Known as the Marauder, the B-26 could absorb significant battle damage and still stay in the air. The aircraft featured here is similar to the B-26 in the Hudson ad discussed earlier, and probably illustrates the same incident. However, in this version the observation bubble atop the plane appears to be shot away, and a crewman is poking his head through the opening. Courtesy, Chrysler Corporation

De Soto
HELPS MAKE THEM

This B-26, badly riddled by anti-aircraft fire in a raid on Nazi installations, returns safely to its Tunisian base. — International News Photo.

B-26 —"The Marauder"

It's a beautiful and powerful all metal monoplane, and some of the world's keenest pilots are its masters.

At Midway and in the Aleutians, these Marauders carried torpedoes; at Soputa, they dropped parachute bombs; at Buna *"they flew low and fast, their guns blazing."*

With its heavy armor and tremendous fire power, the B-26 can take mighty good care of itself. Seldom does it need fighter escort. It's a fighter on its own account. It's big and powerful and faster than most ships the enemy can send against it.

Yes, De Soto helps to build these B-26 Marauders. De Soto makes the big fuselage and nose sections on long assembly lines,

manned by many of the same craftsmen who made fine cars for you every day in peacetime.

When De Soto delivers these nose and fuselage sections, it means that wiring, sound proofing, trim, tubing, functional mechanisms, most of the instruments and all of the controls are in their proper place.

De Soto takes pride in the fame of these B-26 Marauders as reports from the battle fronts tell of their terrific striking power, their fleetness, maneuverability, and success.

DE SOTO DIVISION OF CHRYSLER CORPORATION

WAR BONDS
They are Your Personal Investment in Victory.

DE SOTO WAR PRODUCTION includes the precision building of airplane wing sections—bomber fuselage nose and center sections—vital assemblies for Bofors anti-aircraft guns and General Sherman Tanks—and a wide variety of special manufacturing services to a large portion of American war industry.

DE SOTO DEALERS throughout America remain strongly at their posts of service, maintaining the De Soto products of peace with essential parts and service.

bombing campaign "would be focused on the morale of the enemy civilian population and in particular, of the industrial workers." Terror bombing by any other name, but perhaps understandable after what Germany had done to Britain's civilians during the blitz.

The Americans believed that strategic bombing could significantly weaken the Axis and shorten the war by destroying vital German industries. The cost was high. The Germans possessed the best antiaircraft gun of the war, the legendary 88 (it was also a superior artillery weapon and tank cannon), and when combined with the skill, experience, and courage of the Luftwaffe defending its homeland, Allied aircrew and aircraft casualties became unacceptably heavy. It was terrible on the ground, also.

On July 24, combined British night raids and American daytime raids devastated and incinerated the city of Hamburg in northern Germany. The air temperature reached 1,000 degrees Fahrenheit, creating a firestorm that was uncon-

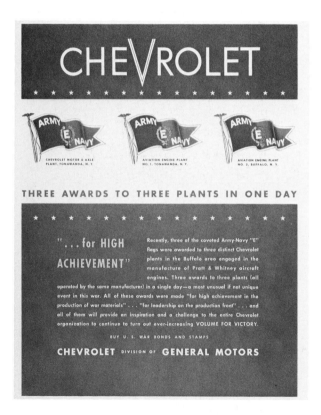

The Army-Navy E banners were eagerly sought by defense manufacturing leaders as proof of superior production achievement. Just about every major company qualified for the flags, and used them extensively in their advertising to showcase government approval of their work. This Chevrolet ad showed the banners in full color, and note the large "V"—as in Victory—in the Chevrolet name atop the ad. Courtesy, Chevrolet Division, General Motors Corporation

trollable, and 30,000 to 50,000 Germans, mostly civilians, died in the fires. Only eight days later, 177 American B-24 Liberator bombers flew from airfields in North Africa to cripple the vast oil refineries located at Ploesti, Rumania. Among British aviators billeted at their own bases near the American fields, there was a perception that US security was lacking, and that Arab agents working for the Germans were certainly aware in advance of the mission destination. Be that as it may, this initial raid on Ploesti knocked out 42 percent of the refinery production for several months, but at a price of fifty-four bombers, 31 percent of the attacking force, each with ten men aboard.

Another air war disaster occurred shortly afterward when 60 B-17 Flying Fortresses out of 291 dispatched from Eighth Army Air Force bases in England were shot down and another 138 damaged in the October 14 raid on the ball-bearing works at Schweinfurt, Germany. Six hundred casualties suffered in one afternoon! There were many bad afternoons in 1943 for the Eighth Air Force: 22 of 66 B-17s lost over Kiel on June 13, 24 lost out of 92 over Hanover, and 22 out of 120 over Berlin, both in July.

During the week of the Schweinfurt Raid, the Mighty Eighth lost 148 bombers and crews over Germany. Such losses led to a hiatus of long-range bomber missions in Europe until the availability of long-range fighter protection became a reality. It came in the form of the beautiful P-51 Mustang fighter, the scourge of the Luftwaffe in 1944 and 1945 over Europe. But for the present, even though the Allies dropped 200,000 tons of bombs on Germany in 1943, armament production still rose 50 percent for the year. While the tide of war seemed to be turning against the Axis, there was still a lot of war to be fought.

On the home front, the conflict dragged on with no end in sight. Several fine books were published in 1943, including *The Human Comedy, The Fountainhead,* and *A Tree Grows in Brooklyn,* as well as *Guadalcanal Diary,* which relived that recent island battle. All were instantly turned into movies.

Automobiles needed tender loving care, and gas and tires were difficult to procure. Civilians

Next page
Central to this advertisement was an American submarine under attack by enemy surface ships, but the theme quickly turned to the social and economic message projected by Nash-Kelvinator in its 1943 ads. In this instance, the auto manufacturer made no claim regarding submarine contracts. US submarines were used mainly in the Pacific, where they sank 1,100 Japanese merchant ships at 4,700,000 tons in addition to dozens of enemy war ships. Courtesy, Chrysler Corporation

I WANT UP!

It's dark down here.

It's quiet down here.

It's lonely down here.

No light. Just the glow of emergency bulbs. No noise. Just the ebb and flow of air in our lungs. No talking. But a lot of thinking.

We're "on the bottom."

They're waiting for us up there. They're listening for us up there. For the turn of a screw, for the clang of a wrench on the deck to tell their next depth bomb where to go.

We're waiting, too. For the sound of their engines to die away or—for the gagging stink of chlorine gas that lets us know our hull is cracked, the batteries are flooded and we're going down in a bubble of air and oil to drown!

Somehow, sweating it out down here in the cold and the dark and the fear, it seems to me I get things straighter than I used to. I see things clear.

I know now what this war's about. I know what this war is being fought for. I want this war over quick—and when it's over, I want up!

That's what I'm fighting for—up!

For the right to stand up in the world with my bride by my side and her hand on my arm.

For the right to speak up in my town and have my say and then sit down.

For the right every night to run up the steps of my house back home and pick up and hold a son of my own.

For his right and her right and mine to grow up, to work up in the same America I left behind . . . where there's freedom to breathe . . . freedom to move up to new and better things . . . to look up to the skies and recognize that in America there will always be a limitless opportunity to rise as high, to go as far as courage and strength and ability can take me!

That's how I remember America.

Keep it that way . . . until I come back.

Here at Nash-Kelvinator, we're building 2,000 h. p. Pratt & Whitney engines for Navy Vought Corsair fighters . . . making intricate Hamilton Standard propellers . . . readying production lines to build Sikorsky helicopters for the Army Air Forces . . . doing our part to keep for our boys while they're away the same America they've always known . . . a land of progress and enterprise and equality for all.

NASH-KELVINATOR CORPORATION
Kenosha · Milwaukee · DETROIT · Grand Rapids · Lansing

were prosperous, earning more than they ever had before, although it was impossible to buy a steak for dinner, and meat ration points went unused because meat just wasn't available. Paper was also in short supply, resulting in very few Christmas cards being sent that year. The scarcity of metal resulted in wooden toys for the children that Christmas. Actually, the demand for services, products, and food was high because people had more money than ever before, and could afford to buy what had been unattainable in their lives before the war.

The prosperity of middle America extended to people who had never previously known it. Counted in this group to some extent were poor blacks who had left the rural South to work in the big-city defense plants up North. Detroit overflowed with transplanted blacks jammed into sub-

standard housing. There was trouble brewing for some time in that city. Blacks across the nation had a taste of social and economic freedom brought about by the war, and were no longer isolated, or afraid to demand equality in practice. The Detroit police force, short of men due to military service, faced a black community rankled by injustice but also responsible for 65 percent of the crime in the city. Segregation was the rule, including the armed forces, and even the Red Cross segregated blood donations.

It didn't take much effort to start trouble, and it began on a steamy Sunday night in June. Picnickers, mainly black, were returning to the city by car and on foot via the bridge from Belle Isle when a fight broke out between a white sailor and some black teenagers. Approximately 200 sailors from the nearby Navy Arsenal came to the sailor's aid, and the deadly brawl was on. Drinkers in the black bars in Paradise Valley were incited by false rumors that a black woman and her baby had been thrown off the bridge by whites. Similarly, whites were aroused by a false story that a white woman had been raped and killed on the bridge by blacks. Battles raged all night and into the next day. Blacks beat up 50 whites in a streetcar on their way to work. In retaliation, whites attacked blacks who were leaving a movie theater and had no idea what was going on in the city. Stores were looted, especially pawnshops in the black sections that were owned by whites, and mobs roamed the streets looking for members of the opposite race to beat or kill.

During Detroit's Bloody Week, 34 people died, 25 of them black, and 800 were injured. More than 1,000 citizens were arrested, while property damage was in excess of $2 million.

The absentee rate at local defense plants exceeded 20 percent, and two million work-hours were lost in two days. War production dropped 6 percent. Of those arrested, 60 percent were under thirty-one years of age and 48 percent were under twenty-one. While black and white church and civic leaders tried to restore peace to the ravaged city, there was only an ominous silence from the leaders of the business community. Although industry needed black workers to fulfill its wartime contracts, they were engaged most reluctantly

This German Heinkel 111 medium bomber, peppered from nose to tail by cannon and machine-gun fire, must have been attacked while on the ground. It does not seem possible to sustain that much damage while airborne and still be able to land intact. Pontiac takes some credit here for its role in Allied forces scoring such kills. The Heinkel 111 was armed with five machine guns and a 20mm cannon in a vertical gondola on the underside of the aircraft. It had a 750 mile range with a 4,500lb bomb load. Courtesy, Oldsmobile Division, General Motors Corporation

Next page
Because it was a mobile system, the 90mm was considered a medium antiaircraft gun. As the war progressed, electronic tracking and range-finding increased the efficiency of these weapons, and by the end of the conflict antiaircraft guns were scoring one hit for every 1,500 projectiles fired. This Fisher ad notes that the company "did not make all of [the gun]," but that several manufacturers' cooperative spirit of war production made it possible. Courtesy, General Motors

BUY
WAR BONDS
AND STAMPS
TODAY
·
*Keep America
free*

Body blow *by Fisher*

The Army-Navy "E" flies above three Fisher plants for excellence in aircraft production and from two others for tank production, while the Navy "E," with three stars, is flown by still another Fisher plant for its naval ordnance work.

IT'S bad news for enemy planes—this 90-millimeter anti-aircraft gun. Here are a few notes for the record—time and place deleted.

A four-gun battery of these "nineties" brought down sixteen high-altitude bombers in twelve days.

"Body blow" was right!

Fisher is proud of this gun, although Fisher did not make *all* of it. Like most armament, it is a fine example of the cooperative spirit of American industry, with many manufacturers contributing to the finished product.

Perhaps Fisher's most notable contribution to this national effort is craftsmanship well directed. Precision men and precision methods help to give Fisher tanks, bombers, anti-aircraft guns and delicate aircraft instruments a technical plus. All the unusual crafts and special skills we have developed are trained on this target.

In war as in peace, craftsmanship is our goal. And we do our best to make the Fisher name on armament mean an ace in the hole when the going gets tough.

armament
BODY BY *Fisher*

DIVISION OF GENERAL MOTORS

and with little real social acceptance. It was something for a nation fighting for democracy to ruminate upon, when many of its own citizens faced so little democracy in their own country.

Similarly, the arrest of a black woman in New York's Harlem by a white police officer caused a riot that claimed six lives, more than 500 hurt, and $1 million in damages. The Army and the police could quell the riots, but they couldn't change the underlying social conditions that caused them. The seeds of civil strife had been sown for a bitter harvest in the years to come.

By the spring of 1943 the United States had lost 18,000 servicemen and women, with an additional 94,000 injured–and yet the toughest battles still lay ahead. In the Pacific, the Marines invaded Tarawa in the Gilbert Islands, a bloody con-

frontation described by an American general as "76 stark and bitter hours." The cost, again, was high.

The Marines suffered 3,301 casualties, with more than 1,000 dead. The defending Japanese, who rarely surrendered, lost 4,690 out of 4,836 soldiers engaged. By this period in the war, escaping prisoners, guerrillas, and intelligence missions into enemy territory had given the Allies quite a bit of information about the brutal treatment of Allied soldiers and civilians who had been captured during the early months of the conflict. The beheadings, tortures, rapes, and beatings were common knowledge to the soldiers in the field. It has been suggested that the American Marines and soldiers in the Pacific, in retaliation for the horrors perpetrated by the Japanese, would not let them surrender. Thus, the vaunted

The Bell P-39 Airacobra featured a 20mm or 37mm cannon in its nose, which fired through a hollow propeller shaft. The twelve-cylinder engine was located behind the cockpit, using an eight-foot extension shaft and a reduction gearbox. The P-39 incorporated a tricycle landing gear due to the weight of the cannon and munitions in the nose, which also housed four .50 caliber machine guns. With a range of 600 miles, it attained speeds of 368mph. More than 10,000 Airacobras were built, with many being shipped to the USSR and designated the P-400. The Soviets used it extensively for anti-tank operations against the Germans. Courtesy, Cadillac Division, General Motors Corporation

The US Coast Guard cutter Spencer sank a German U-boat in the North Atlantic in early 1943 while on convoy duty, forcing it to the surface with depth charges and then raking the superstructure with 20mm cannon fire. The Germans were thus prevented from returning fire with their deck gun and were forced to abandon ship. Germany launched 1,172 U-boats during the war, out of which 789 were lost, often with the entire crew going down with the ship. Hudson manufactured 20mm Oerlikon guns for the Navy, as well as landing craft engines and wings for Helldiver aircraft. Courtesy, Chrysler Corporation

The Bofors gun, with its superior fire power, could fire 120 40mm rounds per minute. It was used by every major Army in World War II except the Soviets, who already had a 37mm Bofors gun in their arsenal. The Navy used the Bofors with great efficiency against Japanese aircraft attacks on US ships, as the American military machine drove inexorably closer to the Japanese home islands. Courtesy, Chrysler Corporation

Pontiac received the first government contract for the 20mm Oerlikon gun, and in this ad credits its product as decisive in the sinking of a German submarine by the US Coast Guard cutter Spencer. Hudson claimed the same battle credit in an earlier advertisement in this section. Pontiac also manufactured aerial torpedoes for the Navy, a process that used 5,000 parts in 20,000 separate operations. Courtesy, Pontiac Division, General Motors Corporation

Japanese fanaticism was reinforced by their enemies' battle philosophy of "no quarter."

Elsewhere the British and Americans had stopped the Japanese in Burma, short of India. With the often lackluster aid of the Chinese under Chiang Kai-shek, the Allies began to reconquer of mainland Southeast Asia, seeking springboards for the air war against Japan itself. Among the leaders were Lord Louis Montbatten, US Gen. Joseph "Vinegar Joe" Stilwell (he referred to Chiang Kai-shek as the "Peanut"), British Major General Orde C. Wingate, who led the Chindits, a unit of British and Commonwealth troops used for long-range penetration of enemy territory (the group's name is derived from the Burmese name for the winged lions that guard Buddhist temples), and Brigadier Frank Merrill, leader of the Marauders, an American unit much like the Chindits. They all gained a measure of military reputation there as did the intrepid fliers supplying them across the Hi-

malayas, "flying the Hump." On the Eastern front, six million Soviets pushed three million Germans back into Germany. The ferocity of that war continued to the end, but the USSR, so close to annihilation, was saved.

Defense production soared in 1943, peaking in October, but with cutbacks starting in December. Advertising had played a role in relaying the production message to the American people, and also the government's philosophy toward the war and the postwar world. One magazine's idealistic editorial halfway through 1943 said, "But make no mistake, advertising has arrived in this war."

Next page
From the appearance of his uniform, former Studebaker employee Harry Ryan served in the infantry. The B-17 Flying Fortresses in the background are powered by engines built on assembly lines run by his father and other skilled Studebaker employees. Studebaker continued its generational advertising campaign throughout the war. Courtesy, Dresser-Rand

© 1943, The Studebaker Corporation

'You purr just like those engines Dad builds!'"

They're Studebaker-built Wright Cyclones for the famous Boeing Flying Fortress

SOLDIER HARRY RYAN and his father were fellow craftsmen in the Studebaker factory prior to Pearl Harbor.

They comprised one of the many father-and-son teams that have been a unique Studebaker institution since the business was founded in 1852.

Today, all over the world, large numbers of young men who once were Studebaker craftsmen, are engaged in using military equipment instead of building it.

In many instances, their fathers, and other older members of their families, are producing Flying Fortress engines, multiple-drive military trucks and other war matériel in the busy Studebaker plants.

For generations, one family after another in Studebaker's home community has maintained a tradition of Studebaker employment. This has resulted in a quality of craftsmanship unmatched in the automotive world.

That craftsmanship is now being utilized to the limit, on behalf of our Nation and its Allies, in the production of large quantities of military equipment. And you may be sure that it will provide finer Studebaker motor cars and motor trucks than ever before for civilian use, after victory comes.

BUY U. S. WAR BONDS

STUDEBAKER

Builder of Wright Cyclone engines for the Boeing Flying Fortress, big multiple-drive military trucks and other vital war matériel

"Always give more than you promise

That Studebaker watchword has been faithfully o served for 20 years by craftsman Henry C. Ryan. Toda he is helping to build Flying Fortress engines in o of Studebaker's aircraft engine plants. On some no too-distant tomorrow, he and his soldier son, Harr hope to be building Studebaker cars again for yo

98

*In a rare departure from its usual bland defense pro-
duction advertising, Chrysler portrayed the Japanese
enemy as "rats in a trap," and caricatured this Japanese officer by emphasizing his oversized, thick eyeglasses
and prominent buck teeth. Racial denigration was used
by both the American and Japanese governments for
propaganda purposes against each other during the
war, but was not often used by American manufacturers–with the exception of a few specific organizations.*
Courtesy, Chrysler Corporation

Our government faces a problem–inflation, for example. In such a matter the interests of every
separate group are in conflict with our interest,
as a whole people. How are we going to behave
and vote? As members of small groups, farmers,
unionists, merchants, manufacturers? Or as citizens of a great nation, intent upon the common
good. Perhaps the only force that can lift us above

*During late 1943, Ford abruptly changed its defense-
oriented advertising focus to visions of the future peace.
As military success seemed ultimately ensured but a
long way in the future, many manufacturers looked for
a significant lessening of the government regulations required in wartime. Understandably, they anticipated
an outpouring of civilian goods, especially cars, to meet
the pent-up demands created by wartime restrictions.*
Courtesy, Ford Motor Company

"IT WASN'T JUST DARK.... IT WAS BLACK AS TOJO'S HEART!..."

Then suddenly our searchlights swept across ten miles of midnight...and
pinned that Jap cruiser in a blinding glare of light...we could see those Japs plain
as day, scurrying around like rats in a trap!"...

Now, the light that caught those Japs came partly from the inside of a
Chrysler engine...Sounds funny, doesn't it?...But the Superfinish process that
gave Chrysler engine parts the smoothest surface in the world is today polishing metal
reflectors for searchlights...polishing them to a mirror-like smoothness that can
send a sharp beam of light up to twenty-five miles without distortion.

CHRYSLER

Who wouldn't like to be in these shoes?...

Important dates in American Progress...

'CHUTING THE FIRE-POWER
TO OUR PARATROOPS

75mm H.

Illustration based on a recent on-the-spot report of an actual airborne invasion.

Invasion from the skies! Men, artillery, ammunition . . . wave after wave of billowing parachutes dropping with dramatic suddenness in the rear of the enemy's lines. Pack howitzers are quickly assembled. 75 mm. shell are unpacked and rushed to the gun crews. Even before the last 'chute has touched the ground, Fire-Power that dropped from the skies is sent hurtling toward the enemy . . .

We at Oldsmobile receive a special thrill from the news of such spectacular airborne assaults. Not only because they demonstrate the strength of Allied arms and give some indication of the tactics that will lead to

final Victory. But also because they afford a dramatic example of how the type of Fire-Power we build for Army Ordnance is being delivered to our fighting men. It's good news to us every time to hear that our products are performing well in action— whether it's high-explosive shell such as those being dropped from the sky in the illustration above, or automatic aerial cannon for America's fighter planes, or tank cannon for the armored forces. Every *new* report of Oldsmobile products in action is *new* incentive for us to "Keep 'Em Firing!"

FIRE-POWER is Our Business!

Do a little "shooting" yourself!

You can help provide the Fire-Power our fighters need . . . help produce it . . . help deliver it . . . by getting your money into the fight.

★ BUY WAR BONDS ★

OLDSMOBILE DIVISION OF GENERAL MOTORS
KEEP 'EM FIRING

Pack Howitzers gave the airborne troops mobile artillery that could be parachuted or flown by gliders with them into enemy territory. Colored parachutes identified supply drops and were more easily sighted by the receiving troops on the ground. They were also useful in bartering with the native inhabitants, both primitive and sophisticated. Oldsmobile manufactured forty-eight million rounds of artillery ammunition during World War II. Courtesy, Oldsmobile Division, General Motors Corporation

100

our petty, separate interests is national advertising. It has the power, if anything does, to persuade us to work together, to forget our conflicting interests for the wartime, and to strive for the common safety of us all." Lofty sentiments, full of hope.

Across the channel from Fortress Europe, England was so jammed full of soldiers, sailors, aviators, trucks, tanks, planes, and all the accoutrements of war that the pundits said the only things keeping the island from sinking were the thousands of barrage balloons that were tethered all over the country to deter Luftwaffe air attacks! The second front, the cross-channel invasion, was coming soon. Everybody knew it and most looked forward to it, especially the British.

The people of the United Kingdom appreciated that America had come to their aid, and looked forward to fighting shoulder to shoulder against the Axis enemy until victory was won. However, British gratitude did not extend to the sometimes boorish behavior of Americans living in their country during the seemingly interminable occupation. According to a popular phrase in Great Britain in late 1943, the only thing wrong with Americans was that they were "oversexed, overfed, and over here."

Civilian trucks provided essential services to a nation restricted by tire and gasoline shortages, but were in turn affected by the same shortages. In the eastern United States, milk deliveries were cut to every other day, and some commercial vehicles resorted to wooden wheels in order to stay on the road. Newspaper deliveries to newsstands were limited to once a day, which created a quandary for papers with morning and evening editions. Eggs were plentiful during the war years, but chickens were a different story. Midway through the war, the Army resorted to highway roadblocks in the New York-New Jersey area to intercept poultry trucks suspected of black-market connections, as local military bases faced severe shortages due to unscrupulous merchants. Courtesy, GMC Truck Division, General Motors Corporation

The apparent advanced age of this doctor about to make an evening house call in nasty weather reflected the fact that most younger doctors were in military service. DeSoto's message stressed the durability of its vehicles over its twenty-year history, while subtly suggesting that these would be good cars to own when peace was established again. Nearly five million of the 27.5 million cars registered in 1941 were out of service by the end of 1943. Courtesy, Chrysler Corporation

Fighting craftsmanship
by Fisher

*The Army-Navy "E" flies above four
Fisher plants for excellence in aircraft
production and from two others for tank
production, while the Navy "E," with
four stars, is flown by still another Fisher
plant for its naval ordnance work.*

THIS new naval dual-purpose 5-inch is bringing added advantages in fire power to our armed forces at sea and on invasion coasts.

Here at Fisher, we take particular pride in it, even though we do not make *all* of it.

For the skills we have developed go into it. All the crafts we have mastered are concentrated on it. It represents the many kinds of Fisher craftsmanship combined in a fighting tool that gives our men the all-important edge.

We believe in armament that holds an actual combat advantage within itself. That's why we throw our reserve of fighting craftsmanship into every tank, bomber or gun we build. And our fighting men tell us that it's an added advantage when the going gets tough.

Every Sunday Afternoon
GENERAL MOTORS SYMPHONY OF THE AIR
NBC Network

armament
BODY BY *Fisher*

While there was less direct naval gunfire against enemy ships in World War II, as air power gained ascendancy, the 5in gun maintained its usefulness against enemy planes and shore installations. The biggest US naval guns were 16in models, while the Japanese had 18in guns on several of their battleships. The latter were a direct violation of prewar naval treaties between Japan, Great Britain, and the United States which were designed to forestall an arms race between the potential adversaries. Courtesy, General Motors

CHAPTER 4

Oversexed, Overfed, and Over Here: 1944

All manner of troops, equipment, and supplies were pouring into England in early 1944 as the Allies prepared for the long-awaited invasion of the European continent.

Major upgrading of both the quality and the quantity of Atlantic convoy escort ships and planes ensured the continuation of this massive build-up. American shipyards produced an astonishing 1,949 ships in 1943 alone. By the end of the war that figure reached 5,600 merchant ships, many of them Liberty ships built by Henry Kaiser, and whose total construction could be completed in just twelve days. The Battle of the Atlantic was being won by the Allies, who actually planned and succeeded in the capture of an intact U-boat; it is presently on display at Chicago's Museum of Science and Industry. While the Germans remained a menace at sea, they were no longer a threat to sever the supply lines across the Atlantic.

The American automotive industry led the way in production of military hardware and equipment carried by the convoys in 1944. While several companies, led by Ford, Pontiac, and Chevrolet, had been producing military equipment prior to the US entry into the war, the changeover of the entire industry to military production was utterly fantastic and completed in record time. The car manufacturers were building fighter and bomber aircraft, tanks, trucks, ambulances, jeeps, artillery, naval guns, machine guns, antiaircraft weapons, and ammunition in every caliber and size. The list goes on and on.

The lack of experienced, skilled workers makes this feat even more astonishing. During World War I, American industry was unable to gear up its production resources effectively before the end of the war, and Americans often fought using European guns, tanks, and airplanes. This was certainly not the case during World War II.

The US was truly the "arsenal of democracy," and its industries ultimately trained thousands of workers in high-skilled jobs, jobs whose skills could be put to use in civilian positions once the war ended.

While the automotive manufacturers enjoyed unprecedented production success, they faced internal problems that needed to be addressed. The Ford Motor Company's difficulties are a prime, if unusual, example. Heir apparent Edsel Ford had died in 1943 at age 50, and his father, Henry Ford, relied to a large extent on Harry Bennett to run the company. This was potentially troublesome since Bennett had many enemies within management and had also alienated the labor unions. In March of 1944 several of the company's designers left, including Bob Gregorie and Lawrence Sheldrick. Their loss would be keenly felt when postwar car production demanded new ideas and leadership. Another major executive, Charlie Sorensen, left Ford the same month to become the head of Willys-Overland, mainly because he had been passed over for the presidency of the company. That position was reserved for Henry Ford II, who was given an early release from the Navy so he could return to Dearborn and help his aging father run the family business. Bennett also left the Ford Motor Company shortly after the war ended, realizing that he too was being passed over by the new emerging leadership at the giant car company. Within the automobile industry these were major occurrences, but the daily life and activity of the average American worker was still dominated by the war overseas.

Meanwhile, in mid-January of 1944, the Allies launched another amphibious invasion in Italy, this time at Anzio in an attempt to outflank the Gustav Line, an unyielding German defensive position that stretched across the waist of Italy.

With America's naval resources at a low ebb in the early years of the war, survival for pilots forced down at sea was a grim prospect, although there were some remarkable rescues of aviators missing after the battles of Coral Sea and Midway. As more surface ships, planes, and submarines joined the fleet, US forces intensified and organized their efforts to recover downed airmen, utilizing subs and picket lines of surface ships stationed along flight corridors, as well as amphibious aircraft. Courtesy, Chrysler Corporation

This action was unsuccessful as the Wehrmacht counterattacked in violent fashion, preventing a breakout by the combined US and British forces and pinning them in their coastal bridgehead. It was a costly campaign, controversial in its strategic necessity as well as in the destruction of the 1,400-year-old Benedictine monastery on Monte Cassino (ostensibly a German artillery observation post), and culminated in the fall of Rome on June 4, 1944. The Gustav Line was not broken until September of 1944.

On the last day of January, American Marines on the opposite side of the world successfully invaded Kwajalein Atoll in the Marshall Islands after an intense naval and air bombardment. In defeat, the Japanese lost 4,650 men killed, and only 50 survived to be taken prisoner. US forces lost 174 killed and 700 wounded. The following month a series of raids by US carrier-

A Mickey Finn, named for a nefarious New York bartender in the nineteenth century, was an alcoholic drink that had been drugged in order to render the drinker unconscious. The victim would then be relieved of his wallet and other valuables and dumped in the gutter. Alcohol was an important component of ammunition, and shortages of drinking liquor were rampant in 1944 as a result of defense needs. White advertised its tanker truck as the "World's Largest Cocktail Shaker," and noted that each shipment of alcohol was accompanied by an armed guard. Courtesy, Volvo GM Heavy Truck Corporation

based aircraft devastated Truk, the huge Japanese naval bastion in the Caroline Islands. Dozens of enemy ships were sunk and hundreds of aircraft were destroyed in these raids by Task Force 58, soon to be a legend in the Pacific war. Gen. Douglas MacArthur was also hard at work in the war against Japan, attacking northward from New Guinea and invading the Admiralty Islands,

Next page
Studebaker moved from the Army to the Marines to feature the Lukavich family as part of its continuing father-son advertising theme. This young man joined the Marines just in time for some of the bloodiest campaigns of the Pacific war, including the invasions of Saipan, Guam, Peleliu, Iwo Jima, and Okinawa. Courtesy, Dresser-Rand

© 1944, The Studebaker Corporation

When the Marines got Lukavich they took a good man

But his team-mate father still builds Cyclone engines at Studebaker

...debaker-built Cyclone engines keep swarms of ...ing Fortresses flying—And Studebaker craftsmen ...ild much other vital war matériel, including vast quan...ies of heavy-duty war trucks. Studebaker is proud ...its part in our country's war production program.

TWENTY-ONE years ago this January, a mechanic named Paul Lukavich signed his first pay voucher as a Studebaker employee.

His son, Steve, now in the Marine Corps, was then a chubby baby two years old.

In September 1940, in keeping with a custom that's generations-old in South Bend, the Lukaviches became a Studebaker father-and-son team.

And not long after that, the two moved from the automotive shops to the great modern aircraft engine plant where huge quantities of Studebaker-built Wright Cyclones that power the Boeing Flying Fortress are being produced. A year ago this month, Steve Lukavich joined the Marines.

Today, the record shows that Studebaker is one of the world's largest builders of engines for warplanes—one of the largest manufacturers, too, of big multiple-drive military trucks, tens upon tens of thousands of which are in the far-flung transport service of the United Nations.

Many Studebaker fathers and sons have parted company for the duration—but the solid principles of Studebaker craftsmanship endure.

When peace comes, that craftsmanship, tested and proved anew in the flaming crucible of war, will be back in civilian service to give the world the highest quality motor cars and motor trucks ever manufactured.

BUY U.S. WAR BONDS

STUDEBAKER

Builder of Wright Cyclone engines for the Boeing Flying Fortress—big multiple-drive military trucks—and other vital war matériel

QUIZ for plane-minded readers

If you can answer nine of these questions correctly, you're good!

A score of eight correct answers is fair, and seven is average.

1. What fighter plane earned the name "B-40" by dropping 1,000 lb. bombs on Jap targets in Burma?

2. What plane has been called "the world's fastest fighter?"

3. What is conceded to be the "fastest bomber in the world?"

4. What is the name of Britain's heaviest bomber?

5. What fighter plane became known as the "tank buster" in the North African campaign?

6. Who powers the Mustang, Warhawk, Hurricane, Mosquito, and Lancaster—and the famous PT boats?

7. What is the finest surface measurement used in making Packard-built Rolls-Royce aircraft engines?

8. What enables the Mustang P-51 to fight 2 miles higher than before?

9. What does a two-stage two-speed supercharger do?

10. The top speed of blades in a Packard-built supercharger equals: an express train? A rifle bullet? Sound?

11. What famous fighting boats depend for their speed on aircraft-type engines?

12. "A" weighs twice as much as "B". Is "A" only twice as powerful as "B"? 8 times? 10 times?

PACKARD-BUILT ROLLS ROYCE ENGINE — A

PACKARD CAR ENGINE — B

13. Can new methods used in making war engines (like nitriding, above) help to build better postwar cars?

ANSWERS:

1—P-40 Warhawk. **2**—Mustang P-51. **3**—Mosquito bomber. **4**—Lancaster 4-motor bomber. **5**—Hurricane. **6**—Packard (Rolls-Royce engines for the planes; Packard marine engines for PT's). **7**—Millionths of an inch. **8**—A Packard-built 2-stage 2-speed supercharger. **9**—Engines, like people, "run out of breath" at high altitudes. Packard-built 2-stage 2-speed superchargers compress thin air, permit high-power performance even in the stratosphere. **10**—A rifle bullet and sound. **11**—Navy PT boats (powered by Packard marine engines of aircraft-type design). **12**—"A" is 10 times as powerful as "B". **13**—Yes, many of them. Your future Packard will be better built, longer lasting, and more economical as a result.

ASK THE MAN WHO OWNS ONE

PACKARD
Precision-built-Power

MUSTANG fighter

WARHAWK fighter

HURRICANE fighter

LANCASTER bomber

MOSQUITO fighter-bomber

NAVY PT boats

Packard's defense production accomplishments were impressive, especially in building precision Rolls-Royce engines for American and British planes. According to the ad, this engine was twice as big, but ten times more powerful than a Packard car engine. Courtesy, Dresser-Rand

106

As the war dragged on with no new cars in sight, DeSoto stressed the durability of its prewar models and their contribution to the nation's domestic transportation needs. Note the ornate gas pump globes at the station where E.H. Krug gets his ration of gas. Courtesy, Chrysler Corporation

Nash was relentless in its continuing demands for an America worthy of its soldiers' sacrifices. Its ads targeted emotions rather than simply touting the company's wartime equipment production. The copy in this ad refers to the Marines' 1943 invasion of Tarawa in the Gilbert Islands. Many landing craft were unable to reach the beach due to off-shore reefs, and the troops had to wade in from 600 yards out while under heavy enemy artillery and machine-gun fire. They took severe casualties, but ultimately destroyed the Japanese garrison in a bitter three-day battle. Courtesy, Chrysler Corporation

as his troops edged closer to their goal of liberating the Philippines. The American strategy of "island hopping" in the Pacific was designed to minimize US casualties by isolating, actually bypassing, fortified Japanese-held islands in the march toward the Philippines and ultimately the home islands of Japan. With their supply lines choked off by American aircraft and submarines, these outposts held little threat for the advancing US forces and were unable to contribute materiel to Japan's defense.

In the skies over Europe, however, the Luftwaffe very ably defended the German homeland against the Allied air war. By the beginning of 1944, the British had already lost more than 38,000 aircrew, and bombed the enemy only at night in an attempt to reduce their own casualties. The US daylight precision bombing campaign also suffered painful casualties and was not always precise. In the spring of 1944, American bombers mistakenly hit Schaffhausen, Switzerland, killing 40 and wounding 240 neutral Swiss. The United States paid more than $20 million in

war reparations to the Swiss nation for the error. It happened again in 1945.

The daylight bombing offensive culminated in the Big Week in February of 1944, when the Eighth Air Force, operating out of bases in England, flew 3,800 sorties during the week, mainly

Next page
Hudson built the wings for the Helldiver, which replaced the Dauntless as the premiere US Navy dive-bomber. With a range of 1,925 miles, it could carry 1,000lb of bombs and had two 20mm cannons in its wings, as well as twin machine guns fired by a rear gunner. Its top speed was 294mph. Hudson ads said, "Our plants are dedicated to war production...our dealers to maintaining war transportation." Courtesy, Chrysler Corporation

..AND THEY ALL CAME BACK!

Last Christmas morning—just 44 days after they had given Jap warships a terrific beating at Rabaul—new Navy Helldivers swarmed over Kavieng, second most important Jap base south of Truk. Down dropped their lethal cargo, destroying 6 Jap ships and 8 planes, and badly damaging others. Then back, "all safe", leaving Kavieng harbor a mass of wreckage!

Blinding speed and heavy fire power *make the Aira-cobra a dreaded enemy wherever it takes the air. Among Hudson's important wartime tasks is the quantity production of cabins for Bell fighters, one of which is shown here, loading bad news for the Axis at an African air base.*

"ALL HELLDIVERS returned safely!" That was the good news to thousands of Hudson employees. It outshone the stirring story of victory over Kavieng harbor.

This was one of the first battle tests of the deadly new Navy Helldivers—and in it, *planes* as well as *pilots* won lasting glory.

At Hudson, we feel we have a personal stake in the lives of these heroic fliers, for we are mass-producing wings for the planes they fly—along with other important tasks for the Air Forces, Navy and Army.

We are thankful for an organization that believes *they have to be built right,* whether the product is war *matériel* or motor cars. Thankful, too, that Hudson had 32 years

of high-precision experience to put to work after Pearl Harbor.

The cars we built in those years are proving their inbuilt ruggedness today, and our nationwide distributor-dealer organization is fulfilling its pledge to keep 'em rolling.

Until the day when our *combined* war and peacetime experience can bring you finer-than-ever Hudsons, see your Hudson dealer for a new car, a used car or service on your present car.

Hudson Aviation Division Wins Second Army-Navy Award for Meritorious Service on the Production Front

HUDSON
MOTOR CAR COMPANY
DETROIT 14, MICHIGAN
34 Years of Engineering Leadership

BUY YOUR EXTRA WAR BOND TODAY

THEY HAVE TO BE BUILT RIGHT

Through a hail of flak *on an Italian run known as "Powder Puff Lane" came the Marauder bomber "Shark", riddled from stem to stern. But, by expert handling, its gallant pilot landed it on one wheel, without injury to a single member of its crew. Hudson is proud to be in large scale production of fuselage sections for these tough Martin Marauder bombers.*

Endurance, proved in peace and war! *Before Pearl Harbor, Hudson cars won and held more than 80 stock car records for per-formance, endurance and economy —more records than were held by any other make of automobile. Hudson owners are profiting today by the kind of engineering and workmanship that gave these cars their ability to GO and KEEP ON going.*

OUR PLANTS ARE DEDICATED TO WAR PRODUCTION...OUR DEALERS TO MAINTAINING WAR TRANSPORTATION!

39

108

Every American had a relative or friend in the service, and understood a mother's concern for her son flying bombers against resolute enemies somewhere overseas. The sentiments expressed in this woman's letter were very real to millions of her fellow Americans. Buick manufactured the 1,200hp radial engines that powered the B-24. Courtesy, Buick Division, General Motors Corporation

Pontiac saluted the men and women of all branches of the armed forces, represented by attractive young people in this ad and pointedly lacking in any minority representation. In prewar America, blacks were considered a servant class, and other racial minorities garnered little attention, except possibly suspicion, from the majority of white Americans. In subsequent magazine issues, each of the services featured here became a full-page Pontiac advertisement as a follow-up to this ad. Reprints of this and the subsequent ads, all using portraits by Bradshaw Crandell, were available from Pontiac. Courtesy, Pontiac Division, General Motors Corporation

against German aircraft factories. Losses were high (244 bombers with ten men in each, and thirty-three fighters), and would have been worse except for the presence of long-range P-51 Mustang fighters that were finally available to escort their "big friends" all the way to their targets and back. This offensive was decisive in the European air war, as German fighter production never again caught up with Allied bomber production. It led ultimately to Allied air domination, so necessary for the upcoming invasion of the Continent and the destruction of German industrial capacity.

The bomber missions were mentally and physically exhausting, flown against highly trained, courageous, and motivated German aviators defending their homes and homeland. Luftwaffe tactics were innovative and effective. Its pilots liked to attack the bomber formations head-on, both for the swift rate of closure and the lack of significant firepower available from the front of the American formations. The United States countered this tactic by installing a "chin turret" on the nose of the B-17 with two additional .50 caliber machine guns. Unfortunately, when a bomber lost an engine over Germany, the increased aerodynamic drag of the chin significantly lessened the chance of getting back to England in the damaged plane.

These youthful aviators, sometimes referred to as a "controlled mob," were the bane of military disciplinarians, but their courage in enemy skies on mission after mission was indeed great. They looked upon the "brass" as warily as they did the Germans, and one of their favorite expressions about airbase discipline and regulations was "Shot at and missed; shit at and hit!"

An aircrew member had to fly twenty-five missions in order to be rotated home. This was

"MOM..."

He was a thorn in their side . . .

All morning long, his accurate mortar fire kept them from forming up, smashed their supply trucks, broke the spearhead of their attack . . .

So, they went all out to get him . . . And finally, a sniper shot him.

Then they laid down a cross fire that was death to defy. I know . . . because one of our men tried. But it was damned hard to lie there and hear him call "Mom" . . . and cry and call "Mom" again . . . like a kid who'd been hurt, he didn't know just how or why.

And all we could do was just lie there . . . and grind our teeth together and tighten our guts because each time he cried "Mom" . . . it tore out our insides.

When I couldn't stand it any more, I got up and ran . . .

And when they saw me coming and the Red Cross band of the Medical Corps on my arm, they held their fire until I knelt down beside him. I put a syrette into his arm and then another, and he relaxed and his head fell back and his eyes were still wide but I could tell he thought his mother was there by his side . . .

Listen, America . . .

Open your hearts, wives and daughters! Open your pocketbooks, fathers! Give your blood, brothers and sisters! Give your money . . . give your work!

So the freedom you want . . . So the country you want . . .

So the future you want . . . Will be there when we come back.

Here at Nash-Kelvinator we're building Pratt & Whitney engines for the Navy's Vought Corsairs and Grumman Hellcats . . . Hamilton Standard propellers for United Nations bombers . . . governors, binoculars, parts for ships, jeeps, tanks and trucks . . . readying production lines for Sikorsky helicopters. All of us devoted 100% to winning this war . . . to speeding the peace when our men will come back to their jobs and homes and even better futures than they had before . . . to the day when we'll build for you an even finer Kelvinator, an even greater Nash!

NASH-KELVINATOR CORPORATION
Kenosha · Milwaukee · DETROIT · Grand Rapids · Lansing

Members of the armed forces were suffering and dying all over the globe for American ideals, but many civilians did not want to be reminded of their sacrifices. Nash-Kelvinator would not let anyone forget, and its ads emotionally demanded that Americans give more hours, more money, and more blood. Courtesy, Chrysler Corporation

Oldsmobile ran a series of advertisements that featured the insigne of various Air Force squadrons that were using aircraft built in part by the automobile manufacturer. The P-38 Lightning, which was especially effective in the Pacific due to its long range and armament, is represented in this ad by the 84th Fighter Squadron. Courtesy, Oldsmobile Division, General Motors Corporation

In 1943, Ford curtailed advertising its defense contributions and instead focused on the peace that lay ahead. In 1944, the manufacturer presented a collection of ads about Henry Ford's personal accomplishments and the general history of the Ford Motor Company. In this example from September 1944, Henry Ford meets the great inventor, Thomas Edison. Ford and Edison became good friends and had homes near one another in Key West, Florida, where Ford studied various rubber trees and rubber compounds in an attempt to develop a domestic rubber supply. Courtesy, Ford Motor Company

upped to thirty-five in the spring of 1944 in Europe, and later to fifty missions. Many crew members had specific rituals—such as sitting in the same seat at target briefings or playing the same phonograph record—that they would superstitiously complete before or after missions to ensure their survival in their own minds. One pilot was said to have put on a brassiere over his flak jacket as he approached the target area. The average survival rate was about eleven missions, which was not great for morale. Some aircrews decided these odds were too great, and headed for neutral Sweden or Switzerland. Many of them were in damaged aircraft that could not make the return flight to safety, and the escapes to a neutral country saved the crews from imprisonment or death. However, more than 400 American planes, mostly bombers, chose this alternative during the war, and the High Command was concerned to the extent that verbal orders were given to some fighter escort commanders to shoot down

any undamaged American planes that appeared to be leaving the war voluntarily.

At home in the motor city, American automobile manufacturers continued their production miracle. Radar (a Navy acronym for radio detection and range finding) played a major role in defeating Japan and Germany. Chrysler Corporation was a leader in the development of the SCR-584 radar set, which was standard issue to medi-

Next page
During the 1940s American boys built "soapbox" racers and "box" cars from whatever materiels were available, and a smooth ride was not usually a consideration. The focus of this General Motors ad is on youth, the nation's hope for the future. This ad is quite different from previous GM ads touting its tremendous military production. Courtesy, General Motors

Pulling a smoothie

That's right, buddy. Smooth up the ride. Make that car drive easier. Tinker with it till you've got something better. And you'll go places!

General Motors engineers decided long ago that a new type of front springing was necessary if cars were to have the best possible riding qualities.

It took years to develop one. But when they got it, they not only improved your car but, as it turned out, solved a pressing war problem.

Their solution, of course, was Knee-Action, or independent front wheel suspension. Standard on all General Motors cars, it is recognized as one of the notable engineering advances made by GM's effort to provide more and better things for more people.

When war struck, there was great demand for vehicles that could travel fast and smoothly over all kinds of going. The "ride" that General Motors engineers had worked so long to provide for you now was called on to help our men in battle.

On today's war fronts, many kinds of vehicles — some weighing high in the tons — employ Knee-Action. They get smoothness, speed, flexibility and freedom from break-downs due to rough going from this peacetime development.

America has such vehicles today largely because of the experience and "know-how" built up by General

Motors men in their efforts to improve peacetime wares. And our country is rich in such experience chiefly because Americans always have been able to earn fair rewards by accomplishing useful things.

This idea helped make prewar America a fine place in which to live. It has proved immensely valuable in war. And it will continue to provide more and better things for more people in the good years ahead.

GENERAL MOTORS
"VICTORY IS OUR BUSINESS"

CHEVROLET · PONTIAC · OLDSMOBILE · BUICK · CADILLAC
BODY BY FISHER · FRIGIDAIRE · GMC TRUCK AND COACH

Every Sunday Afternoon
GENERAL MOTORS SYMPHONY OF THE AIR — NBC Network

KEEP
AMERICA
STRONG
★
*Buy
War Bonds*

More B-24 Liberators were built during World War II than any other type of American bomber. The aircraft had its flaws, and crew members believed that if a B-24 caught fire near one of its fuel tanks the plane would probably blow up in less than ten seconds. A Liberator from the 460th Bombardment Group took a hit in the number three engine over Italy and caught fire, prompt-ing the waist gunner on that side of the aircraft to buckle on his chest parachute and dive out the gunner's window on the opposite side. However, the fire went out of its own accord and the B-24 continued on course for home, as the hapless gunner, shaking his fist at the bomber formation, floated down into enemy territory. Courtesy, Buick Division, General Motors Corporation

um and heavy antiaircraft batteries for tracking enemy planes. Germany was unable to keep up with the Allied development of short-wave radar, and the Japanese were barely participating in the contest. Chrysler's Dodge Division built 2,092 short-wave radar sets at a cost of $9,386 each, saving 57 percent ($15 million) of the initial cost and fee contract price. Ultimately, the Army and Navy spent $2.7 billion for radar equipment during World War II.

Another of Chrysler's contributions to the war effort was 5,500 gyro-compasses, originally designed by Sperry Corporation for the Navy. Weighing 1,300 pounds, the Dodge-built systems cost only 55 percent of the original cost estimate of $42.7 million, a savings of $19.2 million. By March 1943, thirteen months after accepting the contract, Dodge was building eight gyro-compasses a day. Sperry had estimated it would take the car company eighteen months to build the first model. For the life of the contract, Dodge aver-aged six compasses a day, a tribute to the precise skills of the auto maker's work force.

Elsewhere in the States, a war-weary and increasingly cynical populace exhibited a growing irritation with consumer shortages by dealing more and more with Mr. Black, the euphemism for buying rationed goods on the black market. The tremendous surge in production during 1943

Next page
Lack of experience in the workplace restricted opportunities for women early in the war, but by mid-1944 they had made appreciable gains and undertook more leadership roles. Unfortunately, women who wanted to continue working in peacetime were often let go in favor of returning servicemen. This ad, while honoring women's contributions to the homefront effort, almost gasps in astonishment that "Miss Elsa Gardner trains soldiers!" Courtesy, Oldsmobile Division, General Motors Corporation

113

Doing a Man's Job

— TRAINING FIGHTING MEN!

THE GARDNER FAMILY OF BUFFALO have no sons of military age. But they do have a *daughter* to lend to their country. Today, she is doing a job as important to winning the war as anything she might do if she were a man. Miss Elsa Gardner *trains soldiers!* At Camp Bell, New York—operated by the Bell Aircraft Corporation—Miss Gardner instructs Army Air Force mechanics in pre-flight inspections, servicing and maintenance of Airacobra fighter planes, as capably as any man. She has earned the highest esteem of her associates, and of the soldiers she trains. And she has never failed to report for duty. Although there is no direct bus service at the hours Miss Gardner goes to work, she always gets there *on time*. Her transportation is her 1935-model Oldsmobile. She couldn't do so much to Keep 'Em Flying without it.

ARMY AIR FORCE MECHANICS receive first-hand experience in the maintenance of "Airacobras" in their training at Camp Bell. They go to all fighting fronts to Keep 'Em Flying.

THIS AIRACOBRA FIGHTER PLANE at Camp Bell was built from salvaged parts by some of Miss Gardner's students. It is used for instructional and ground training purposes.

IT'S AN OLDSMOBILE-BUILT CANNON these Camp Bell instructors are studying. This advanced technical training school teaches maintenance of the entire Airacobra plane, including its cannon.

ANOTHER WAR BOND for mother. Miss Elsa is the only member of the Gardner family of working age. She is investing every cent she can save, in War Bonds.

AUTHORIZED OLDSMOBILE SERVICE keeps this 9-year-old Oldsmobile in fighting trim. Miss Gardner teaches mechanical maintenance, knows how important it is.

OLDSMOBILE DIVISION OF GENERAL MOTORS

had led to an initial easing of many shortages. Many people thought the war was won and practically over. However, expanding military demands caused by multiple campaigns during 1944 overstressed US production capacity, once again causing shortages.

Meat was the most desired item on the black market. More than 60 percent of the prime meat and 80 percent of the "utility" cuts in the country went to the armed forces. Meatless days, a throwback to the First World War, were considered patriotic and necessary. Demand was frantic. There were reports of cattle rustling in the West, and horsemeat went on the market, with more than twenty tons being sold in St. Louis. Four tons were sold in a day and a half in Milwaukee at the aptly named Man O'War Meat Market. Country folk had access to wild game and could raise their own livestock, but city dwellers had to rely on their relationships with their local butchers.

Ice cream was limited to eight flavors, and sliced bread was discontinued for pricing reasons, but the housewives demanded and got a retraction of that OPA (Office of Price Administration) order. Because tin was needed by the military, canned beer was replaced by bottled beer. Nylon and rayon goods were nonexistent and leather shoes were not only tough to find, they were rationed to two pair a year.

But the biggest complaint from the people was the lack of automotive gasoline. Counterfeit ration coupons started to appear. It was estimated that 30 percent of the gas coupons in New York City were fake. Gasoline coupons were stolen from OPA offices, twenty million gallons' worth in Washington, D.C., and five million gallons' worth in Cleveland. Arrests were made, with 4,000 gas stations losing their licenses and more than 30,000 drivers forfeiting their ration cards. Normally law-abiding businesses were involved in wartime ration irregularities. Allegedly 20 percent of the businesses in the nation received warnings regarding illegal activities, and better than 7 percent were charged with illegal transactions.

Many members of the military and civilians still plugging along in their prewar civilian occupations were patiently dealing with the problems and frustrations brought about by the war. To a certain extent, they resented the financial success of war workers in the defense plants. Some also envied the fast and loose social life available to the more restless elements of the work force. Evidence also existed that a minority of defense workers stole precision tools from their factories and resold them on the street, which did not endear them to more honest workers. Anguished families who lost a loved one in battle or through the inescapable wastage of war could not help but

With visions of peace on the horizon, many young people who had delayed marriage plans took the plunge. A June military wedding was and still is considered classic. This also gave DeSoto another opportunity to praise its long-lasting prewar cars and encourage servicing from authorized dealers. Courtesy, Chrysler Corporation

view this new class of blue-collar workers as slackers or draft-dodgers, even though some war workers were prohibited from enlisting because of their necessary civilian skills.

Black Americans gained a degree of economic independence during the war heretofore unavailable to them. It was estimated that 700,000 blacks, 400,000 of them from the South, moved to the West and East coasts, and also the Midwest, to find defense-related work. Interestingly, two of

Next page
The Hinkle boys were certainly long gone from their old assembly line in South Bend, Indiana. The young flyer featured here wears the gold bars of a second lieutenant, the shoulder patch of an Air Force headquarters unit, and the silver wings of a pilot, but his brother, a corporal based in the Fiji Islands, probably had the better assignment. Flying unarmed transports across the Himalayas to China was dangerous duty, and the chances of survival slim if weather or other problems forced the plane down in the mountains. Courtesy, Dresser-Rand

© 1944 The Studebaker Corporation

Tom Hinkle's boys do him proud in the Army
just as they did on their Studebaker jobs

IT'S a long way from the Fiji Islands to the Studebaker factories where Wright Cyclone engines for the Boeing Flying Fortress are built.

It's still farther to the American air bases in India from which vital war cargo is flown into China across the towering Himalayan "hump."

But there's a link that spans those distant spots where Tom Hinkle's boys are now stationed and their father in South Bend. That link is a comradeship in craftsmanship which had its beginning when all three were working close together in the Studebaker plants.

Like large numbers of other Studebaker automobile craftsmen, Tom Hinkle is now building aircraft engines while his sons serve their country in combat areas overseas. Instead of manufacturing Studebaker

Champion, Commander and President cars as a family team, they're working together for victory although many miles apart.

For over 92 years, the tradition of fine craftsmanship has been fostered in many families like the Hinkle family in Studebaker's home community. The painstaking efforts of many such father-and-son teams have been considerably responsible for the surviving soundness that puts so much solid wartime value into Studebaker motor cars and trucks.

STUDEBAKER

Builder of Wright Cyclone engines for the Boeing Flying Fortress — big multiple-drive military trucks — and other vital war matériel

Lieutenant, corporal and craftsman—the Hinkles still "work together"—Tom Hinkle now builds Flying Fortress engines at Studebaker where his record as a motor car craftsman goes back nearly 23 years. At last reports, one son, George, is an Army Air Forces lieutenant in India, Bill Hinkle, Tom's other son, is a Coast Artillery corporal in the Fiji Islands.

BUY MORE AND *MORE* WAR BONDS

the five areas with the largest increases in black population, Hampton Roads, Virginia, and Mobile, Alabama, were in the South. The other three cities were San Francisco, Los Angeles, and Detroit. As in the case of women, many blacks were the first to lose their jobs when production demand dropped off.

However, the auto industry was among the first to rehire blacks, albeit in the unskilled labor force, when the war ended and the demand for new American cars accelerated.

The spirit of sacrifice that prevailed early in the war had to some extent dissipated by early 1944. Many goods were in constant short supply, and working conditions were often not ideal. Large numbers of war workers had to commute long distances or at great expense, and people moved restlessly from job to job for several reasons, including housing, commutation, and especially the thirst for adventure.

American women became more and more vital to the civilian economy as military casualties and commitments further drained American men from the domestic work force. Females were recruited for any number of jobs. They represented 40 percent of the employee group in aircraft assembly plants and 12 percent in the shipyards, and in one barrage balloon factory women made up 90 percent of the production force.

Even Ford Motor Company, traditionally reluctant to employ women in any capacity other than clerical positions, utilized women for 40 percent of its Willow Run assembly line. (Some companies tried to restrict the wearing of sweaters by women on the assembly line because such activity created a so-called safety hazard for the male workers.) Physically small women, as well as midgets and dwarfs of both sexes, could fit into tight spaces in planes and other vehicles to complete intricate or space-restricted tasks, welding being one of them. Many employers felt that women were more dexterous than men for small detail work, and many also assumed that women were better able to handle the monotonous work of the assembly line.

While women had a higher rate of absenteeism, they also brought a cultural influence to defense plants that was lacking in an all-male work force. Fashion designers such as Lily Dache created feminine uniforms for several companies. In a well-publicized incident, movie actress Veronica Lake, whose hairstyle was copied by many young women in the 1940s, cut off her famous peek-a-boo wave as a safety example for America's factory women who worked with industrial machinery.

The War Labor Board also decreed equal pay for equal work, resulting in women being paid the same as men for the same job performance. However, on average, they were usually paid less than men for the same work because they had less job seniority, having been hired last. They were also the first fired, as twice as many women as men were let go in 1944 when defense production requirements decreased.

As citizen cynicism increased, President Roosevelt nationalized the railroads due to a threatened wage strike, and also as a warning to other labor groups. The war was costing $315 million a day, and by midyear the national debt reached $260 billion. Total salaries rose from $52 billion in 1939 to $113 billion in 1944, and savings increased from $6 billion to $39 billion in the same period. Even with special taxes being levied, such as the 5 percent Victory Tax and the 10 percent increase (later 20 percent) in the Federal Amusement Tax, spending was still rampant. Civilians

CHEVROLET

Farm life was not idyllic during World War II, as the shortage of workers created real problems at harvest time. Sons and daughters were also absent for at least the duration, leaving the burden on the middle-aged and the elderly. Help came in the form of young volunteers and Axis POWs from the many military prison camps located in the United States, as more production was needed than ever before to feed the nation and her allies. Modern communications were few, and the average farm in the 1940s was quite isolated, a tough and lonely existence. Courtesy, Chevrolet Division, General Motors Corporation

A Jap bayonet put him out of the fight — but not for long!

BUNA, NEW GUINEA, December 20—For 3 months, Pvt. Charles Turner's infantry company had been slugging it out with the Japs in a life-and-death struggle.

Finally, in one of the bitterest hand-to-hand encounters, Turner went down, with severe bayonet wounds.

But you can't keep a man like Charlie Turner out of the fight—not for long.

After his honorable discharge from the Army, Turner came back to the U. S. to continue the fight—as one of America's war production workers.

Today, along with some 36,000 other war workers here at Packard, over 700 of them war veterans, he is staying on the job—helping to turn out Packard marine engines for PT boats, and Packard-built Rolls-Royce engines for fighter planes and bombers.

Charlie Turner knows—because he has *seen* the need—how even *one* extra piece of fighting equipment can help shorten the war by perhaps a week, a day, or an hour.

He knows, too, that in the crucial months ahead, the struggle for Victory is one in which every loyal American can, and *must*, take part.

Are you doing *your* share to help make this the year of Victory? Are you doing

not just as much as you can—*but more than you ever thought you possibly could?*

Let's do more in '44!

●PVT. CHARLES TURNER, awarded the Purple Heart for wounds received at Buna, is now an aircraft engine parts assembler at Packard. Such men are an inspiration to do more—turning out Packard PT-boat engines, Rolls-Royce aircraft engines, and vital parts to keep America's essential transportation system rolling. These veterans are a constant reminder that Victory depends, in great part, on *how much* America can produce, not tomorrow, but *today!*

with money to spend wanted new clothes, but cloth, especially wool, was hard to procure. Most men's pants did not have cuffs or pleats, and the Office of Price Administration ordered that women's skirts end one inch above the knee to save material.

America's music changed also. There was still defiance of the enemy in such songs as "Let's Put the Ax to the Axis," "Slap the Jap Right off the Map," and "Der Fuehrer's Face." However, sentimental ballads like "I'll Be Seeing You," "Long Ago and Far Away," "We'll Meet Again," and "I'll Never Smile Again" were increasingly popular. Movies, too, were changing from the propaganda

genre of the early war years to sadly realistic movies like *The Story of G.I. Joe,* with Robert Mitchum and Burgess Meredith.

Hollywood still vigorously supported the war with more than 6,000 entertainers, led by Bob Hope, traveling all over the globe to perform for the troops. It is estimated that actress Dorothy Lamour sold more than $350 million in war bonds. Another popular actress, Carole Lombard, was killed earlier in the war in a plane crash while on a bond tour, and Hedy Lamarr bestowed kisses on those who bought $25,000 war bonds. One of the most prominent actors in the military was Jimmy Stewart, who earned a Distinguished Flying Cross as a pilot over Germany.

Farms and farmers were dramatically affected by the war; nearly 5.5 million farm people moved to city jobs and another 1.5 million entered the military, leaving a shortage of workers for the annual harvest. California was especially hard hit when Japanese-Americans were required to leave the coastal zones sensitive to possible enemy infiltration where they had been major contributors to the local economy as farmers and

Dodge spotlighted its last car built before the war, an effort aimed at keeping the company name before the public. Four years of deprivation became the marketing tool for postwar sales. Halfway through 1944, the only mention of the war is "Back the Attack," the national slogan for buying war bonds. Courtesy, Chrysler Corporation

Mail call was, of course, enormously popular with the troops far from home. Along with news of families and friends came word that this G.I.'s prewar Pontiac is still running and waiting for him. In the background is the ubiquitous Jeep. The end was in sight, but not just yet. Courtesy, Pontiac Division, General Motors Corporation

tenant-farmers. Among those who helped bring in the crops were the Women's Land Army, the High School Victory Corps, the Volunteer Land Army, and both the Young Women's Christian Association (YWCA) and Young Men's Christian Association (YMCA).

Severe labor shortages were also addressed by using German POWs as farm workers. By late 1944 there were 130,000 Axis prisoners housed in 666 camps in the United States. For example, German prisoners worked on 196 different farms in Fairfax County, Virginia, in 1944, replacing state convicts who were sent back to jail. It appears that the nation felt safer having enemy prisoners bring in the harvest than its home-grown criminals. The United States fed the free world during World War II.

While Americans bemoaned their shortages and separations in 1944, the plucky British could take pride in the knowledge that they had suc-

The B-29 Superfortress, twice as heavy as a B-17, was designed as a high-altitude pressurized heavy bomber. Its defensive machine guns were fired by remote control through periscopes. It had a 3.250 mile range with a 10,000lb bomb load, and was first deployed in China to attack Japan's bases there and in the home islands. After the capture of the Marianas in July 1944, the 300 B-29s of the Twentieth Air Force operated out of Saipan and Tinian against Japan. Hudson manufactured wing and fuselage components for the B-29, which did not serve in Europe. Courtesy, Chrysler Corporation

cessfully thwarted a German invasion of England during the dark days of 1940. They did not, however, fare as well against an invasion by their American allies. Yanks were everywhere in the UK, often arrogant and overbearing, drinking in every pub, pursuing every available woman, and spending their money lavishly. This overwhelming presence was the precursor of Operation Overlord, the cross-channel invasion of the Continent, which finally took place on D-day, June 6, 1944.

Involved were two million men, 5,000 ships, and 8,000 aircraft. Except at Omaha Beach in the American sector, casualties were surprisingly light, with less than 3,000 killed the first day. Troops and equipment poured ashore, leading to a break-out from the beachhead in mid-July. Gen. George Patton's Third Army charged across France, capturing thousands of cut-off and disheartened German soldiers along the way. However, heavy casualties could not be avoided, as the Wehrmacht was still a tough and powerful opponent. Fighting in the Normandy hedgerows prior to the break-out, the US 90th Division had to replace 100 percent of its enlisted soldiers and 150 percent of its officers due to battle action.

Whatever jubilation the Allies did feel due to their lightning advance across France was also tempered by Germany's successful V-1 rocket attacks on English cities that killed 2,700 civilians in less than one month that summer. During August, an Allied army invaded the south of France near St. Tropez, and soon joined forces with Patton's Army. Despite the combat losses, a favorite slogan that summer was "The Hun Is on the Run!" The final push in Europe was about to start, and the Allies were confident of victory.

The war in the Pacific was also going well. Shortly after the US Army and Marines' June 15 invasion of Saipan in the Mariana Islands, Navy pilots of Task Force 58 annihilated a Japanese naval force in what was called the Marianas Turkey Shoot. Two enemy carriers were sunk and 200 enemy planes were destroyed at a cost of 26 American pilots. During its withdrawal the next day, the Japanese fleet was again pursued by the US fliers, with another Japanese carrier sunk and two additional damaged. Realizing that his aviators would be returning in the dark and low

Next page
Nash toned down its message somewhat as victory seemed assured, a direct result of America's overwhelming defense production. The company still lectured on postwar responsibility and obligations, pledging itself to help provide a better life for all men and women. Refrigerator manufacture had been banned during the war, and probably as many Americans wanted a "fridge" as wanted a new car. Courtesy, Chrysler Corporation

"I SAW A MIRACLE..."

I got in early . . .

So I know how it was.

And I tell you, it was a miracle.

Because I remember when broomsticks were our rifles and we threw tin can grenades . . . and propped up stove pipes and painted signs that said, "This is an eight-inch gun" . . . "This is a howitzer" . . . and we threw tarps over trucks and made out they were tanks.

And though we laughed about it and kidded about it, we were ashamed . . .

And then they hit us . . .

And America went to work and performed a miracle.

I know because I was at Kasserine when tanks and guns, American-made, rolled them back and broke their backs in the passes and we and the British smashed their Mark IV's and their 88's under the weight of our attack . . . and drove them out and pinned them like rats between Cap Bon and the sea.

And I was in the first wave in Sicily, and when we cracked the iron ring at Anzio and killed the hard spirit of their Elite Corps with more bombs and shells than they had ever dreamed of before . . .

And I was with them on invasion day . . .

It was a miracle. And now seeing here the endless miles of tanks, the long railroad trains of guns, the flying fields carved out of every corner to hold the overflow of planes . . . I know my country has found again the strength that made us great . . .

Has found again in this mighty power to destroy . . . the power to create . . .

And I see how this miracle . . . this mighty power, this energy used now for war . . . can, after Victory, create a new and finer life than we have ever known before . . .

New cities, new farms, new homes, new industries . . . new opportunities for me, and every man, to plan and work and grow . . . to build a new and greater America. . .

The way we want it to be . . .

The way it's got to be!

* * *

Here at Nash-Kelvinator, when our war job is done, it will be our obligation to convert all the new strength, all the new power to produce, all the new ability and skill and knowledge that have come to us so quickly under the driving necessity of war to production for peace.

That means more automobiles than we have ever built before . . . automobiles even finer than the great Nash cars that are today proving their outstanding quality and economy. It means an even greater Kelvinator refrigerator than we produced before . . . finer home freezers, electric water heaters and electric ranges than have ever served in any household.

This is our program. This will be our part in the building of a greater, happier nation. For we believe all of us owe to those who have fought to preserve it a strong, a vital, a growing America where all men and women will have the freedom and the opportunity to make their dreams come true.

The Arma Nava G servorless to Nash-Kelvinator Corp. Propeller Division.

NASH-KELVINATOR CORPORATION
Kenosha · Milwaukee · DETROIT · Grand Rapids · Lansing

NASH N·K KELVINATOR

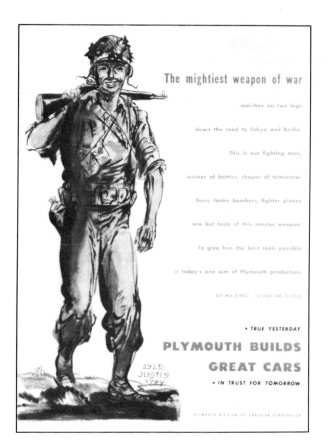

The mightiest weapon of war

marches on two legs

down the road to Tokyo and Berlin.

This is our fighting man,

winner of battles, shaper of tomorrow.

Guns, tanks, bombers, fighter planes

are but tools of this master weapon.

To give him the best tools possible

is today's one aim of Plymouth production.

• TRUE YESTERDAY

PLYMOUTH BUILDS
GREAT CARS

• IN TRUST FOR TOMORROW

"Gee! you surely took care
of my Pontiac!"

PONTIAC MOTOR DIVISION
General Motors Corporation

Plymouth saluted the American fighting man, armed in this illustration with the standard eight-shot M-1 Garand rifle, a ten-pouch cartridge belt, and a spare bandolier of ammunition across his chest, all very heavy. This is an extremely basic ad that thanks the soldiers and notes Plymouth's contributions. Courtesy, Chrysler Corporation

This advertisement appeared to be a continuation of a theme expressed in a previous ad, where Pontiac featured a young soldier overseas reading a letter from home about his car. Having survived his military situation, he has now come home to his car and the hope of a peaceful life. However, with no new models yet available, preventative maintenance is still the important message. Courtesy, Pontiac Division, General Motors Corporation

on fuel, Vice Adm. Marc Mitscher ordered the lights in the fleet turned on to guide them home, a gallant but risky gesture of life-saving importance to the pilots and crews. Many were forced to land in the ocean, but were saved by American rescue submarines and picket ships. When returning downed aviators to their carriers, rescuers were usually rewarded with ten gallons of ice cream!

Saipan was secured on July 9 at a cost of 3,000 US lives and 30,000 Japanese. That island and neighboring Tinian provided the air bases needed to launch the B-29 strategic bombing campaign against Japan's home islands.

During the pivotal summer of 1944, the Axis suffered defeats on every combat front. While it is improbable that Germany and Japan could have reversed the course of the war at that time, the possibility of stalemate did exist if the Allies' inexorable advance could have been thwarted on some of these far-flung battlefronts. But that was not to be, and the noose continued to tighten.

The shortages facing civilians in the United States that summer were baseball players and liquor. More than 4,000 players out of the 5,700 in the major and minor leagues entered wartime military service. Many of them were "Tunney-fish," recruited by the Navy as physical education instructors under the leadership of boxing champion Gene Tunney, but hundreds saw combat and several were killed. For some, the war robbed them of the best years of their careers. Old men

Next page
Normandy was the site of the Allies' June 1944 invasion of Festung Europa, Hitler's fortified coast of France. This beach on the home front provided a different scene, with happy-faced Americans of all ages enjoying hot dogs on the sand. What "helped us take the beachheads in Normandy"? "The American Way," according to this ad. Grandpa must have been a little warm with his jacket and tie. Courtesy, Chrysler Corporation

It helped us take the beachheads in Normandy!

Where but in America could you see a sight like this? . . .

Cars by the thousands on the roads . . . new, sleek, powerful machines driven, not alone by bankers and millionaires . . . but by 30 million average Americans.

It was the wonder of the world . . . and you made it possible.

For you had a restless, burning ambition for better and still better things . . . you forced American industry to fight for your favor . . . by improving, expanding, searching for new ways to give them to you.

That is "The American Way."

It inspired Chrysler engineers, for example, to invent improvements for your peace time cars that helped our fighting men take beachheads in all parts of the world, press on to Victory on land, sea and in the air.

It gave us, and the rest of free American industry, the will and heart to grow big, strong . . . until we were ready to out-produce the regimented Axis nations at their own game of war.

You were the driving power . . . you

were the driver. And, because this is "The American Way," you will start again asking us to give you even better cars than before.

And you will get them!

CHRYSLER
DIVISION OF CHRYSLER CORPORATION

Buy more War Bonds than ever before

51

123

Willys aggressively explored civilian markets for its famous vehicle as the war neared its conclusion, and farming was a prime target. Mindful of the fact that Ford built thousands of Jeeps under government contract, Willys reminded the public that only its company produced the real *Jeep. The ad stressed the Jeep's versatility by showing it involved in insect control, road repairs work, plowing snow, and doing general farm work. Courtesy, Chrysler Corporation*

Dodge produced engines for the B-29 Superfortress. After moving its base to the Marianas, the Twentieth Air Force initiated high-altitude bombing raids against Japan that were not very successful, due mainly to tremendously high winds at those altitudes over Japan. Gen. Curtis LeMay instead ordered low-level nighttime raids utilizing incendiary bombs, and in one raid on Tokyo by 334 B-29s in March 1945, burned 16 square miles of the city and killed 80,000 people. It was the most destructive attack of the war, and the forerunner of the strategic bombing campaign against Japan. Courtesy, Chrysler Corporation

and young boys populated the big leagues, and the St. Louis Browns even had a one-armed outfielder named Pete Gray. But baseball was still the national pastime, and served to take people's minds off their worries and troubles.

Many Americans looked to alcohol to perform the same relaxing service, but they were often disappointed by liquor shortages in 1944. In 1942 all liquor production had been commandeered for the war effort, and since that time Americans had managed to drink up the reserves, imbibing 190 million gallons a year–50 million gallons a year more than the prewar average consumption. Some Americans started making their own whiskey, just as they had during Prohibition. In Brooklyn, fourteen people died from drinking wood alcohol dispensed by a local distiller of illegal spirits. During August of 1944, the government allowed the liquor companies one month of production to ease the shortage, but for many

Americans their only refuge was beer or domestic wine.

There were other tragedies on the home front that summer. Train wrecks were all too frequent due to worn-out equipment and overscheduling for the war effort. In Hartford, Connecticut, a circus tent went up in flames during a performance, and 168 people died, with another 400 injured.

Next page
DeSoto continued its durability campaign with the now familiar slogan, "Seven out of Ten Still Running." This happy family is preparing for Thanksgiving with a turkey and pumpkin for a pie. The leg room in this back seat is unimaginable by today's standards. Courtesy, Chrysler Corporation

Of all the De Soto cars ever built, 7 out of 10 are still running

16 YEARS AGO the first De Soto cars rolled off the line. De Soto grew up in a tough decade, with a tough creed: "Make a better car or get out of business." Engineers gave De Soto a long list of brilliant "firsts," among them floating power, fluid drive, superfinished parts, safety-steel bodies. And De Sotos sold fast. When war came,

we had a bigger job. Bomber sections, airplane wings, guns. Other war materials pour out of De Soto factories. Meanwhile, we're glad we built De Sotos to endure— and thousands who know that 7 out of 10 are still running will be glad to decide on De Soto.

DE SOTO DIVISION, CHRYSLER CORPORATION

Tune in on Major Bowes, every Thursday, 9:00 to 9:30 p. m., Eastern War Time.

BACK THE ATTACK—BUY MORE WAR BONDS THAN BEFORE

De Soto
Designed to Endure

125

Fisher provided the automatic loader and rammer for the 120mm gun, which could fire an antiaircraft shell nearly twelve miles into the air. Powder charge and shell casing are separate components for this weapon. By this point in the war, Fisher's Army-Navy "E" banner bears five stars for its excellent production work. Courtesy, General Motors

Thought to have been started by a discarded cigarette, it now appears from recent evidence that a teenage runaway started it deliberately. Two years earlier, the Coconut Grove Nightclub fire in Boston had taken almost 500 lives.

More ominous than these conflagrations, however, were the racial fires burning in American hearts and minds. Pearl Harbor was the scene of several racial disturbances during the war, as were many mainland cities, especially those heavily involved in defense contracts and overflowing with relocated war workers.

In California, 50 black sailors were convicted of mutiny for refusing to load ammunition ships. In their segregated role as support units, they had suffered heavy casualties when a munitions ship blew up as it was being loaded near San Francisco. Two ships were sunk, and debris almost hit a plane flying 12,000 feet above the scene. Of the 320 dead, 202 were black. When ordered back to their assignments a few weeks later, more than 200 black sailors refused their

orders and were court-martialed. The leaders went to prison and the rest received bad-conduct discharges. Their claims that they were forced to do this dangerous work because of their color fell on deaf ears. Military men and women were dying all over the world, and segregation was not enough of a reason for an exemption from danger in 1944.

Still, there were some bright spots in the struggle for equal rights, as several laws that prevented black voting were struck down by the courts. The National Association for the Advancement of Colored People (NAACP) grew in membership from 100,000 before the war to 500,000 by 1944. The war was changing America at a tremendous pace, and race relations at home could not be ignored by a nation so immersed in a fight for freedom and equality elsewhere in the world.

One inescapable arena of equality was the ubiquitous draft board. All men between eighteen and thirty-eight who didn't enlist in the service, regardless of race or creed, ultimately received "greetings from Uncle Sam." As the war stretched out chronologically and geographically, the availability of young men for the meat grinder lessened substantially. There were different status classifications, depending on age and marital status, and thousands of men had war-work deferments, whether they wanted them or not. In addition, the Army was a bureaucracy of the highest order, with the administrative "tail" wagging the combat "dog."

Less than 20 percent of the 11 million men in the Army were in combat divisions, and fewer than 700,000 of these were in the infantry. The real casualty rates, which were horrendous in line companies, were hidden statistically in the larger, overall number of soldiers involved.

It is curious that in late 1944 the Army allowed all draftees still stationed stateside and over thirty-eight years old to apply for hardship discharges, and plenty did so successfully. This occurred at a time when the war was going well for the Allies, but certainly was not nearly over, as the planned invasion of the Japanese home-

Next page
The Northrop Black Widow was the first aircraft specifically designed as a night fighter. Officially the P-61, it carried a crew of three, including a radar operator. Armament consisted of four 20mm cannons and four .50 caliber machine guns. The Black Widow had a large fuel capacity and flew at 415mph. Oldsmobile manufactured the cannon shells. The ad said Oldsmobile also produced other equipment including "other 'censored' weapons which are already doing much to 'Keep 'Em Firing?' "Courtesy, Oldsmobile Division, General Motors Corporation

The Black Widow[*]
SNARES AN AXIS "FLY"!

* *Black Widow is the name of America's newest, most deadly night fighter . . . the cannon-firing P-61*

An Axis raider drones toward its target, unaware that far ahead . . . the Black Widow is waiting! Busy Axis hands prepare to release their cargo of destruction. Straining Axis eyes peer out into the night . . . where the Black Widow is waiting! But they see nothing, no sign of danger, until suddenly . . . a huge, dark shape appears from nowhere! There's a burst of cannon fire, a blinding explosion, an Axis plane flaming downward . . . the Black Widow has struck!

The P-61 Black Widow is the first American plane to be designed, from the very beginning, as a night fighter. It has everything . . .

speed to catch an enemy unawares, electronic devices to search in the dark, fire-power enough to pulverize anything that flies!

Fire-power is our specialty at Oldsmobile. Automatic aircraft cannon, such as we have built by the tens of thousands, help give the Black Widow its "poisonous sting." Other Oldsmobile war products include cannon for tanks and tank destroyers, high-explosive and armor-piercing shell, parts for aircraft engines and heavy-duty military vehicles . . . plus other "censored" weapons which are already doing much to "Keep 'Em Firing!"

The Widow's MIGHT is Fire-Power!

The Black Widow packs the Fire-Power of fast-firing 20 mm. automatic aerial cannon that can smash any enemy plane that flies.

YOUR BONDS HELP PROVIDE IT

Give our fighting men the Fire-Power they need to fight with. Buy more War Bonds and Stamps to Keep 'Em Firing.

OLDSMOBILE DIVISION OF GENERAL MOTORS
FIRE-POWER IS OUR BUSINESS!

✳ IMAGINATION IN PRECISION

Chrysler built and Superfinished this big Navy searchlight reflector

HOW IMAGINATION HELPS CHRYSLER BUILD BETTER PRODUCTS FOR YOU!

Imagination looks in a mirror and sees a polished piston, so shining smooth it outwits wear and adds extra life to engines.

Imagination at Chrysler found a way to mirror-finish moving parts with the world's smoothest surface, used also on this searchlight reflector.

Imagination spurs Chrysler Corporation's constant search for precision methods that can build longer life and better performance into cars or trucks — or weapons of war.

Imagination made possible the long list of car improvements introduced by Chrysler Corporation: the combination of Floating Power and Fluid Drive that gives you such effortless, quiet performance, the long life that comes from Superfinished parts, and many others.

Here at Chrysler, imagination stimulates the search for new methods and improved products. And all the Corporation's divisions work together to share their experience and findings, strengthening *each* with the strength of *all*.

Chrysler imagination quickly applied our precision methods to building tanks, aircraft engines and other war equipment. After the war, the same kind of imagination will once again help make better cars and trucks for you.

✳ IMAGINATION IS THE DIRECTING FORCE AT

CHRYSLER CORPORATION

PLYMOUTH	**AIRTEMP** Heating, Cooling, Refrigeration
DODGE	**CHRYSLER** Marine and Industrial Engines
DE SOTO	
CHRYSLER	**OILITE** Powdered Metal Products

YOU'LL ENJOY MAJOR BOWES THURSDAYS, C.B.S. 9 P.M., E.W.T.

land still lay ahead. Another disturbing aspect regarding combat availability is discussed in *Don't You Know There's a War On?*, where author Richard Lingeman states, "there were estimates that as high as one-half of the combat-trained troops avoided battle by 'psyching out,' getting a dishonorable discharge and the like."

It would appear that not quite all Americans were willing to participate in the times in which they were living. The "doggies" in the front lines didn't understand it all, but they realized they were in a kill-or-be-killed environment, and the only way out was death, wounds, or the end of the war. Many could laugh at themselves through Bill Mauldin's famous *Up Front* cartoon characters, Willy & Joe, those tired, dirty G.I.s doing a dirty job with resigned humor, and George Baker's cartoon, *Sad Sack,* who looked a lot like Kilroy. The boys smoked their favorite Camel cigarettes, sneaked a drink whenever they could, and tried to survive the savagery of modern combat.

The fact that women on the home front were too tired from their defense jobs to bake many cookies or cakes anymore, and that the enthusiasm for victory gardens was on the wane, didn't bother them much. Their problems were much more immediate, and their enemies could get very personal. American soldiers knew that the Germans had better tanks and artillery, and that some other US equipment, such as antitank mines that blew up unexpectedly when handled in freezing weather, was inferior.

They also knew that they had a great rifle in the eight-shot M-1 Garand (four million were manufactured), and that the Allied air forces owned the skies over Europe. And they knew that if they died, the family back home collected a $10,000 life insurance policy from the government, $55 a month for twenty years or $36.80 a month for life. The G.I.s even invented some words to explain their situation. The most famous of them was SNAFU, which meant "situation normal, all [———] up," and FUBAR, "[———] up beyond all recognition."

One snafu that had a direct effect on the soldiers' life expectancy was Eisenhower's decision to redirect gasoline and supplies from Patton's hard-driving Third Army to the British forces under the leadership of Gen. Bernard Montgomery. This was done in the name of Allied unity and cooperation, but led directly to a slowdown of the offensive against the Germans and gave them a chance to regroup their defenses. Patton was only 71 miles (115 kilometers) from the Rhine River when he was halted. It should not be forgotten that the Russians attacking from the Eastern front were not yet in Germany, and had Patton been allowed to continue his advance, the Western powers may have been able to end the war without having to divide up Europe with the Soviets nine months later. Approximately two-thirds of the Allied losses suffered in the liberation of the Continent, as well as uncounted thousands or even millions of European deaths, occurred after September 1944.

Facing a possible stalemate with winter coming on, the Allies attempted a daring airborne assault that was designed to capture a series of bridges behind the German lines. A British armored column would then smash through on the ground to link the isolated airborne units and cre-

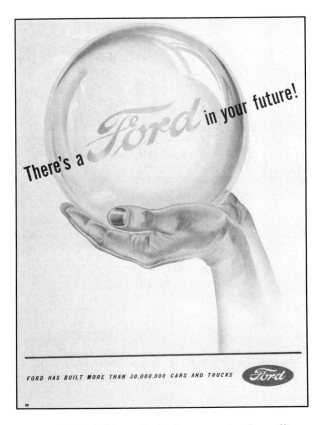

A crystal ball holds unlimited opportunity for millions of Americans freed from the rigors and uncertainty of wartime. This ad is incredibly spare and simple, yet this slogan was one of the most famous and successful in the history of advertising, and encompassed the hopes of several generations of Americans emerging from World War II. Courtesy, Ford Motor Company

*Automotive manufacturers had been silent on the sub-
ject of Christmas in the earlier, uncertain years of the
war. By the end of 1944, nearly everyone expected the
troops home by Christmas. Barring that as unrealistic,
the population was still ready to return to civilian pursuits and holidays with a flourish. Except during
wartime, Hudson owners apparently turned their cars
over for new ones with frequency. This ad notes that
when the Hudson was bought three years earlier, "[per-
haps] you didn't dream you would have to drive it so
long or so far."* Courtesy, Chrysler Corporation

ate a corridor into Germany. Code named Mar-
ket-Garden, the assault failed when the ground
forces were unable to relieve the British para-
troopers at the Arnhem Bridge over the Rhine in
Holland, made famous in the book and movie, *A
Bridge Too Far.*

Battles were raging in all the zones of this
global conflict in the fall of 1944. Having finally
broken through the Gustav Line in Italy, the Allies found themselves brought up short by another set of imposing German defenses called the
Gothic Line. In Poland the Soviets stopped on the
outskirts of Warsaw, encouraging the partisans
in the city to revolt against the hated Germans.
When the Poles did so, the Soviets halted their
own offensive and left the erstwhile civilian irreg-
ulars to be crushed by the Axis troops in the city.
It was just another step in the planned occupation of Eastern Europe by the USSR once the war
was over.

In the Pacific, however, the picture was
brighter. Encouraged by their success in the Marianas and New Guinea campaigns, the American
leadership moved up its invasion of the Philippines by two months. General MacArthur fulfilled
his promise to return. The islands were retaken,
but at a cost of 3,500 American lives. The Japanese, who usually chose to fight to the death, lost
80,000 men. Ominously, while the naval Battle of
Leyte Gulf in the Philippines was a decisive US
victory, it marked the first appearance of Japanese "kamikazes," enemy pilots who sacrificed
themselves by crashing their explosives-laden aircraft into American warships. This suicidal campaign would grow in intensity and destructive-
ness in the months to come.

The Japanese mainland was now the target of
American bombers. Giant B-29 Superfortresses
staged from China to bomb Japanese cities and
military installations from very high altitudes.
This campaign was not very successful, as the B-
29s had to fly three supply missions from India to
China in order to support each bombing mission
over the enemy's homeland. The Japanese, however, viewed the threat differently and attacked
the B-29 bases in China with ground troops, capturing all but two of the airfields used by these
huge bombers. The American effort then shifted
to bases on Saipan and Tinian in the Marianas to
carry on the B-29 offensive against Japan.

As 1944 drew to a close, the German Army
made one last desperate attempt to throw back
the Allies poised to overrun its homeland. Attacking in winter conditions through the Ardennes
Forest in Belgium, the Wehrmacht broke through
American lines and drove toward the sea. The
fighting was relentless, brutal. Prisoners were
machine-gunned by both sides, although the
Malmedy Massacre of eighty-six American POWs
is the atrocity remembered by history. Courage
was commonplace, and so was cowardice. Confusion was paramount. When a surrounded US
paratroop command was called on to surrender by
the Germans, Gen. Anthony McAuliffe's response
was "Nuts!", yet at another point in the battle,
9,000 Americans surrendered en masse.

But the Wehrmacht had gambled and lost.
When the weather cleared in mid-December, the
Allied air forces threw their weight against the
German advance and forced it back. The Ameri-
cans took 77,000 casualties, the Germans suffered
125,000.

The Battle of the Bulge was a sobering experience for those Americans who viewed the war as
nearly over, but optimism regarding an early victory still ran high, and much of the home front
advertising in late 1944 reflected this thinking.
Many companies focused on the peace that was

sure to come soon, realizing that people were impatient to spend their pent-up earnings.

The Ford Motor Company produced a series of ads that featured historic moments in the company's early years, as well as incidents in the personal life of founder Henry Ford. Pontiac focused on a young soldier's dreams of his car waiting at home, and Dodge spotlighted the durability of its All-Fluid Drive. Willys-Overland touted its Jeep's civilian uses, but Oldsmobile continued to fight the war in its product advertising, as did Buick, Nash, and Chevrolet.

With paper quotas at 75 percent of prewar availability, there was stiff competition for advertising space and magazines enjoyed unusually high popularity among both corporate advertisers and the reading public. The pessimism of the early war years was replaced by a "home for Christmas" philosophy. Companies were anxious to keep their defense contributions in the public eye, but did not want to miss postwar marketing opportunities.

In a September editorial, *Collier's* threw some cold water on this optimism, stating that automobiles were wearing out at a rate of 150,000 a month. The same editorial said that American cars needed 45 million replacement tires in 1944, but only 20 million were available, and labeled the conservation of tires and gasoline as an "urgent patriotic duty."

After three years of war it was apparent that advertising, the magazine industry, and the federal government had formed a wartime alliance that persuaded and molded public opinion, enumerated war goals, and praised patriotic production. This was a far cry from the hostility that permeated prewar relations between government and business in the nation, and at least stilled for a while the radical elements in the US government who had foreseen and still foresaw a very different world than most of America's citizenry.

November in America marked the election of the ailing Franklin D. Roosevelt to a fourth term as president of the United States. Although the Republicans took control of the House of Representatives in the 1942 elections, FDR was a formidable political force and was also the commander in chief. Some felt that Wendell Wilkie, the Republican standard-bearer in 1940, had a good chance to defeat Roosevelt, but he bowed out of the race after a poor primary showing. Wilkie died of a heart attack less than a month before the 1944 election. Tom Dewey, a well-known New York district attorney, won the Republican nomination but never had a chance in the general election. The vote in the Electoral College was Roosevelt 432, Dewey 99.

Elsewhere on the home front, there were at least plenty of eggs available in the stores. Conversely, a story came out of Florida that a chicken farmer located near a military base had converted his coops into $3 a night bedrooms, and he wasn't checking for luggage. A person could not stand up in one and they smelled terribly of disinfectant, but for couples about to be separated by the war, the coops were at least private.

The bad news on the domestic front was that there was barely a cigarette to be had anywhere that Christmas season. The military services received 30 percent of them, and production had just not kept up with demand, so the smoking pipe was reborn. Another major shortage in the face of a bitter winter was the lack of heating fuel. Stores were closed at dusk by government decree, and schools in the Northeast were shut down. (The government also closed the horse and dog tracks, but nobody knew why. They didn't reopen until the following May.)

Another tragedy struck home that December when popular band leader Glenn Miller disappeared in a small military aircraft over the English Channel. Miller had joined the Army and recruited his famous US Air Force Band to entertain the troops. Now he was gone. In 1985, a former RAF pilot disclosed that his bomber squadron returning from a mission on the same day that Miller disappeared had jettisoned unexploded bombs in an unauthorized area of the Channel. Flight crew members saw them blow a small Allied aircraft into the sea, the same type in which Miller was flying that fateful day, December 15, 1944. The incident was not reported at the time because the squadron had been in violation of orders. It joins the list of other possible explanations for Miller's disappearance.

In the far-off China-Burma-India (CBI) theater, the forgotten war was being waged. British General Wingate and his Chindits, American General Stilwell and his Marauders, and the famous air commando of the youthful Air Corps Col. Phil Cochran, fought the Japanese in the mountains and jungles of Asia. The men and women of the CBI did not get the same wartime publicity as some other units and theaters of operations, but they did gain enduring fame via Milt Caniff's well-known comic strip, *Terry and the Pirates.*

Easily recognizable were Phil Cochran as Flip Corkin and Casey Vincent as Vince Casey. And who didn't love the Dragon Lady, with her overtones of the Japanese radio propagandist Tokyo Rose? However, for most of the young Americans fighting a determined Japanese enemy in what appeared to be a backwater of the war, it seemed that the conflict would never end, and the chance to see the States very soon was remote. Their plaintive battle cry was "The Golden Gate in '48!"

CHAPTER 5

"The Golden Gate in '48": 1945

The first day of 1945 witnessed a major German air attack in Allied-occupied Europe. As the battered Wehrmacht retreated from its December defeat at the Battle of the Bulge, the Luftwaffe staged one of its most effective tactical air strikes of the war in the West when it attacked 17 Allied airfields on the Continent and destroyed 156 American and British planes on the ground. The price, however, was too high, as 200 German aircraft failed to return from the raid, pilots Germany could ill afford to lose as the Allies continued their constant aerial bombardment of the Reich.

Germany was devastated, its civilian industries in ruins and its people hammered mercilessly on all sides by their enemies. Transportation was practically non-existent for civilians, and the few cars on the road were often powered by wood-burning engines. The situation in the US was not quite as bad, although to listen to the general driving public, it might seem so.

With no new cars manufactured since the beginning of 1942, the average car on America's roads in the spring of 1945 was seven years old. According to one major oil company, automobiles were going permanently out of service at a rate of one every 22 seconds, nearly 4,000 a day, more than a million a year. Another petroleum giant reported that private cars ran nine times more passenger miles a year than bus and rail combined, and without cars the nation's transportation system would collapse The public was reminded that if new car production started immediately, it would take four years to match the demand for new vehicles. It was obviously in the drivers' best interest to take excellent care of their existing vehicles, because it would be a long time before any new ones would be available. DeSoto capitalized on this concern by announcing that "Of all DeSoto cars ever built, 7

out of 10 are still running," effective advertising for the postwar market.

US auto manufacturers were fully aware of the potentially lucrative sales opportunity that would come at war's end, but in most cases were unable to design new cars for the future because of the present demands placed on all their resources by military production and the general war effort.

In other parts of the world, such as Japan, postwar cars were not a priority.

On December 7, 1944, the third anniversary of the Japanese attack on Pearl Harbor, Tokyo had been severely damaged by an earthquake. It was a harbinger of things to come as Japan was about to undergo a trial by fire, the destruction of its cities from the air by the B-29 Superfortresses of Gen. Curtis LeMay. The B-29 was the premiere bomber of the war, able to fly higher and faster than any other bomber while carrying a formidable bomb load of 20,000 pounds. However, the winds at 40,000 feet over Japan often reached 200mph, reducing the effectiveness of strategic precision bombing which in turn was disappointing the US High Command.

General LeMay, operating out of the recently captured Mariana Islands of Saipan and Tinian, only 1,250 miles from Japan, was given command of the operation. LeMay had been a tough, resourceful, and successful bomber commander of the Eighth Air Force in Europe, and now was asked to destroy Japan's industrial capacity to wage war.

He did so with a campaign of low-level incendiary area attacks by as many as 800 B-29s on a single mission. More than sixty Japanese cities were engulfed by fire. In a May 25 raid by 300 B-29s on Tokyo, 25 percent (18 square miles) of the city was burned and more than 100,000 people were killed. The Japanese Broadcasting Company estimated that 2,726,000 people were homeless as a result of the bombing, and 130,000 structures were destroyed. By the end of the war, more than half of Japan's urban areas were destroyed by firebombing. It was an awesome display of America's ability to wage merciless war on a determined enemy.

On the ground, the US Army under the supreme command of Douglas MacArthur invaded Luzon in the Philippines on January 9. It was the decisive battle in the retaking of that island nation, one that MacArthur fiercely desired to win as a result of his own defeat there in 1942. The general was also eager to free the thousands of sick, starving, and brutalized American prisoners still in the hands of the Japanese, fearing for their survival when the Japanese were forced to retreat. The battle for Luzon resulted in 8,000 American dead and 30,000 wounded, while the Japanese lost 170,000.

Once the Philippines were secured, Japan would be next, and the Japanese knew it. A major element in their plan of defense was the kamikaze, meaning "Divine Wind." Just such a wind, a typhoon, had destroyed the enemy invasion fleet of Kublai Khan in the thirteenth century. Now it took the form of suicidal Japanese pilots in aircraft filled with explosives purposely crashing into American warships and transports. The tactic was terribly successful and led to the loss of forty US ships in the Philippine area alone, but it could not stave off an American victory there. MacArthur had returned, just as he had promised in the dark days of 1942.

It was sometimes difficult to recall that three years earlier, America had been in desperate straits militarily. What occurred since those days had not only been a production miracle, but a technological miracle as well. The response by manufacturers, especially in the automotive industry, was incredible by any standards. By 1945, production of most war materiel had actually been reduced, but in both quality and quantity the United States was far superior to just about anything produced by either ally or enemy.

The B-29 was the best strategic bomber, followed by the B-17 and the B-24. Tactically, the B-26 and B-25 bombers were modified to undertake a variety of missions and proved their excellence. The P-51 Mustang was probably the best fighter to come out of World War II, while the Navy flew the Hellcat and Corsair, both of which had superior kill ratios against the Japanese in the Pacific. Trucks by the thousands, Jeeps, large-caliber artillery and equipment of every variety dominated the resources of the enemy. There were exceptions, such as the German Tiger tanks which were better armed and armored than the American tanks, but even in those instances the num-

This farmer appeared to be showing his seed corn to the county agent, who probably was not affected by gas rationing when he drove about his district. Hudson included in this ad some information about its company symbol, the Hudson triangle, as it prepared for the postwar automotive market share battle which had been suspended since early 1942. Courtesy, Chrysler Corporation

bers were so heavily in favor of the US forces that they were able to overwhelm their opponents.

There are many reasons for this preeminence in the worldwide conflict, not the least of which is that the war was not fought in most instances on American soil, and the population did not undergo the terror and destruction that devastated most of the warring nations. Additional reasons were superior resources, ample numbers of troops, and training. But American manufactur-

Next page
Seabee was an acronym for C-B, construction battalion. These sailors created construction miracles throughout the war, often while under enemy fire. They were justly famous for their role in the Pacific campaigns, where they built airfields on coral atolls and made desolate backwaters habitable for thousands of Americans and their allies. Studebaker continued this father-son advertising campaign into early 1945. Courtesy, Dresser-Rand

"Seabee" Balaban and his father helped build many a Studebaker in peacetime

And they're comrades in craftsmanship still

Studebaker's Joe Balaban has another son and a daughter in the Navy—Like thousands of Studebaker automotive veterans, Joe Balaban is doing his share for the war effort in one of Studebaker's aircraft engine plants. Other Studebaker automotive employees are busy building big multiple-drive Studebaker military trucks and Weasel personnel and cargo carriers.

KEEP ON BUYING WAR BONDS AND KEEP ALL THE BONDS YOU BUY!

THE whole nation is justly proud of the accomplishments of our Navy's Seabees, the fighting construction battalions on whose banners is blazoned: "We do the difficult immediately—the impossible takes a little longer."

One fine example of the resourceful Seabees at their best is First Class Seaman Milan Balaban of South Bend, Indiana. He learned his way around with tools as an apprentice millwright in the Studebaker automotive plants—working close by his father who has been a Studebaker employee for more than 26 years.

Today, Joe Balaban, the father, is putting his skill and experience to good account in the Studebaker Aviation Division—from which tens upon tens of thousands of Studebaker-built Wright Cyclone engines for the

famous Boeing Flying Fortress have been steadily streaming forth.

It's largely because of the painstaking craftsmanship in peacetime, of numerous Studebaker father-and-son teams like the Balabans, that wartime America is getting such dependable performance from Studebaker Champion, Commander and President passenger cars and Studebaker trucks and commercial cars.

Awarded To All  *Studebaker Plants*

STUDEBAKER

Building Wright Cyclone engines for the Boeing Flying Fortress—multiple-drive military trucks—the Weasel personnel and cargo carrier.

134

ing production, led by the automobile companies, must receive a large share of the credit. Without them the cost in blood, lives, and treasure would have been much greater, and the achievement may well have been less.

In the United States that January, there were shortages of cigarettes, liquor, automobile tires, and shoe leather, to mention a few. The nation's motto became "Use it up, wear it out, make it do or do without," and it permeated magazine advertising. Companies tried to keep waving the flag, but the longing for peace and a return to normality was constant and impossible to ignore. Thus, advertising in 1945 started focusing on the desire for abundance and prosperity which peace was bound to bring to the nation.

The Northeast suffered through a bitterly cold winter with severe shortages of home heating oil, forcing the closure of schools and businesses. To add to the burden, cities on the East Coast were warned of the "probability" of rocket attacks by the Germans. It seemed as if it would never end, even though the Germans were reeling back in defeat on every war front, and the Japanese

Empire was facing fearful civilian as well as combat losses and a serious economic blockade by American submarines and surface ships. German civilians were suffering also, as the advancing Russians paid back in full the brutal treatment accorded their citizens during the German invasion and occupation of the USSR. On January 30, a Russian submarine torpedoed the *Wilhelm Gustloff* crowded with German refugees in the Baltic Sea and sank it, with a loss of 7,700 lives.

FDR, recently reelected to a fourth term and possessed with grand plans for a prosperous America in a world at peace, met increasing resistance in Congress from old enemies who surfaced with the end of the war hopefully in sight. He had dropped Vice President Henry Wallace as too progressive for the American voter, and added old-line Missouri politician Harry Truman in his place. Shortly thereafter Roosevelt met with Churchill and Stalin at a place called Yalta, in the Russian Crimea on the Black Sea, where the division of postwar Europe was decided. FDR accepted, welcomed America's new international political role, and was justifiably proud of the birth

Defense production diminished rapidly as the war headed for its conclusion, and companies were proud of their achievements. Chevrolet cited some of its major contributions, which included 400,000 trucks, 54,000 *aircraft engines, 3,000 90mm antiaircraft guns, and 50,000 tons of aluminum forgings from just one plant in less than two years. Courtesy, Chevrolet Division, General Motors Corporation*

135

Even Nash acknowledged that the war was winding down, as the company logo featured a scene from civilian life, a Nash driving down a snowy country lane. This G.I. dreamed of a Christmas homecoming to his wife and children, while realizing his commitment would not end until victory and peace were secured. Courtesy, Chrysler Corporation

Willys compared its Jeep's role in the liberation of the French city of Orleans to Joan of Arc's great victory there in 1429. According to the copy in this ad, the French people cheered their nation, the American soldiers freeing their city, and the Jeep with equal fervor. "Vive le Jeep!" Courtesy, Chrysler Corporation

of the United Nations, purportedly one of the main reasons for the conference, which received its approval at Yalta. His critics, however, felt that he abandoned the small countries of middle and Eastern Europe to the Communists.

It must not be overlooked that very few Americans were willing to prolong the war by fighting the Soviets for the liberation of nations already under Stalin's control, some of which had sided with the Germans during the war. The Big Three also made a secret pact to give the Soviets territorial concessions and railroad rights in Manchuria in return for their intervention in the war against Japan. The agreement to allow free elections in Europe was also disregarded immediately by the Soviets in territory they controlled, and realists at the conference knew that guarantees and safeguards were a farce even before they sailed for home. The concept that there is no morality in international politics loomed large at Yalta.

On the Western front, the Wehrmacht attempted a counterattack in the Alsace region following its retreat from the Bulge. When it failed, the American Army started its victorious drive for the Rhine River and the German heartland. Early February found the Soviet armies only thirty-eight miles from Berlin. The Russians wanted revenge and certainly achieved it in their occupation of Germany as the war progressed, but they also asked the British and the Americans to assist them by destroying the city of Dresden from the air. For two days and nights the Allies devastated this beautiful city which had no military significance, killing 135,000 people. It was terror bombing at its worst. Author Kurt Vonnegut was an American POW in Dresden during these attacks, and wrote about his experiences in his book *Slaughterhouse Five*. Clearly, Germany was swiftly losing the war at this time, and it is difficult to justify Dresden as either a tactical or strategic target.

The air war over Europe was still a savage contest as the Germans fought desperately to de-

136

Mercury had not advertised in the national magazines since 1941, mainly because Ford had not chosen to portray its divisions individually during wartime production. This ad noted that "Today—a big, new, handsome Mercury must necessarily remain a dream to you and countless others. But the day is steadily drawing nearer when you'll see that dream come true." Mercury manufactured 86,603 cars in the 1946 production year, offering six models priced from $1,448 to $2,209. Courtesy, Ford Motor Company

Oldsmobile maintained its emphasis on defense production in its ads, continuing its popular series featuring Air Force unit insigne. Powered by two 2,000hp radial engines, the Black Widow was first assigned to combat in May 1944. Its radar capacity allowed the P-61 to intercept enemy aircraft on the darkest of nights, and Oldsmobile provided the 20mm cannon shells. Courtesy, Oldsmobile Division, General Motors Corporation

fend their homeland. Luftwaffe Gen. Adolf Galland described his fighter pilots' tactics in attacking American bomber formations as "controlled suicide." The British policy of "carpet bombing" was not expected to be very accurate. A survey of their results indicated that only one in five bombing attacks came within five miles of its target. Still, Bomber Command suffered a 54 percent casualty rate.

One of the ominous developments in Europe at this juncture was the arrival in battle of the German M-262, the first jet fighter operational in the war. While it was extremely effective against the American bombers on an individual basis, there were too few of them to make a significant difference against the overwhelming number of attackers pounding Germany. Had they been committed a few months earlier, the M-262s probably could have seriously crippled the bomber offensive, creating an unacceptable casualty rate.

In the Pacific, the B-29 bomber raids on Japan necessitated a 2,500 mile round-trip from the Marianas. Many damaged planes failed to make it back to base, and the High Command believed that one solution to these losses was an emergency landing field closer to Japan. Iwo Jima in the Volcano Islands was targeted for this purpose, as well as being another step on the road to Japan, and Iwo was invaded by US Marines on February 19. Probably the most famous photograph of the war was taken here of several Marines raising the American flag atop Mount Suribachi, the island's highest point. A brutal battle raged in the caves and bunkers of this volcanic hellhole, ultimately resulting in the death of 5,000 Marines and 25,000 Japanese.

Ernie Pyle, a war correspondent loved and respected by the troops, was killed by a Japanese machine gunner in April on one of the other small islands nearby. But in the several months remaining before the end of the war, no fewer than 2,400 crippled B-29s would make emergency landings on Iwo Jima, doubtlessly saving count-

Cadillac

Peacetime Power *with a* Wartime Job!

When Cadillac discontinued motor car production, its engine assembly line continued to roll. For the famous Cadillac V-type engine, and Hydra-Matic transmission, had been adapted to war.

This Cadillac "power-train" was first used in the M-5, a light tank designed by Cadillac under the direction of Army Ordnance technicians. Thousands of these tanks—as well as its companion, the M-8 Howitzer Motor Carriage—were produced by Cadillac, and are fighting in battles all over the world.

Finally, out of this experience, came the M-24—the powerful, hard-hitting weapon illustrated above.

The M-24—like its predecessors—is powered by two Cadillac V-type engines, driving through two Cadillac Hydra-Matic transmissions. Actual battle experience has proved these to be the most practicable power units ever used for tanks of this type. As a result, these power units have been adopted by the Army as standard for all light tanks.

The Cadillac-built unit that powers the M-24

tank has been vastly improved over its peacetime prototype. It is of the same basic design, but it has been hardened and toughened to meet demands that would never be made of an automotive power plant.

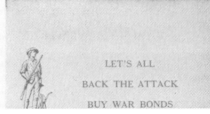

LET'S ALL
BACK THE ATTACK
BUY WAR BONDS

Every Sunday Afternoon . . . GENERAL MOTORS SYMPHONY OF THE AIR—NBC Network

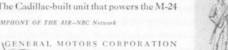

CADILLAC MOTOR CAR DIVISION — GENERAL MOTORS CORPORATION

less lives as each aircraft carried a crew of up to eleven, and also saving the aircraft itself.

Back in the forty-eight states, civilians struggled along as their fathers and brothers, sisters and friends fought the war on foreign shores. Many a family had a world map on the kitchen wall or door, with colored pins marking the progress of the Allies and especially the locations of their loved ones. Cigarettes were impossible to find. Other scarce items were coffee and butter, as well as many soaps. There was often a shortage of bread in the stores because the ingredients were not available to the bakeries. Women's girdles had no rubber in them, somewhat defeating their purpose, and golf balls were impossible to obtain.

Even though the war was clearly being won by the Allies, the threat of danger on the home front had not disappeared. Children in school still had air-raid drills and bought defense stamps through their teachers, and schools were the depository for the aluminum foil that all children saved for the war effort. They also collected and saved old newspapers in their neighborhoods for

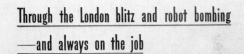

Nash advertisements throughout the war were harshly realistic, and it is therefore surprising that this "homecoming" type ad ignored the continuing struggle in the Pacific. At the time, most US leaders believed it would be necessary to invade the home islands, with great loss of human lives and materiel, in order to defeat Japan. Nash's logo was becoming more domestic, this time showing the returning soldier with his family, while the central character in this illustration has put the war behind him. Courtesy, Chrysler Corporation

Even as the war in Europe neared its conclusion, the Germans continued to attack British cities from the air. They used a 13.6-ton ballistic missile called the V-2 (Vengeance Weapon #2), which carried a ton of high explosives. When fired at London from Peenemunde on the Baltic, a distance of 183 miles, the missile would land within a rectangle measuring 16 miles by 13 miles. More than 10,000 V-2s were built, and 1,115 of them were fired against England. An additional 1,341 V-2s were targeted against Antwerp, while Paris was hit fifteen times. This ad touts the reliability and durability of Packards used by the American Ambulance Corps in London. Courtesy, Dresser-Rand

the ubiquitous scrap drives. There was very little metal available for toy manufacture, thus inadvertently leading to the creation of the plastic toy industry.

Among the popular authors that winter and spring were John Hersey, the war correspondent who wrote *A Bell for Adano,* and Ben Ames Williams with his best seller, *Leave Her to Heaven.* People hungry for entertainment and companionship packed the movie theaters every night, viewing such classics as *The Story of G.I. Joe, The Lost Weekend, A Tree Grows in Brooklyn,* and *National Velvet.* Two popular movie musicals that year were *Anchors Aweigh* and *Meet Me in St. Louis.*

Interestingly, the cataclysmic events associated with world war, so destructive of societies and economies, actually *strengthened* the capitalistic

system prevalent in the United States. The depression of the 1930s created doubt in the minds of many that free enterprise could or should survive. The president had been elected three times prior to the war on a platform that business executives were convinced would lead to socialism, and many of his public works programs for economic rehabilitation were indeed socialistic. Certainly many officials in FDR's administration were in favor of government intervention in the marketplace, including the banning of product advertising as wasteful, fraudulent, and unnecessary.

For all of the bureaucracy that surrounded America's war efforts, the production miracle achieved by the nation's manufacturers, farmers, and businesses convinced the general public that the best future for themselves and their country was through private enterprise. Once again the automobile manufacturers had led the way, overcoming all obstacles in their path to provide the equipment and munitions needed to win the war.

By 1945, General Motors' corporate ad campaign centered on the home front, and especially the peaceful pursuits of children. The crooked wooden fishing pole in the boat, however, seemed a little extreme, even in an economy facing wartime shortages. The aircraft pictured in the upper right corner is the OS2U-3 Kingfisher, which was used extensively as a naval scout plane that could be catapulted from ships at sea. There were many stories of heroic rescues effected by these versatile planes, including that of Eddie Rickenbacker and his crewmates when a Kingfisher taxied forty miles across the sea with the rescued men lashed to the wings. Courtesy, General Motors

This advertisement is reminiscent of the hurricane that battered New England in 1938, and included a testimonial from a mail carrier in Natick, Massachusetts. Plymouth was proud of its cars' ability to last through the war years and revived the company's 1941 slogan, "The Car That Stands Up Best!" Courtesy, Chrysler Corporation

140

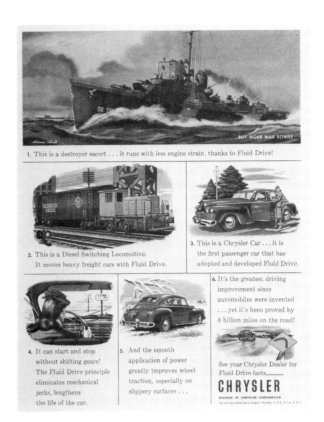

Ford continued its crystal-ball series of ads, looking into the future after victory was secured. A new Ford and a peaceful family life was "a promise to be fulfilled only when Victory is accomplished...Meanwhile, the full Ford resources will continue to be engaged in helping speed the victory." What could be more American than a boy going fishing with his dad? Bait-casting reels, metal rods, and black linen fishing line were the state of the art in 1945, while today they are sought as antiques. Courtesy, Ford Motor Company

Chrysler featured its fluid drive transmission in a variety of products as advertising started to stress postwar markets. The company maintained civilian car design departments throughout the war, but most of the planned changes were not brought to fruition. For several years after 1945 Chrysler cars were updated versions of 1942 models, and the same can be said for most automobile manufacturers. Courtesy, Chrysler Corporation

Events in Europe were moving swiftly to their conclusions. Believing that the two recent winter offensives by the German Army, even though they had failed, would slow down the British and Americans, Hitler stripped the Western defenses of equipment and troops to meet the massive Soviet onslaught in the East. He also counted on the V-2 rocket attacks on England and on the Allied supply port of Antwerp to hinder the offensive activities. Thus, the Western front was open to exploitation by Patton's fast-moving Third Army and the much slower, but powerful, offensive of the British Army under Montgomery. In early March Cologne was captured, and on March 7, the Ludendorff Railroad Bridge over the Rhine, the famous Bridge at Remagen, was taken intact by the advancing American Army.

Most professional German military leaders realized that the war was lost, but fear of Hitler's reprisals against themselves personally and their

families (demonstrated the previous July when thousands of innocent Germans were brutally executed in revenge for the failed attempt on Hitler's life), as well as concern for their fates under the "unconditional surrender" edict of the Allies, kept them fighting. By this late date, Hitler sought a miracle to save Germany, and, always something of a mystic, had taken to reading horoscopes to divine the future. Most shocking to the advancing Allies was the discovery of the concentration camps on German soil, with their thousands of dead and dying civilian inmates. While there had been rumors about these camps, this was the first real proof to the fighting troops of just what horrors the people of Europe had been subjected to under the Hitler regime.

Horror continued in the Pacific also as US forces invaded Okinawa on Easter Sunday, April 1, 1945 (also April Fool's Day). An island seventy-five miles long with a civilian population of 500,000, Okinawa was an integral part of Japan, not a colonial outpost. Military planners viewed it as a staging area for the invasion of the Japanese

Of all the De Soto cars ever built, 7 out of 10 are still running

A husky youngster of a car was born in Detroit 17 years ago. De Soto . . . born of brilliant engineers whose sole aim was *to make a better car.* As De Soto grew, these engineers gave it advantages that made De Soto famous . . . floating power, fluid drive, superfinished parts, safety-steel bodies. Which helps explain why so many De Sotos are rolling up 100,000 . . . 200,000 miles . . . and more. Today, we're making bomber sections, airplane wings, parts of anti-aircraft guns, and other war goods. But watch for the day when we'll again be making De Soto cars for you . . . cars *designed to endure.*

DE SOTO DIVISION, CHRYSLER CORPORATION

Tune in on Major Bowes' Program every Thursday, 9:00 to 9:30 p. m., Eastern War Time.

BACK THE ATTACK—BUY MORE WAR BONDS THAN BEFORE

DeSoto
DESIGNED TO ENDURE

As the end of the conflict approached, Americans again started families with the expectation that life would shortly return to normal. This little girl was obviously unhappy to see a younger brother join the family. For many years afterward, children born between 1942 and 1945 were called "war babies." The ad noted, "Today we're making bomber sections, airplane wings, parts of anti-aircraft guns, and other war goodies. But watch for the day when we'll again be making De Soto cars for you." Courtesy, Chrysler Corporation

142

home islands, and the Japanese defended it furiously, but with a major difference from other campaigns. Approximately 12,500 Americans were killed, with 36,500 wounded (the worst losses of any Pacific campaign), and 110,000 Japanese lost their lives. However, more than 7,400 enemy soldiers surrendered, something that had never happened before in the Pacific war.

These island combats were usually fought with "no quarter given" by either side. For a country that prided itself on its humanitarian attitude toward other people, it is an unfortunate truth that US postal censors were constantly removing the skulls of enemy soldiers from the mails sent home by young servicemen, young men who until only recently had been the "kid next door, the paper boy, or the local soda jerk."

Some soldiers and Marines pulled the gold teeth from the mouths of dead Japanese soldiers. Word of the shocking treatment of captured civilians and military personnel by the Japanese early in the war had much to do with these barbarities,

but both sides in the conflict portrayed their opponents as subhuman, murdering brutes. Politics mixed with the ferocity of modern war resulted in some shocking behavior by the combatants.

Militarily, the Japanese reacted violently to the Okinawa invasion with massed kamikaze attacks known as *Kikusui*—Floating Chrysanthemum. In just two days in early April, thirteen US destroyers were either sunk or badly damaged by these suicide flights. The US Navy in the Okinawa campaign actually suffered more fatalities (4,907) than the Army (4,379) or the Marines (3,440). During the ensuing three months, the Japanese mounted 1,500 kamikaze attacks against the US fleet, sinking 34 American ships and damaging 368. American aviators were also busy, sinking the world's largest battleship, the *Yamoto*, in April. This Nipponese behemoth displaced 70,000 tons and carried nine 18in guns compared to the 16in guns of the largest American battleships. Another positive factor from the Allies' point of view that April was the increasing-

Buick surrounded this superb 1942 model convertible with images of battle and victory, including the Coliseum in Rome and the Eiffel Tower in Paris. On the home front, the ad said, "the bustle that now enlivens Buick's factories is the make-ready process for getting back into the production of cars." *Buick postwar production began in October 1945, but only 2,482 cars were produced before the end of the year. Courtesy, Buick Division, General Motors Corporation*

This is the NEW
DODGE
Everything but the Beauty

Jimmie Lynch at the wheel.

ENGINE High compression power,— built in Dodge engine factories to the extreme precision standards further advanced by vast Army and Navy requirements.

ALL-FLUID DRIVE Dodge all-fluid drive entirely separates engine from the rest of the car. Gives cushioned, liquid smoothness to all performance, at all speeds.

DRIVING Driving the new Dodge is largely a matter of steering. All-Fluid Drive eliminates most clutching and shifting, giving the driver complete freedom of mind.

BRAKING These new Dodge (Four-Wheel Hydraulic) brakes bring the car to rest from any speed, on any grade, surely and softly, with *one-third less* foot pressure than before.

It Is The Finest Car in Dodge History—Fully Tested and Proved in Performance and Economy,—for Your Complete Protection

This is the straightest possible answer to the Nation's urgent question,—"What's Dodge going to do?"

What Dodge has done is to fully protect you by avoiding experiment, and by giving you its finest product, fully tested and proved.

If you obtain one of these cars, you may drive it happily for as many years as you like.

This new Dodge gives you the superb qualities of the new (gyrol) All-Fluid Drive, the most important mechanical development in the history of the motor car.

It affords you greater safety, better braking, easier steering and car control than you have ever known.

When you see the new bodies, you will know that beauty, comfort and safety are the companion qualities to these extremes of speed, power and economy.

ECONOMY Gasometer tests again show extreme gas economy. In certified tests, the last prewar Dodge cars *averaged* better than twenty-one miles to the gallon.

RIDING Equa-balanced car weight and fully synchronized springs give constant unison of all riding action. Aero hydraulic shock absorbers assure full rhythmic control.

Listen to "The Music of Andre Kostelanetz" with leading Personalities of the Entertainment World as Guest Stars, Thursdays, CBS, 9 P.M., E.W.T.

K E E P   O N   B U Y I N G   B O N D S

144

Previous page
Dodge used an imaginative approach to its unsolved
postwar design changes, promoting every aspect of its
models except their still-unplanned exteriors and in this
case, the back seat, which appeared to be a rather tenu-
ous perch. A "gasometer" atop the dash reported fuel
mileage of more than 21 miles per gallon (mpg). Cour-
tesy, Chrysler Corporation

ly effective naval blockade of Japan, cutting the
island nation off from raw materials, food, and
other badly needed supplies.

While the Japanese faced calamitous conditions at home and on the battlefield, Americans
also endured a calamity. President Franklin Delano Roosevelt, age sixty-three, died from a massive cerebral hemorrhage while vacationing in
Warm Springs, Georgia. He had been sworn in for
his fourth term as president only a few months
earlier. Although FDR had many bitter enemies
within the American political establishment, the

people had rallied behind the president to "win
the war." For three days and nights, American
radio stations limited their transmissions to religious music and news broadcasts. An untried, un-
known, and relatively uninformed vice president
named Harry Truman became the president of
the United States.

FDR's arch enemy, Adolph Hitler, did not out-
live the president by very long. He observed his
fifty-sixth birthday on April 20, a few days after
Vienna fell to the Soviet Army. Five days later,
advancing American troops linked up with the
Soviets at the Elbe River. By this time, the German Army was fighting desperately in the East
and perfunctorily in the West, with the hope that
most of Germany would be occupied by the
British and the Americans, while also allowing
thousands of their refugee countrymen and
women to escape the clutches of the dreaded
Russian troops. The USSR lost twenty-six million
people in World War II, mainly in conflict with

This April 1945 ad shows that Pontiac finally dropped
its depictions of antiaircraft guns that had dominated
its advertising since the beginning of the war. The many
technical innovations and inventions spawned by four
years of conflict made the world a smaller place, dra-
matically illustrated in this ad. Car makers continued
to urge readers in every ad to buy more war bonds.
Courtesy, Pontiac Division, General Motors Corpora-
tion

Military marriages were popular as the war wound
down and young people considered their chances of sur-
vival much improved. This depiction is understandably
short of automobiles, although it features a DeSoto wed-
ding car. It is, however, populated by some interesting
characters, including inquisitive children and dogs. The
woman in the window in the upper left corner does not
appear at all interested in the proceedings. Street lights
such as these have long since disappeared from the
streets of America. Courtesy, Chrysler Corporation

Willys still retained some vestiges of the battle Jeep in this ad, but mainly concentrated on its potential as a farming vehicle. A Jeep was capable of hauling an 800lb trailer load cross-country, or 1,200lb on an average road. As depicted in this ad, Jeeps were seen as vehicles versatile enough to be driven like trucks or do field work like tractors. Courtesy, Chrysler Corporation

Germany. Its soldiers committed untold thousands of atrocities against German civilians, which to their minds were just retribution for what their own people had suffered at the hands of the Germans.

On April 30, Hitler married his long-time mistress, Eva Braun, and the next day they both committed suicide in his bunker in Berlin. A few days prior to his death, the fuhrer appointed Adm. Karl Doenitz as his successor. Two days earlier, Italian dictator Benito Mussolini and Clara Petacci, his Rumanian mistress, were shot by a partisan firing squad and their bodies were hung upside down in a public square in Milan. Within those few days, two of the three worst dictators in the world violently lost their lives, much as they had lived. Germany surrendered to the Western Allies on May 4 and 5, and May 8 was declared V-E Day (Victory in Europe).

America went wild! On May 9, the German Army on the Eastern front surrendered to the Soviets, who proceeded to forcibly remove two million German soldiers and civilians to a life of slav-

This June 1945 ad reminds readers that Plymouth "told you so" regarding its car's durability. It also shows a car full of commuters who car pool to save gas. Plymouth's postwar civilian car start-up production in 1945 was limited to only 770 cars in the calendar year, ranking twelfth overall. All were Series P-15 cars, which used styling carried over from 1942. Truly new styles weren't introduced until the 1949 model year. In 1946, production jumped to third place with 242,534 cars. Prices ranged from $1,089 to $1,539. Courtesy, Chrysler Corporation

ery in the salt mines of the USSR. Left behind in the ruins of Berlin were 50,000 German orphans, wounded, maimed, and in many cases, insane. The Third Reich was finished.

Germany may have been knocked out of the war, but Japan had no plans to quit. One bizarre weapon brought into use by the Japanese in late 1944 and 1945 was the balloon bomb. More than 32 feet in diameter and filled with hydrogen gas, these balloons (9,000 of them were launched) carried incendiary and high-explosive bombs across the Pacific (winds aloft often reached 200mph) to the northwest coast of the United States in the hopes that they would start multiple forest fires and otherwise disrupt the country and the citizens' morale. In fact, parts of these devices were found in twenty-six different states, as far east as Michigan and Iowa. A few small fires were start-

BLOWING A BLOCKHOUSE TO BITS—

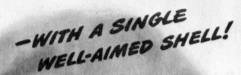
—WITH A SINGLE WELL-AIMED SHELL!

THROUGH A HAIL OF ENEMY FIRE, behind a screen of covering tanks, our heavy "Long Tom" cannon rolls forward to attack an "impregnable" blockhouse . . .

ONE VULNERABLE SPOT is found! A solid steel "back door" guards the enemy guns. Still covered by tanks, we line up this door at point-blank range . . .

This scene is based on an actual battle technique developed by American forces fighting their way through the Siegfried Line. The success of such a daring operation depends entirely on careful planning, split-second timing . . . *and perfectly functioning equipment.* That's where American industry comes in. It's up to us on the production lines to supply our fighters with weapons which will never let them down. At Oldsmobile, for example, we realize that many lives may depend on any one of the millions of heavy caliber shell we produce for "Long Toms" and other guns. This knowledge serves as a constant incentive to put into every shell . . . and every rocket, tank cannon, aircraft cannon, aircraft engine part, and heavy forging . . . all the "know-how" and skill at our command. *Fire-Power* is our business at Oldsmobile. *And we mean business!*

BUY WAR BONDS . . . TO KEEP 'EM FIRING!

"FIRE!" — and the whole hilltop erupts. Driving straight through the door, our shell explodes inside the pillbox, building up terrific pressure . . .

CONCUSSION ALONE does the rest, shredding a reinforced concrete structure into fragments so small that a soldier can hold them in his hands!

OLDSMOBILE DIVISION OF GENERAL MOTORS

The 155mm Long Tom cannon fired a 95lb projectile up to fourteen miles. It was transported by the M-40 gun motor carriage, which had six crew members and a top speed of 24mph. By war's end, 311 M-40s had been built. Oldsmobile produced millions of the heavy caliber shells for the big gun, and used this ad to show the Long Tom destroying an enemy bunker. Courtesy, Oldsmobile Division, General Motors Corporation

147

ed, but the government asked the news media to suppress any reports about the balloon bombs. Unfortunately, a minister in Lakeview, Oregon, and his wife took five Sunday school children on a picnic on May 5, 1945. The children and the wife found one of the balloon bombs and detonated it by accident, killing all six of them.

There was deep concern among Allied military leaders about the expected casualty toll in the upcoming invasion of Japan. A *Collier's* editorial from late 1944 was entitled "Don't Forget the Japs!" and discussed the huge enemy army, fresh and ready for battle, in China and Manchuria, as well as the people of Japan, not very well understood but fearfully respected, who were fully prepared to fight for their nation and their emperor. The editorial also warned that for all of the brav-

ery and sacrifice on the part of US forces in the Pacific battles, they were just nibbling around the edges of the Japanese Empire.

From intelligence analysis and reports by American spies in Japan, it was known that the Japanese had held back thousands of planes and weapons from the island battles in the Pacific to use in defense of the homeland. (At least one Caucasian, Frank Schuler, who parachuted into Japan in July 1944, successfully performed his mission as a spy and survived the war in the enemy's country with the help of missionaries. The five other Americans on the mission were

Packard-built Rolls-Royce engines power the Mustang fighter, Mosquito fighter-bomber, and Lancaster heavy bomber. U. S. Navy PT boats and Army rescue boats are powered by Packard super-marine engines. Packard has produced nearly 65,000 precision combat engines.

What every motorist can learn from a Mustang pilot

The P-51 Mustang fighter was the premiere Allied fighter aircraft of World War II. Packard built the Rolls-Royce Merlin engine which gave the aircraft superior performance and range, allowing the Mustang to escort US bombers to any target in the Third Reich, and protect them from enemy aircraft. The Mustang performed the same mission against Japan in the Pacific. It was armed with six .50 caliber machine guns, attained speeds of 437mph, and had a range of 2,080 miles when fitted with drop tanks. Packard was the only independent auto maker that was free of debt at the end of the war, and ranked eighth in 1945 production with 2,722 cars for the calendar year. In 1946, Packard built 42,102 cars but dropped in rank to fourteenth. This June 1945 ad does not contain copy urging people to buy War Bonds, one of the first to run without that familiar reminder. Courtesy, Dresser-Rand

Studebaker Weasel proves a "Champion" in hard going

The Weasel was a tracked, amphibious personnel and cargo carrier. Its speed was 33mph over land and 25mph in the water. Powered by Studebaker's six-cylinder engine, the Weasel weighed 2.5 tons and carried two crew members. Studebaker was slow in reviving civilian production, building only 651 cars in late 1945. In 1946 the company ranked tenth in production with 77,567 vehicles priced from $1,002 to $1,097. Studebaker was able to offer a completely new car in late 1946, as its design work was done by an outside consulting firm known as Loewy Associates, and thus had not been hampered by a total dedication to defense work. Courtesy, Dresser-Rand

captured and executed. There were even American business executives still freely doing business in Japan at this late date.)

Two million soldiers, 250,000 militia, and millions of civilians were committed to dying for the emperor. Potential invasion beaches contained tunnels packed with supplies and ammunition, and the Japanese had manufactured V-1 rockets, designed by Germany, to use against US forces. School children were mobilized as suicide troops to stop the enemy at the water's edge. Nobody doubted the courage, determination, and ferocity of the Japanese. Planners expected at least one million American casualties. Enemy radio signals intercepted by an Army Signal Corps listening post on a mountaintop in Ethiopia indicated also that the Japanese knew about American attempts to build an atomic bomb as a result of German spy activity. (In fact, they might have known about it before the new president, Harry Truman, did. The White House had kept him in the dark about the project until after FDR's death.)

The Japanese desperately wanted a V-2 rocket, armed with an atomic warhead, which could fly from Tokyo to American-occupied Manila at 1,500mph. Hitler declined to give them a V-2, but did supply the Japanese with the data, uranium, and "heavy water" needed to build an atomic weapon. The last such shipment left Norway onboard the German submarine U-234, in April 1945, with enough raw material to build two atomic bombs. When all German ships at sea were ordered to surrender by Admiral Doenitz at the conclusion of the European war, U-234 surrendered to an American destroyer, the USS *Sutton,* off the northeast coast of America in May. Two Japanese officers onboard the sub committed suicide, hara-kiri, rather than fall into American hands. The ferocity of the enemy at Iwo Jima and Okinawa was also fresh in the minds of American military planners, and all these factors conspired to affect the decision to use the atomic bomb, which had just been successfully developed by an international collection of scientists working in New Mexico.

As the Allied leadership pondered the fateful decisions to be made, the war dragged on, causing casualties and heartbreak. In Burma, Allied

Dodge created a vision of small-town America with this ad describing a performance test conducted four years earlier, a month prior to the debacle at Pearl Harbor. By the end of 1945, the auto maker had built only 420 of *its 1946 cars, but in calendar year 1946 it jumped to fourth place in total production with 156,126 autos. Prices ranged from $1,229 to $1,743.* Courtesy, Chrysler Corporation

149

troops toiled through heavy jungles, dragging their heavy weapons up and down trackless hills and ridges, mainly being resupplied by air. In the China-Burma-India war theater, artillery soldiers were known as "two percenters" because that was the percentage of the shells fired that were expected to fall short among their fellow soldiers. It was a bloody, exhausting campaign with little publicity when compared to the other major theaters of war. The highest ranking American in the CBI was outspoken Gen. Joseph "Vinegar Joe" Stilwell, who still referred to the Chinese Generalissimo Chiang Kai-shek as the "Peanut" and whose abrupt, often rude mannerisms did little to make him popular with Chinese military and government leaders.

The pilots flying the Hump with the supplies of war had a thankless task, and many aircrews disappeared into the Naga Hills, never seen

again. US carrier-based aircraft, as well as the dreaded B-29s, bombed the Japanese home islands at will, and naval task forces swung in close to shore to bombard Japan with their large-caliber shipboard guns. Japanese aviators fought back courageously. In the last few months of the war, 5,000 "special attack" pilots were killed attacking the American fleets and installations.

On the Eastern front, literally millions of repatriated Russians were murdered or shipped into slavery, including soldiers who had surrendered to the Germans earlier in the war, and almost one million who had formed an anti-Communist army under Soviet Gen. Andrei Vlasov to fight with the Germans, ostensibly for the freedom of their homelands within the USSR.

Displaced Russians who had fled to Western Europe to escape the Communists after the 1917 Revolution were rounded up by the thousands and deported to Russia to be executed or enslaved, and Stalin took the opportunity to destroy ethnic minorities such as the Cossacks that he saw as a threat to his regime. There are still

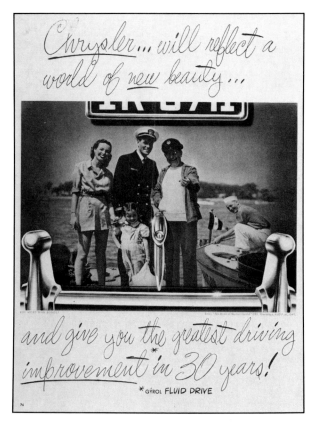

Chrysler created a memorable image incorporating a returning naval officer, his family, and an enjoyable day near the water, all reflected in the mirror finish of the trunk on a Chrysler car. The company placed last in 1945 civilian production with only 322 vehicles, but climbed to eleventh in 1946 with 76,753 cars ranging in price from $1,753 to $3,875. The Town and Country model, utilizing wooden side panels, is indeed a classic. The simple reminder—"Buy More War Bonds!"—has been reduced to tiny type in ads like this as peacetime approaches. Courtesy, Chrysler Corporation

Armed with his K-bar knife, cartridge belt, canteen, and baseball bat, this young man is undergoing the measurement ritual so well known to the youth of every generation. The family DeSoto waits in the driveway to transport him to camp and summer fun. DeSoto built 947 cars in calendar year 1945 and 62,860 in 1946, ranking thirteenth. Prices varied from $1,331 to $2,193. Courtesy, Chrysler Corporation

First glimpse of cars to come

A hint of glamor is coming 1946 Hudsons
. . . caught by the camera of John Paul
Pennebaker, nationally famous photographer

You have waited long for new motor cars. Soon they
will be here.

That they are urgently needed goes without saying.

But, more important, their manufacture is one means that
will speed America back to normal living when final
peace is won.

The famous Hudson Triangle—glimpsed here as it will
appear on the 1946 Hudsons—is more than a promise of
glamorous beauty, new styling and appointments.

It is the symbol of great factories which, after four years of
the most exacting war manufacture, will be ready to build in

large volume—to highest quality—for old friends and new.

It is the mark of an organization with a 36-year record of
progressive engineering—which has introduced scores of
important "firsts" for the benefit of the motoring public, and
which has an old tradition of performance, endurance and
safety to uphold.

It is the emblem of a company that is rich in experience,
competitively alert, confident of its future.

A company that is planning great things for you!

Look for the fine Sixes and Eights that will wear the
Hudson Triangle—in a new dress, for a new day.

HUDSON
HUDSON MOTOR CAR COMPANY, DETROIT 14, MICHIGAN

*Hudson obviously did not know what its 1946 cars were
going to resemble and used a theatrical curtain raiser
on the Hudson triangle as an advertising gambit. "A
hint of the glamor in coming 1946 Hudsons...caught by
the camera of John Paul Pennebaker, nationally famous photographer." The advertising focus has left the
war behind and is now addressing the exciting cars that
will come from the factories that pumped out military
goods. Hudson manufactured 4,735 cars in calendar
year 1945, and though the company had trouble obtain-
ing steel, turned out 90,776 in 1946 priced from $1,481
to $2,050. Courtesy, Chrysler Corporation*

many unanswered questions about the many
thousands of American and British POWs who
were in German camps captured by the advancing Soviets and not, at least initially, repatriated
to the West. Allegations persist that many were
shipped off to Siberia to provide slave labor for
the USSR. The few small voices that called for an
investigation of their fates were overwhelmed by
the massive events still engulfing a world at war.

Tragedy and uncertainty still affected the
daily lives of thousands of Americans both home
and abroad, but many millions were buoyed up by
the vision of victory and peace which now seemed
attainable. Sons and daughters, fathers and
brothers were coming home. Some, however, were
only scheduled to transit America as they re-em-
barked for the Pacific and the upcoming invasion
of Japan.

IT'LL BE THE PRIDE OF THE FAMILY

There's a *Ford* in your future!

COUNT on it! One day, you too will know the joy of owning a new Ford
—a car that will be eager to take you traveling in style. . . . Then you'll
look with pride at a car that's big—inside and out. It will be smart
appearing. You'll listen, to a motor that whispers of power. . . . And when
you get underway—what pleasure! It will be so smooth and easy-riding—

wealthy with comfort. Thrifty and reliable, too, as all Ford cars have been
for more than 40 years. . . . More Ford cars are coming soon. Production
has started but is very limited. America needs all available transportation,
so keep your present car in good condition by seeing your Ford dealer
regularly. *FORD MOTOR COMPANY*

"THE FORD SHOW". Singing stars, orchestra and chorus. Every Sunday, complete NBC network. 2:00 P. M., E. W. T., 1:00 P. M., C. W. T., 12:00 M., M. W. T., 11:00 A. M., P. W. T.

*By August 1945, when this ad appeared, Ford's crystal
ball encompassed a civilian family, including Grand-
mother. There's no mention of war or War Bonds. "More
Ford cars are coming soon. Production has started but
is very limited." Ford jumped out to the lead in calendar
year 1945, producing 34,439 cars. In 1946, the company
built 372,917 vehicles and placed second to Chevrolet.
All models fell into the $1,074 to $1,982 price category.
Courtesy, Ford Motor Company*

A group of pilots being re-trained in Nebraska
for this campaign used a B-25 bomber to fly back
East for a weekend liberty. One pilot was flying
the plane in heavy fog from Boston to Newark,
New Jersey, to pick up the rest of the group for
the return trip to their base when he flew into the
side of the Empire State Building in New York
City on Saturday morning, July 28. Because it
was a weekend with few workers in their offices,
casualties were not excessive, but fourteen people
died, including the pilot and two enlisted men onboard the bomber, and there were several hair-
raising escapes. On the seventy-ninth floor of the
building a blackened and burnt section of wall
under the windows on the northwest side remains
as a reminder and a memorial.

The easing of restrictions on consumer spending and the availability of more products for purchase resulted in a drop in individual savings ac-
counts in the United States from $38.9 billion in
1944 to $35.3 billion in late 1945. If people had a

How New will your New Car Be?

A flier . . .

An infantryman . . .

A Navy gunner . . .

A tank commander . . .

A torpedo man . . .

If you knew as well as they do the great engines, the precise mechanisms, the most dependable machines ever built for war or peace . . . what kind of an automobile would you expect for your next?

How new would that new car have to be to satisfy you?

It would have to be a car with a one piece, one-unit welded body and frame that has the lightweight structural toughness of a Mustang or a Hellcat fighting plane.

A car with beauty and strength, lightness and grace, yet with plenty of power and speed, because the rocket and torpedo have taught you to prize the clean engineering that eliminates dead weight.

An automobile designed to go farther on less rubber, less oil . . . that will deliver 25 or 30 miles to a gallon of gas at normal highway speeds.

A car that's compact and maneuverable but big inside because combat has made you hate the heavy and the clumsy . . . and hours in a cockpit or a tank turret have given you a craving for elbow room and lots of it.

An automobile with the kind of conditioned air system that gives you volumes of fresh, filtered, thermostatically controlled air under pressure that forces stale air out and banishes drafts forever . . .

A car that travels in sound-proofed quiet on a new kind of four-wheel coil spring suspension that rides smoothly on corduroy roads as well as on concrete . . .

That's how new your new car can be . . . if the name of your car is Nash!

Nash Motors, Division of Nash-Kelvinator Corporation, Detroit, Michigan.

Nash
will be the News when the News is New Cars

Tune in Nash-Kelvinator's hit musical program Sundays 4:30 p. m., E. W. T. American Broadcasting Company.

Nash refused to relinquish its servicemen image that had highlighted its advertising throughout most of the war. The captain and the lieutenant portrayed here are using their technological know-how sharpened by wartime experience to decide on the car designs they want when they get home. Nash was third in 1945 production with 6,148 vehicles, but fell to eighth in 1946, producing 98,769 cars. Nash's special automobile after the war was the Sedan Suburban, trimmed with wood and priced at $1,900. But because they were labor intensive, only 272 Suburbans were built in 1946. The lowest priced Nash that year cost $1,293. Courtesy, Chrysler Corporation

152

place to spend their money after four years of war, they were only too happy to do so. On the negative side, large numbers of defense plants were closed down since many did not manufacture viable products for peacetime consumption, and most women were put out of their wartime jobs when the positions were given to the returning servicemen.

The automobile industry was one element of the defense production consortium that had definite postwar plans. With cash in their pockets and bursting with anticipation, returning soldiers and civilians alike impatiently awaited whatever Detroit could produce in the way of new cars as soon as possible. Many business executives and government officials predicted that it would take more than two years to meet the pent-up demand for new automobiles. Even if people were willing to purchase last year's models, the cars did not exist, and had not since 1941. Most design modifications had been in abeyance for the war years, but restyling did not matter as people just wanted new wheels.

Indeed, to the average driver a 1941 Ford and a 1946 Ford were the same car (but one was new), and the other manufacturers were in the same situation.

Nothing stays the same, especially after conflict, and all of the car companies faced difficulties adjusting to the civilian economy and the permanent changes, most noticeable in the work force, brought about by the war. Women and minorities, being the last hired and having the least political clout, had been the first employees to experience the reductions created by peace. Although the auto companies were in the forefront regarding the rehiring of blacks as the economy converted to civilian status, these employees had the least seniority and entered the company on the lowest pay scales. Among women, there were plenty who were perfectly happy to return to the traditional homemaker role, but for many others it was bitter medicine to be cast aside now that the victory was achieved.

Management also underwent change. Several key executives switched companies. At the Ford Motor Company, Henry Ford had stepped aside, and his son, Edsel, an engineer of great promise for the industry, died in 1943. A few new stars, or better yet meteors, such as Henry Kaiser, that fabulously successful builder of Liberty ships, appeared on the horizon. Kaiser believed he could manufacture cars in conjunction with his associate, Joseph W. Frazer, but their success could be called at best, limited. Preston Tucker designed a prototype called the Torpedo, using an air-cooled engine, but did not start production for several years after the war and only built fifty-one Tucker cars.

On the whole, car companies were about to enter a fabulous decade of sales, with great strides as well in design and performance. But much turmoil also lay ahead for the industry, and many companies would not survive the competition in the years to follow.

On June 26, 1945, the United Nations charter was signed in San Francisco. FDR had not lived to see it, but Harry Truman was there. Two weeks later, the United States successfully tested the atomic bomb at Alamogordo, New Mexico. Although there was a peace party attempting to gain status in Japan, American political and military planners believed that the militarists were firmly in control in Japan and would fight a protracted and costly war to the death if their home-

Cadillac treasured its reputation as a quality-crafted luxury car and wished to maintain that status in the industry and the nation after the war. However, sex has always been an integral part of advertising, and the allure of an elegant woman with money to spend was an enticement to all those Americans who made a lot of money on the home front, no matter what their social background may have been. Cadillac continued to promote War Bonds and to fly its "E" flag in ads like this, which appeared in August 1945. Cadillac produced 1,142 cars in 1945 and 28,144 in 1946, ranking fifteenth. Only Lincoln manufactured fewer cars that year. The price of a 1946 Cadillac ranged from $2,200 to $4,669. Courtesy, Cadillac Division, General Motors Corporation

land was invaded. The US casualty count would be unacceptable to Americans and the Allies in general. Other political factors demanded consideration, including the agreement made at Yalta for Russia to enter the war in the Pacific, and the fear that the USSR would swallow Manchuria and its immense natural resources for its own postwar empire. Additionally, the Soviets demanded a place in the postwar occupation of Japan as part of the price for participation.

Thus, for a variety of reasons, the decision was made to drop the atomic bomb on Japan. The mission was carried out on August 6, 1945, by the crew of a B-29 named the *Enola Gay*. The target was Hiroshima, and 80,000 people died. Three days later *Bockscar* dropped a second atomic bomb on Nagasaki, killing 35,000 more. From the view of the governments involved, worse than the deaths was the incredible materiel devastation caused by a single bomb. (Several conventional bombings in Japan and Germany caused more casualties.)

At the same time, Russia entered the Pacific war, engulfing Manchuria and half of Korea, and more than 400,000 Japanese disappeared into Siberia as a result. It was the end for Japan, and the emperor sued for peace.

In the several weeks between the dropping of the bomb and the actual signing of the surrender treaty, Japan prepared in various ways to meet its conquerors. Many fanatical supporters of Japanese expansion, especially among the military, committed suicide rather than face the ignominy of surrender. Thousands of important documents relating to Japanese war activities were destroyed, making accountability difficult. Workers removed the symbol of the emperor, the chrysanthemum, from weapons and equipment to be surrendered to the Allies, not allowing this sacred icon to fall into the hands of the Western barbarians.

Regrettably, the deaths of many Allied POWs occurred at this time. At the prison camp at Fukuoka, Japan, there were at least three differ-

Before becoming the leading postwar auto producer, Chevrolet was a wartime leader, especially in military truck production. Following the war, the Chevrolet once again became the most popular car in America, and it would remain so for the rest of the decade and beyond. Note that this ad avoids reminders of genuine military conflict, choosing to show civilian trucks in use during the war rather than Chevrolet's mighty military trucks. Chevrolet built 12,776 cars in 1945, placing second to Ford. However, it rebounded in 1946, producing 397,104 vehicles and regaining first place in the industry. Like Ford, Chevrolet stayed under $2,000 in price in 1946, starting at $1,098 and ending at $1,712. Courtesy, Chevrolet Division, General Motors Corporation

ent incidents involving the torture and beheading of captured B-29 crews in the days following the emperor's surrender broadcast. Of particular brutality was the treatment of American aviators imprisoned on a small island called HaHa Jima. They were butchered and eaten by the Japanese officers of the garrison. After the war, the men responsible were tried and executed as war criminals.

The Imperial Japanese government surrendered on August 15, 1945. The Western world again went wild with joy. V-J Day was even more tumultuous than V-E Day had been in the United States. A note of tragedy interfered when the American cruiser *Indianapolis,* returning to the West Coast after delivering one of the atomic bombs to the Air Force on the island of Tinian, was sunk by a Japanese submarine. Nobody reported the ship missing, and most of the crew perished in the shark-infested waters of the Pacific before the survivors were located and rescued several days after the incident.

The actual "instruments of surrender" were signed on the deck of the USS *Missouri* (the home state of President Harry Truman) on September 2, 1945. The ceremony was over in a few minutes, ending with Douglas MacArthur's words, "Let us pray that peace now be restored to the world and that God will preserve it always." Looking at the Japanese delegation he then added, "These proceedings are closed." It was over.

Here's where **PONTIAC** Good Will begins...

The war was over, Rosie the Riveter was retired, and the white glove on a woman's hand emphatically stated that it was time to buy a new Pontiac. The company ranked fourth in 1945 with 5,606 cars, and sixth in 1946 with 131,538 cars. Prices ranged from $1,307 to $2,047. Pontiac made a concerted effort to change the appearance of its postwar cars, the first of which were built in September 1945. While maintaining its prewar Torpedo styling and standard three-speed transmissions, Pontiac introduced full-width grilles and triple chrome fender decorations. It also offered all models with either six- or eight-cylinder engines. Courtesy, Pontiac Division, General Motors Corporation

BORN FOR WAR — READY FOR PEACE

Willys Builds the Mighty **'Jeep'**

It seems fitting to end this book about an industry at war with an illustration of the nation at peace. America would never again be as innocent as this September 1945 advertisement suggested, with its peaceful farmland and young boys fishing. However, the future was indeed bright with promise, and the men and women who had fought the war asked only to be a part of it. The Jeep became an integral part of American life, starting civilian production in 1947, and is still popular today. Courtesy, Chrysler Corporation

Epilogue

Six years of world war had ended; years of terror, brutality, destruction, and death. More than 55 million people had died, half of them in the Soviet Union. Germany lost nearly 7 million of its population, while China lost in excess of 7 million. Japan suffered 2.5 million military casualties, and another 670,000 civilian casualties in the US bombing campaign against the home islands. Poland lost 6 million people, most of them civilians and many of them Jews. Poland's Christian and Jewish populations had been marked for extermination, and Poland endured the largest percentage of population loss of any country during the war.

The United States lost 405,400 military personnel killed and an additional 670,850 wounded. Infantry losses accounted for 80 percent of American casualties in World War II. In the air war over Germany, 50,000 young Americans died, and another 30,000 lost their lives in the skies over the Pacific. The famous B-17 bomber suffered a combat casualty rate of 40 percent. (One example of the carnage is the estimate that 7,000 military planes from both sides crashed in Holland alone during the war.) The United States also reported 78,000 soldiers, sailors, and aviators missing in action, the dreaded MIAs.

Allied surveys indicate that it took 25,000 bullets to record one kill during the war. In 1940s dollars, the United States spent $186 billion on ammunition in World War II, and by war's end in 1945 the US Navy had 78,000 active ships, a most formidable armada. The economic cost of the war was great. The emotional havoc wrought was inestimable.

The enemy suffered much more. During the strategic bombing campaign against Germany, bomb tonnage dropped on the enemy accelerated from 40,000 tons in 1942 to 200,000 tons in 1943, and by the last year of the war averaged 80,000 tons a month. Depending on the target, bomb loads were high-explosive, incendiary, or fragmentation. One type of Allied bomb, known as Grand Slam, weighed 22,000 pounds, and a Tall Boy weighed 12,000 pounds. During the March 9, 1945, firebombing raid on Tokyo, US B-29s dropped 2,000 tons of incendiary bombs, killing 83,000 in one night.

The cities and industries of both nations, Japan and Germany, were devastated, although German war production, which was the target of strategic bombing, was not stifled until Allied ground units overran the factories one by one.

American factories only closed down when their immense production accomplishments were no longer needed to win the war. They certainly had been impressive, from ball bearings to bombers, trucks to tanks, and compasses to cannons. The automotive industry had led the way.

General Motors and its various divisions were the biggest contributors, operating ninety-four plants around the country. Oldsmobile alone produced 48 million rounds of artillery ammunition and 350,000 precision parts for aircraft engines, while Buick produced 1,000 aircraft engines a month and Fisher built 16,000 tanks during the war. Of the 2,665,196 military vehicles of all types procured by the armed forces, GM manufactured 854,000 of the trucks. Ford, which built 8,685 B-24 bombers, produced 7.2 percent of all American aircraft engines during the war. Ford also manufactured 93,217 trucks, 277,896 Jeeps, 4,291 gliders, and 2,718 tanks and tank destroyers, plus 12,500 armored cars and 13,000 amphibious vehicles.

Willys-Overland produced 380,000 Jeeps and Chrysler built 20,000 tanks.

All of the automotive companies contributed a great deal to national defense production, as the government poured more than $2 billion a month into the economy. One of the country's problems was what to do with this vast production empire now that the war was over. Fortunately, some $20 billion in defense plant investment was convertible to civilian use, including Willow Run, which became the home of Kaiser-Frazer automobiles.

Most American servicemen had been drafted (66 percent), and they wanted to go home. Returning military personnel brought a variety of diseases back with them. Dengue fever, malaria, dysentery, and respiratory ailments were prevalent, along with the emotional burden caused by fearful combat and the deep-down knowledge that the only way out of a frontline unit was wounding, victory, or death. According to a scientific study taken twenty years after the war, more than 33 percent of US combat veterans suffered in some form from a wide range of neuroses. They came back to a country much changed by the war.

While civilians underwent many trials and privations on the home front, they had more money than ever before, had experienced more freedom, travel, and romance than ever before, and they would never be the same again. Americans had put away more than $140 billion in savings and war bonds during those adventuresome years, and now wanted to cash them in to buy some of the luxuries and necessities unavailable during the war because of rationing and controls.

The advertising industry had redirected its focus midway through 1944, when it became apparent that the Allies were certainly not going to be defeated, and most probably would win the war. Companies were positioning themselves for the postwar demand for goods, cars, houses, and recreation. New kitchens, new clothes, and new products based on wartime technology would start entering the marketplace as the United States continued its boom times, and advertising planned to make them all available.

Servicemen and their wives, mothers, and girlfriends were the main focus. A popular ad featured a soldier and his girl with the slogan, "Back Home for Keeps." The future was bright. Alas, the boom times would not last, at least not at the pace of wartime. By the summer of 1946, the percentage of working women dropped from 36 to 29 percent as defense industries closed down. There was a large excess fleet of ships swinging at anchor, and millions of displaced servicemen were looking for a future in the work force. Still, there was also a wonderful spirit of unity fostered by victory. Most war veterans wanted to restart their interrupted lives as quickly as possible. Higher education was available to them under the newly enacted G.I. Bill, and 7.8 million vets took advantage of the offer, becoming the cornerstone for America's modern affluent middle class.

Returning military personnel were issued a gold eagle insignia, referred to as the "ruptured duck," which they wore proudly as a symbol of their honorable discharge from wartime service. Displaying it was usually good for some free drinks from the 4-Fs (men who failed a military medical examination) and civilians to the young soldiers relaxing in their neighborhood tavern, spending their discharge bonus, telling war stories, and glorying in their freedom from military discipline. The downside to these happy times would appear soon enough.

Factory workers wanted to keep earning their high wartime paychecks, and there were severe labor strikes in many industries. As price controls and restrictions were lifted, inflation became a major concern for the government. Blacks who had discovered some economic freedom during the war were not going to return to their inferior prewar status, and race riots broke out in many cities. It was an ugly return to the reality of domestic problems that had been temporarily postponed and also exacerbated by the war emergency.

The nation needed more than four million new homes and prices started climbing, causing President Truman to ask Congress for price controls on new and existing homes. It was revealed that Lend-Lease had cost the country $40 billion, and the rebuilding of Europe was only just beginning, a project that would cost billions more. The tough job of making government work in peacetime, as well as the United States' new role as world leader and watchdog, made great demands on America's war-weary population.

Detroit was anxious to start civilian car production for 1946. Oldsmobile got a headstart in 1945 by hand-building 1946 models, while Cadillac's first postwar cars had wooden bumpers. Many car manufacturers were able to prosper with their prewar models and designs for several years after the war because of the great demand for *any* new cars.

Ford managed to produce 467,536 cars in the 1946 production year, while Chevrolet brought out 398,028. There were 85,169 Nash production year cars available in 1946, and 91,626 Hudsons, but only 30,793 Packards and 19,275 Studebakers. People had their favorites, but initially the public was not very discriminating, as long as their cars were shiny and new, a precious symbol of peace and prosperity to come.

The first cars produced following the war were, for the most part, slightly updated versions of the 1942 models. Remember, however, that the 1942 models had only been on the market for a few months before the onset of war. The postwar demand for new cars—even with their recycled styling—was insatiable, and the government froze the price of new models to prevent price-gouging. But there were no postwar restrictions on the prices of used cars, which led to some creative pricing schemes. Some enterprising individuals would buy a new car, drive it around the block, then sell it to a used car dealer at a profit. The dealer could in turn sell it as a used car and push up the price to a desperate buyer who needed a new car at any price.

Immediately after the war, car companies' engineers and designers started working to modernize the look of America's cars. For most companies, though, it wasn't until the 1949 models became available in late 1948 that their progress became apparent. As the decade neared a close, practically all of the automobile manufacturers offered cars dramatically different from their first postwar models. Leading the parade was General Motors, who in 1949 presented the first GM Motorama, a traveling new car extravaganza that went well beyond the typical car show.

While car design had been essentially neglected during the war years, the same could not be said for truck design and development. Chevrolet, Ford, Dodge, and International Harvester were able to introduce new postwar truck styling and technology due to their production of trucks for the military throughout World War II. As they produced trucks for military use during the war, they made progress with truck design and technology, and they passed that up-to-date technology on to their consumer trucks at war's end.

Chevrolet's 1947 lineup included a new look—the "Advanced Design" truck—and Dodge converted its military truck assembly line to one producing civilian models within hours of the war's end.

The automobile industry did an outstanding job in providing new vehicles to a car-hungry nation in the postwar years. Many alleged experts had said it would take four years to meet the pent-up demand, but it actually took only two years for most citizens to own a good American car again.

While the war was over, it was not finished, and the Allies had to oversee the governments and occupation of the defeated Axis nations. The victors demanded retribution for the war crimes perpetrated by their enemies, leading to the Nuremberg Trials in Germany and the International Military Tribunal of the Far East.

Many Nazi leaders escaped to other identities, and some had been killed or committed suicide during Germany's last days, but there were still plenty available for trial. Herman Goering cheated the executioner by taking a poison pill in his cell, but several were executed for crimes against humanity and a large number went to prison with lengthy sentences. The trials were very political in nature, and created the precedent that soldiers must not carry out orders perceived to be illegal, even though failure to do so made them traitors to their own countries during wartime and could lead to their own execution or imprisonment.

It was a time of vengeance for the Allies, especially for the Soviets, who had suffered so terribly at the hands of the Germans.

In Japan twenty-eight military and political leaders, but not Emperor Hirohito, were put on trial for war crimes. The emperor asked his people to "endure the unendurable and suffer the insufferable." Because Hirohito was a god to the Japanese people and could to a large extent guarantee their good behavior, he was spared a trial that could have cost him his life, as it did Generals Tojo, Yamashita, and several others. An American Navy dentist named George Foster got into trouble with his superiors for carving "Remember Pearl Harbor" in morse code on Tojo's dentures while he awaited trial. The Japanese nation was very uncooperative during the two-year-long proceedings.

Although more than 3,000 Japanese went to prison for war crimes and another 920 were executed, many hundreds of Japanese soldiers guilty of brutal crimes in the POW camps escaped prosecution.

An open society has its costs, and within the US the FBI apprehended 1,500 spies by the end of the war. There were also other supporters of the enemy within the citizenry of the Allied nations. Among the well-known traitors to stand trial were several propaganda broadcasters like Axis Sally (Mildred Gillars) and the Georgia Peach (Jane Anderson) and Lord Ho-Hum (Edward Delaney) whose allegedly strong anti-Communist beliefs led them to work for Germany against the USSR and the Allies. Another famous propagandist was William Joyce, an Englishman known as Lord Haw-Haw. Most took the defense that they were pro-German and anti-Soviet, rather than anti-British or anti-American. For some it worked and they continued in postwar careers, but for many a jail cell was their reward. The name Tokyo Rose was given to a number of Japanese and Japanese-American women who made propaganda broadcasts for Japan in the Pacific, and one, Iva Toguri D'Aquino, was sentenced to seven years in jail.

The American people wanted the guilty to be punished, but they were much more interested in getting on with their own postwar lives. Vacations were a major priority, with trains, planes, and buses filled to capacity en route to holiday destinations. The airlines matured during the war, and constituted a major transportation force, although it took another thirty years until 50 percent of the population had flown in an airplane. The demand for goods was insatiable, especially cars and appliances. Some backlash occurred when the cost and the results of the war were calculated, especially with the advent of the Cold War.

The federal government had gained an ascendancy over the states that it would not relinquish, and the battle between these different political philosophies continues today. As the Cold War intruded into the lives of Americans, some would wonder if the sacrifices were worth it, to the extent that the Allies were rebuilding Germany and Japan at great cost to the victors, while the Soviets enslaved many of the people the war was fought to free.

But it was done, and it could not be undone, nor would most Americans want it to be undone. The demands of war had opened up the American economy, and also created more personal freedom for individuals than had been available since the closing of the western frontier fifty years earlier. American advertising had played a momentous role in awakening and nourishing the people's will to fight and sacrifice for final victory, and had enjoyed the finest years of its existence. Not only had it fulfilled its mission of distributing information for its corporate clients, but the advertising industry had performed the important public service of government information dissemination through the War Advertising Council, much of it for free.

During 1943, advertisers contributed $300 million in providing government information programs to the public. The industry had indeed matured, and was no longer the target of some reformers who before the war had attacked it as sheer economic waste that forced up the price of many goods. As the people of the US looked hopefully to a new and brighter future, the advertising industry could look to a job well done. It had provided and would continue to provide a glorious and colorful compendium of the United States as the emerging centerpiece of a radically different world from what it had known just a few innocent years earlier.

Index